MILITARY STRATEGY
FOR THE 21ST CENTURY

MILITARY STRATEGY
FOR THE 21ST CENTURY

People, Connectivity, and Competition

Charles Cleveland, Benjamin Jensen,
Arnel David, and Susan Bryant

Rapid Communications in Conflict and Security Series
General Editor: Geoffrey R.H. Burn

CAMBRIA
PRESS

Amherst, New York

Requests for permission should be directed to:
permissions@cambriapress.com, or mailed to:
Cambria Press
University Corporate Centre,
100 Corporate Parkway, Suite 128
Amherst, New York 14226, U.S.A.

Library of Congress Cataloging-in-Publication Data on file.

ISBN: 9781604979503

Table of Contents

LIST OF TABLES

LIST OF FIGURES

ACKNOWLEDGMENTS

We would like to thank a number of individuals and organizations for their support, advice, and comments over the last couple of years. They are too numerous to list in full, but for their encouragement, intellectual thought, and feedback on our manuscript, we extend a special thanks to Frank Hoffman, Celestino Perez Jr., Jay Liddick, John Nagl, and Geoffrey Burn. We would also like to thank special organizations like Spirit of America and University of Notre Dame's Business on the Front Lines Program. We hope more organizations like these continue to work with the military.

We are extremely grateful for the Chief of Staff of the Army Strategic Studies Group (CSA SSG)—now known as the Army Future Studies Group (AFSG). We would like to thank the leadership of the CSA SSG, Colonel Patrick J. Mahaney, Jr., and Dr. Christopher Rice, as well as the current director Colonel Bradley Martsching. The CSA SSG and now AFSG, under the leadership of Lieutenant General Edward Cardon, continues to serve as a critical nerve center for ideas and programs shaping the US national security community.

For Benjamin Jensen this book is for all those who served and sacrificed. Beyond the battlefield, that includes mentors and families who create the space for soldiers to think about the tragedy that is war. Ben could not have worked on this book without the love and support from his family —especially his loving wife, Oksana, and wonderful children, Max and Yana—and the guidance of old souls, true mentors like Abdul Aziz Said, John Richardson, and James Goldgeier who empowered and challenged him at the same time. He also wishes to thank the leadership of Marine Corps University, American University School of International Service, and the Atlantic Council for giving him the time and space to contribute to this important book.

For Charles Cleveland this project is inspired by the soldiers of the US Army Special Forces whose accomplishments and sacrifice remain unmatched. He is grateful to his three talented coauthors, who in their own ways came to believe that America must do better to avoid the waste of blood and treasure and who provided the scholarship and energy to question convention and propose a studied alternative. Most especially though, he is indebted to his wife of nearly forty years, Mary Ann, and their children, Jeremy, Christina, and Matthew, who supported his calling to the Green Berets and loved him anyway.

Sue Bryant would like to thank fellows of SSG Cohort three whose scholarship on the Global Land Power network informed aspects of this book. Special thanks go to Kathryn Hillegass, Angelica Martinez, and Paul Thomas for their efforts and insights. She would also like to thank Dr. Laura Junor, Director of the Institute for National Strategic Studies at National Defense University for her mentorship and support during the process. And as always, she thanks her family who remained patient through weekends lost during the drafting and editing process.

Arnel David would like to acknowledge his genuine gratitude for Colonel Celestino Perez Jr. and his Local Dynamics of War Scholars Program at the US Army Command and General Staff College (CGSC). It was in this rigorous academic program that inspired Arnel and many other students to think more strategically. Many of the lessons from this course are reflected in the book. Unfortunately, CGSC was unable to keep this incredible program going but hopefully books like this encourage its revival. Big thanks to IncoStrat and its unique approach to strategic communications, amplifying indigenous voices and focusing on the micro level of conflict. Their approach is emblematic of many of the ideas portrayed in the book. He is also grateful to Wes Strong, Nick Fitzpatric, Shamaila K. Fitzpatric, Imam Hadji Abduraja Abdulla, Haji Rasol Danial, Stephen Boardman, Christopher Holshek, John Church, Stuart Taylor, Tom Matelski, Jay Liddick, Christopher Stockel, and John Ehrlich Kiley for sharing many of their stories and ideas to help shape parts of the book. He is thankful to his loving family—his wife Katherine and children Erik, Angelina, and Angelo—who have been patient and supportive along this journey. Finally, he is grateful to his parents, Eduardo and Evangeline David, for their encouragement to read.

PREFACE

My professional military life began when America lost its first war. I would retire thirty-seven years later, convinced that our nation has repeatedly floundered in its fundamental approach to conflict short of conventional war. We lack organizations and leadership at the highest levels oriented to the most prevalent forms of conflict: irregular and population-centric.

In this book, my coauthors and I balance our military experiences alongside academic scholarship to build a theoretical foundation on how to define a human domain and achieve a position of advantage through understanding connectivity. War remains political and eternally human. If you don't understand humans, their interests and relationships, you cannot seize the high ground in modern war. We need to build sufficient capabilities to thrive in this space and integrate a human domain construct with the other domains (land, sea, air, space, and cyber). Only then will we be able to develop holistic concepts and better allocate resources for specialized structures, leaders, and processes to operate more effectively amongst the populace.

Time and again, we built ad hoc organizations (e.g., Vietnam CORDS, Afghan PRTs) but did not institutionalize these efforts or cultivate the leaders required to direct this type of war. In the Army, special operations forces (SOF) provide value in the human domain but current structure prevents experienced leaders and requisite headquarters from directing these campaigns. The existing model is increasingly inadequate and fails to achieve political objectives against less capable, irregular adversaries. We squander blood and treasure for limited gains.

The changing character of conflict and competition continues to reinforce the importance of the human domain. Whether we address it or not, it is now a reality of the national security environment with proof worldwide given the depth of SOF operations from the Philippines to Yemen, the Baltics and across Africa. Such campaigns differ significantly from traditional land campaigns, with special-operations raids and US-advised indigenous forces conducting either internal defense and development or unconventional warfare. Influence and information operations, in which the United States continues to struggle, are not organized in an optimal manner.

Enemies determine how they will challenge the US military by identifying our weaknesses. Since America's loss in Vietnam, the US military has repeatedly showcased its technological advantage and superior skills at conventional maneuver, and at the same time struggled in wars where our enemy can operate and shelter among the populace. Learning from both Vietnam and Desert Storm, our state and non-state adversaries have chosen to fight America and its allies through insurgents, terrorists, resistance movements, and subversive campaigns.

The United States must develop the world's best irregular warfare capability to match our dominance in conventional arms (including high-end raids) and nuclear weapons. The centerpiece of irregular warfare is recognizing the human domain and building a strategy to account for people, connectivity, and competition.

I left the service two years ago, believing that over time the irregular efforts of those threatened by our way of life would slowly grow to become an existential threat. Our nation is like a frog in boiling water, ever vigilant to avoid the gigging stick but unaware of the rising temperature. It appears to me that the Army, SOCOM, the Department of Defense, and the rest of the national security enterprise are equally unaware of the rising temperature. The Army fails to understand how significant the differences are between the wars for which its headquarters and units are built and the ones to which they are committed by policy makers. SOCOM does not acknowledge its lead role as America's irregular warfare component and instead invests most of its resources on counterterrorism, particularly manhunting strategies. This prioritization of lethal targeting, often conducted unilaterally by US forces, over the fashioning of indigenous solutions through partnering, engagement, and shaping, to include coalition military operations, leaves a knowledge and capability gap in the US arsenal unfilled by the Army or Marine Corps and only partially addressed by the CIA. Finally, DoD continues to let this gap go unaddressed, forcing neither the conventional force nor SOCOM to address these fundamental challenges.

I had an extraordinary front-row seat, and on occasion even played a role, in most of America's overseas ventures since 1979. I have seen the good, the bad, and the ugly when it comes to US interventions. At some point, I realized my professional military education was designed to prepare my classmates for wars that, thankfully, rarely happened. The system did little to address the wars I actually fought. Through experience, I came away with a basic understanding that insurgencies and other population-centric conflicts are best fought by those indigenous to the area, and only supported to the minimum extent possible by foreign actors and in a manner that is not alien to the culture. Unfortunately, in these local struggles for power and influence, US military options remain consistently biased towards the use of conventional force. And too often, I have been left wondering what "best military advice" was given by military leaders to politicians and their appointees. Who spoke truth to power? What was their basis of understanding conflicts far from America's shores? Were these military leaders and their staffs professionally prepared to provide literate advice about local grievances and networks they didn't understand? Did they have a complete understanding of the local context, and were potential indigenous solutions identified and accounted for in staff estimates?

The United States must continue to connect and expand its networks to win in irregular war. The 2018 National Defense Strategy highlights the "vitality of alliances and partnerships." Those alliances and partnerships are a source of strength our adversaries cannot match. They are a center of gravity. Yet, America's founding principles and resulting way of life that have so inspired the world and led to the spread of liberal democracy have come under increasing threat as the world gets more connected and crowded.

Our adversaries are trying to attack our center of gravity through amplifying grievances and creating rival networks to limit US power and influence. America cannot allow this. The United States should protect and extend our ability to operate in the human domain, extending our network of alliances and partnerships, and creating organizations capable of working by, with, and through local partners, to include conducting irregular warfare, faster than our enemies can respond. These actions should be consistent with another source of strength: the values enshrined in the American constitution. The United States needs an "American Way of Irregular War" that counters adversary efforts to discredit, diminish, and destroy our alliance network and democratic institutions.

To this end, the nation needs to prioritize concepts and capabilities that help us gain a position of advantage in population-centric and irregular warfare. Recognizing the human domain is the first step on this journey, providing the foundation for developing the people, structures, and processes the United States requires to achieve vital national interests.

Thanks for picking up the book to continue the discourse.

—Charles T. Cleveland

MILITARY STRATEGY
FOR THE 21ST CENTURY

Chapter 1

Introduction

> Over the long term, we cannot kill or capture our way to victory.
> Non-military efforts—these tools of persuasion and inspiration—
> were indispensable to the outcome of the defining ideological
> struggle of the 20th century. They are just as indispensable in the
> 21st century—and perhaps even more so.
>
> —Robert Gates, Former US Secretary of Defense[1]

Intrigue before Battle

This book calls for rethinking how the US national-security community approaches population-centric warfare and strategic competition in the twenty-first century. Strategic advantage in the twenty-first century will emerge from mapping human geography in a connected world, leveraging key relationships, and applying a mix of unconventional and conventional methods that put adversaries on the horns of a dilemma. Consider the 216 BCE Battle of Cannae.

The military profession teaches the battle as a masterpiece of ground maneuver. Hannibal used mobile forces to draw out heavier Roman units before enveloping the legions and causing a catastrophic defeat. In the early twentieth century, Chief of the German General Staff Alfred von Schlieffen, of the Schlieffen Plan fame, used the ancient battle as a campaign study to advocate envelopment. Schlieffen argued that modern war, like ancient battle, was a "struggle for the flanks."[2] Similarly, in his famous "Patterns of Conflict" briefing in the late Cold War, John Boyd, the US Air Force pilot and maneuver theorist, used the battle to highlight the importance of unmasking enemy activity and confusing them to open up weak points vulnerable to attack.[3] Mobility allowed a smaller force to fix and flank a larger force.

The traditional focus on maneuver tactics misses the shaping campaign Hannibal waged prior to the battle. Before he could bait the Romans to attack at Cannae, Hannibal had to get rid of Roman dictator Quintus Fabius Maximus Verrucosus, of the Fabian strategy fame. Fabius's delaying tactics, though unpopular, deprived the Carthaginian army, which lived off the land, of much-needed supplies. Hannibal needed to oust Fabius and force the Roman generals eager for a fight into a decisive battle at a time and place of his choosing. To this end, he leveraged knowledge of Roman political and economic networks to undermine support for Fabius from within.[4]

Knowing that Fabius was already politically vulnerable due to the unpopularity of his delaying tactics, Hannibal raided wealthy Roman estates, but, "gave orders for [Fabius'] property to be spared from fire and sword and all hostile treatment whatever in order that it might be thought that there was some secret bargain between them."[5] The resulting uproar in the Senate led to Fabius being stripped of supreme command. Hannibal used a knowledge of Rome's internal divisions to wage political warfare and shape the battlefield.

More than maneuver warfare and the importance of envelopment, Hannibal thus demonstrated the utility of understanding and shaping an adversary's political and economic networks to achieve a position of relative advantage. The Carthaginian used his formations for strategic signaling as much as he did open battle. He set the conditions and defined the tempo of his adversary.

ESCAPING A SERIES OF FAILURES

The United States is constantly engaged in prolonged armed conflicts with few victory parades. Over the last eighteen years as America mobilized to conduct a series of campaigns against terrorist networks and rogue states, the military achieved tactical victories and limited operational successes, but ultimately fell short at the strategic level. After the withdrawal of the US-led Coalition in 2011, Iraq descended into sectarian violence and its major cities fell into the hands of extremist groups within two years. Despite a sustained NATO troop presence, the 2016 and 2017 fighting seasons in Afghanistan were some of the most violent for Afghan forces since 2001.[6] The US national-security community continues a global hunt for suspected terrorists linked to multiple Al Qaeda affiliates and the so-called "Islamic State" (Daesh). Yet, Daesh's defeat in Mosul and Raqqa did little to address the local political and economic conditions that created a convergence of interests between disenfranchised Sunnis and global jihadists.

Great powers similarly flank America and find creative ways to limit her military power and influence. Russia brought war back to Europe through its audacious activity in Crimea and Eastern Ukraine while using cyber intrusions, as a twenty-first-century form of "Active Measures" (i.e., political warfare and propaganda), to undermine the West's democratic institutions and mobilize discontent amongst the population.[7] China is outflanking the United States through expansive economic investments in new trade routes such as the One Belt, One Road initiative while combining soft power, new overseas bases, and military modernization to balance US conventional power.

The character of not just war but strategic competition appears to be changing. Failure to adapt will result in further losses of blood and treasure as well as prestige and influence. Power withers when it proves frail.

This book outlines a new approach to thinking about military art rooted in increasing connectivity and defining a new domain of competition, the human domain. In the twenty-first century, strategic advantage will emerge from how we engage with and understand people and access political, economic, and social networks to achieve a position of relative advantage that complements American military strength. These interactions are not reducible to the physical confines of the land domain, which tend to focus on physical geography and terrain features. They represent a web of networks that define power and interests in a connected world. The state that bests understands local context and builds a network around relationships harnessing local capacity is more likely to win the twenty-first century "struggle for the flanks." In this connected world, even more than before, the decisive battle will occur before the first shot is fired as actors compete to amplify internal divisions and develop key partnerships.

Military power exercised through joint combined-arms is no longer sufficient to compel adversaries or control populations. Just as conventional forces like those of the United States increased their ability for precision strike and lethal fires, competitors opted to shift strategic competition away from direct confrontations to an indirect clash of wills. The weak undermine the strong through mobilizing local populations—often through predation and manipulating grievances—to carry out insurgent attacks, terrorism, civilian massacres, propaganda campaigns, and cyberattacks. The site of this clash of wills, occurring predominantly in civilian populations and their relational networks as opposed to battlefields of old, reduces the US military's comparative advantage in combined-arms maneuver. Military art is practiced increasingly in a human domain.

To be successful in these twenty-first-century struggles, the military profession must recognize and organize for its role in these indirect conflicts and develop appropriate concepts that account for the need to gain a position of advantage in the human domain. Leading military powers like the United States must find a way to maneuver in an inter-connected world of competing influence networks. America's military needs to be part of a global security network optimized for twenty-first century influence campaigns backed by military force as opposed to fighting twentieth-century military campaigns backed by information operations that often do not match the local context.

THE EMERGING HUMAN DOMAIN

In this book, we offer the outlines of a military theory that 1) charts the changing character of strategic competition and conflict and 2) proposes a new operational concept for mapping the human domain, building a global security network, and leveraging these relationships to gain a position of relative advantage. We contend that the emerging character of war is changing how military professionals and policy makers think about civilian populations as well as how they conduct operations around and through them in a connected world. The emergent character of war calls for the recognition of a human domain, a web of interactions, as the central battlefield between rival antagonists. These interactions constitute a global land commons as shifting economic, social, and political networks cluster in time and space, generating key nodes that friendly nations have to access or at least influence to advance their interests. Just as nineteenth-century theorists in the United States and England looked to the sea as a global commons required to sustain economic growth, the intersection of physical and virtual networks create new collective-action challenges.

Future conflicts will likely occur amongst the people, digitally in their social media feeds and physically in proximity to hubs of political and economic power sitting along the spine of global supply chains.[8] Where political institutions break down and populations compete for influence and resources, whether scarce or not, regional actors and great powers will exert their influence. These networks of influence become the key terrain, as much or more so, than prized pivot points in traditional geopolitics. Critical sea lines of communication, like the Strait of Hormuz and Malacca, matter to the extent they connect local actors to global resource networks. New lines of communication linked to the movement of ideas, and the associated internet architecture, and people become as important as sea lines of old. These changes push strategists and military planners to visualize competition in a new domain, the human domain.

Traditionally, military practitioners conceptualize warfare in terms of the physical domains where conflict occurs. Current US military doctrine accounts for five domains: land, air, maritime, cyber, and space.[9] As seen in Table 1, each of these domains is defined by its physical properties.

Our definitions of the world around us change as the struggles we fight evolve. These definitions in turn codify military practice, creating new concepts and organizations. The Greek victory at Salamis in 480 BCE demonstrated the importance of controlling the sea. The growing importance of air operations and their integration with both close air support and strategic bombing in the interwar period necessitated the importance of conceptually defining the air as a domain and organizing forces around this change.[10] The military use of space for communications and intelligence during the Cold War forced strategists to add space as a domain. The transition of commerce, social interactions, and politics, as much as the digital dependence of modern militaries, to cyberspace led to the proclamation of a cyber domain. Each new domain required capability investments and new theories of victory.

Table 1. Domains Defined by Physical Properties.

Domain	US Military Joint Doctrinal Definition (JP 1-02)
Land	The area of the Earth's surface ending at the high-water mark and overlapping with the maritime domain in the landward segment of the littorals (p.141)
Air	The atmosphere, beginning at the Earth's surface, extending to the altitude where its effects upon operations become negligible (p. 7)
Maritime	The oceans, seas, bays, estuaries, islands, coastal areas, and the airspace above these, including the littorals (p. 150)
Cyberspace	A global domain within the information environment consisting of the interdependent network of information technology infrastructures and resident data, including the Internet, telecommunications networks, computer systems, and embedded processors and controllers (p. 58)
Space	The environment corresponding to the space domain, where electromagnetic radiation, charged particles, and electric and magnetic fields are the dominant physical influences, and that encompasses the earth's ionosphere and magnetosphere, interplanetary space, and the solar atmosphere (p. 224)

Source. Joint Doctrine JP 1-02.

The central idea in contemporary Joint US doctrine is that acting in multiple domains against an adversary enables a military force to achieve a position of relative advantage. For example, according to Joint doctrine, full-spectrum superiority (i.e., dominating all five domains) enables US forces to strike at a time and place of their choosing without significant opposition.[11] The Joint Operational Access Concept (JOAC) asserts that the

> future joint forces will leverage cross-domain synergy—the complementary vice merely additive employment of capabilities in different domains such that each enhances the effectiveness and compensates for the vulnerabilities of the others—to establish superiority in some combination of domains providing the freedom of action required by the mission.[12]

By prioritizing an understanding of warfare based on the physical characteristics of domains, US military doctrine misses the fact that modern wars occur, to use Sir Rupert Smith's phrase, amongst the people.[13] The adversaries of the world's preeminent military power choose to fight indirectly. They understand that since Vietnam and further demonstrated by US campaigns against multiple extremist networks, population-centric warfare and subversive influence campaigns limited American military power.

Even nuclear superpowers, like Russia and China, prefer this indirect approach. Russia opts for the Gerasimov Doctrine, undermining American institutions through targeted cyber intrusions and propaganda backed by signaling the risk of military escalation.[14] China focuses on constructing a global economic network to enable twenty-first-century power projection while building a network of area denial capabilities in multiple domains to limit US options. Though both of these nuclear states continue to modernize their military, they choose to compete in the space between peace and war, leveraging social and economic networks to limit American military power.[15]

As a result, war amongst the people is the method states and non-state actors alike opt for to tie the giant's hands, making indirect competition, confrontation, and conflict the preferred strategy in the twenty-first century.[16] In fact, the majority of conflicts since World War II were intrastate struggles defined by the needs and wants of mobilized political actors. In these struggles, there are distinct, local dynamics that define how groups fight.[17] Even contemporary interstate conflicts like Russian action in Eastern Ukraine involve mobilizing social groups, conducting cyber strikes, and waging propaganda campaigns, each defined more by the characteristics of the targeted population than a physical feature of the terrain.[18]

Focusing singularly on the physical effects of terrain tends to strip modern operational art of an appreciation of the needs, wants, and history of local populations through which combatants struggle. We teach that war is a continuation of politics by other means in schoolhouses but reduce our understanding of the struggle from a reciprocal clash of wills to a correlation of capabilities in discrete, physical domains. According to Frank Hoffman and Michael Davies:

> Much of Western military theory focuses on physical domains (air, sea, land, and space). ....American security institutions are largely organized around these physical domains, increasingly now connected by a cyberspace domain.... These domains create a frame of reference that defines the preparation and conduct of war. Each military institution and Service crafts doctrine and platforms that are designed to operate or maneuver in their dominant domain. Little preparation is made to conduct war beyond them. Because of this focus on the physical domains, Americans tend to overlook, and underinvest in, the more important aspects of war and warfare —those best defined as human.[19]

Definitions of domains restricted to the features of physical terrain miss that the object of struggle is human decision. People—not sea lines of communication, mountains, or the clouds above them—are the ones who make decisions. Terrain has important tactical and operational characteristics but is devoid of meaning absent an understanding of the architecture of decision: what you want your enemy, neutrals, and your own forces to do and how best to get them to do it. Domains therefore have little meaning absent the interactions between people transiting them. According to Dorothy Deming:

> all domains of warfare, with the possible exception of land, are fundamentally manmade. The maritime domain would not exist without boats, the air domain without planes, and the space domain without rockets and satellites. Indeed, these domains, along with their respective military forces, were created only after the introduction of naval vessels, military aircraft, and spacecraft, respectively.... Nature, and especially geography, still matter, but none of the traditional domains, including land, can be understood, let alone operationalized, in today's world without accounting

for the artifacts of mankind and the changes man has made to the environment.[20]

Domains are devoid of relevance if they have no material impact on the success of your military campaign. Combined-arms maneuver – the use of tanks, infantry and artillery - remains relevant so long as your adversaries have critical vulnerabilities you can threaten with these formations. These systems are land-domain tools in which the human is secondary other than as an agent that uses the weapon system. Competition in the human domain reverses this logic to focus on the human as the system. Understanding and shaping the needs, wants, fears, and beliefs of people—each of which manifest in networks of relations— becomes more important than any single weapon system. The side that best mobilizes populations gains a position of advantage in the human domain and creates opportunities in other domains that places the enemy on the horns of a dilemma.

Failing to understand the human domain was a recurrent theme in accounts of the Afghan and Iraqi conflicts. A 2015 National Defense University study found that "neither national-level figures nor field commanders fully understood the operational environment, including the human aspects of military operations."[21] A 2014 RAND study led by Linda Robinson came to similar conclusions.[22] According to the study, a major lesson of these conflicts was "the inability of technology to substitute for the sociocultural and historical knowledge needed to inform understanding of the conflict, formulation of strategy, and timely assessment."[23] A 2012 Joint Staff study similarly found that the US military failed to "recognize, acknowledge, and accurately define the operational environment," including "not only the threat but also the physical, informational, social, cultural, religious, and economic elements of the environment."[24] A 2009 Defense Science Board study found that "the US military consistently realized the importance of human dynamics too late in the conflict and often in such an ad hoc manner that concepts and organizations developed to understand and influence local dynamics were abandoned after war."[25]

Senior leaders echoed this emphasis on failing to understand the human domain as limiting the ability to convert US military power into strategic end states. General Raymond Odierno, General James Amos, and Admiral William McRaven saw the inability to understand the human domain as contributing to US military setbacks noting that, "time and again, the US has undertaken to engage in conflict without fully considering the physical, cultural, and social environments...One has only to examine our military interventions over the last 50 years in Vietnam, Bosnia and Kosovo, Somalia, Iraq, and Afghanistan to see the evidence and costs of this oversight."[26] According to Lieutenant General Robert Brown, "it's the ability to work in the human domain that we need to be aware of. We've got to be working out here on the edges, not the center, in order to win our next engagements."[27]

Despite this recognition, there is not a clear understanding of what the human domain is or how to operate therein. Existing efforts to reorient the US military towards the human domain have become stalled in a massive, often paralyzed, defense bureaucracy. Military services cannot agree on whether or not there is a standalone human domain. Whereas the initial Strategic Landpower Task Force Report described a distinct human domain that intersects with land and cyber, current joint doctrine development narrowed the focus to "human aspects of military operations."[28] The discourse of physical domains, with its organizational pull on the military services, appears resilient.

Our treatment challenges the notion of physical domains as the optimal organizing feature for modern conflict. We show how competition, confrontation, and conflict are changing, and as a result, create a need to map the human domain and use this information to achieve a position of advantage by brokering local relationships across a global security network. Strategic advantage in the twenty-first century requires understanding the web of interactions that converge in cyber and geographic spaces and developing the concepts and capabilities required to gain a position of advantage in this human domain.

Understanding enables action. Modern struggles start not with the rapid deployment of expeditionary forces or deep air and cyber strikes on high value targets, but with building and maintaining a global security architecture, a collection of treaties and partnerships that order relations. This network, a twenty-first-century corollary to a Corbettian "fleet-in-being," allows a state to work with partners and to gain a deeper understanding of the roots of crises, confrontations, and conflicts required to act. Like Hannibal, you map the social, political, and economic factors shaping a group and use them to achieve a position of advantage. The US defense community needs new concepts that embrace this broader understanding of struggle. This book does not seek to fundamentally reorient the military so much as recognize that the addition of a new domain requires new concepts for operating therein as well as new structures (i.e., DOTML-PF) to support operations.

Adapting the force starts with concepts. Concepts "describe how military forces operate" in broad terms.[29] For former Commanding General of the US Army Training and Doctrine Command and architect of the AirLand Battle doctrine, Don Starry, concepts were "ideas, thoughts, and general notions about the conduct of military affairs."[30] To propose a new operating concept is to call for a fundamental shift in how organizations define and approach problem solving.[31] In this book, we seek to define the human domain and global security architecture as a means of developing new approaches to conflict prevention, conflict resolution, and warfighting. Without an operational concept for the human domain, future force development will likely stall, leading the US military to once again reject efforts to understand the local dynamics of conflict.

The Changing Character of War

We contend that the US military's failure to understand the human domain and assess the local dynamics of war is a key aspect of recurrent setbacks. The book pivots on the assumption that failing to understand the character of warfare leads to flawed judgment. The idea that war has a changing character unique to each historical period comes from Clausewitz's seminal book, *On War.* [32] Table 2 offers some of the references to 'character' and how these observations inform our approach.

Reading across these passages, one sees Clausewitz's concept of a character of war as an early form of net assessment, the practice of analyzing "the interaction of national security establishments in peacetime and war." [33] The ways and means each actor brings to bear in forging their military strategy are not independent and static. Rather, actors, the belligerents, are engaged in a *werra* struggle relative to one another and informed by a broader context. This context is not reducible to the checklists prevalent in most strategic estimates. [34] The context tends to be emergent and reflects particular configurations of ways and means, as well as prevailing adaptions, how each actor learns from each other and alters its approach to warfighting. [35]

Other authors have similarly sought to identify emergent patterns that define strategic competition and conflict. For historian William McNeill, material factors from technology to economic activity and the environment created different modes of warfare and a unique specialization of violence. [36] William Lind and Thomas Hammes suggested distinct, identifiable generations of warfare paralleling larger technological change. [37] Antoine J. Bousquet proposed that the character of war tends to reflect the dominant scientific paradigm of the period, shifting from the mechanistic Newtonian struggles of Napoleon to complex, nonlinear systems thinking and self-organizing terrorist cells. [38] Regardless of its source, the character of war and resulting specialization of violence shaped the range of choices open to military practitioners.

Table 2. The Character of War.

Section	Passages	Extrapolation
Book I, Ch 10	"From the character, the measures, the situation of the adversary, and the relations with which he is surrounded, each side will draw conclusions by the law of probability as to the designs of the other, and act accordingly."	Measures, as ways and means, and the situation, as the context in which each side defines their ends (i.e., motives) together inform planning for war.
Book I, Ch 27	"Wars must differ in character according to the nature of the motives and circumstances from which they proceed."	
Book VIII, Ch 2	"We shall have to grasp the idea that war, and the form which we give it, proceeds from ideas, feelings, and circumstances, which dominate for the moment."	In any given historical moment, there are prevailing notions about war that emerge through competitive interactions.
	"If we must grant that war originates and takes its form not from a final adjustment of the innumerable relations with which it is connected, but from some amongst them which happen to predominate."	
Book VIII, Ch 3	"In order to ascertain the real scale of the means which we must put forth for war, we must think over the political object both on our own side and on the enemy's side; we must consider the power and position of the enemy's state as well as of our own, the character of his government and of his people, and the capacities of both, and all that against on our own side, and the political connections of other states, and the effect which the war will produce on those States."	The character of a given conflict is relational and defined by both the relative balance of forces and the larger web of interactions that define the appropriate ends, ways and means in a given epoch.
	Tartars, the Republics of ancient times, the feudal lords and commercial cities of the Middle Ages, kings of the eighteenth century, and, lastly, princes and people of the nineteenth century, all carry on war in their own way, carry it on differently, with different means, and for a different object	

Source. These passages and the corresponding book and chapter reference are drawn from Carl von Clausewitz, *On War*, trans. J.J. Graham (London: N. Trübner, 1873), http://www.clausewitz.com/readings/OnWar1873/TOC.htm.

For Helmuth von Moltke the Elder (1800–1890) new material conditions, from railroads to telegraphs, changed the speed of mobilization and
military practice.[39] In the wake of the Russian Civil War, Soviet theorists
from Marshal Aleksander A. Svechin (1878–1938) to Marshal Mikhail
Tukhachevsky (1893–1937) argued that the industrial age created conditions challenging notions about ground maneuver in wide circulation
since the Napoleonic era.[40] The architect of Plan 1919, Major General
J.F.C. Fuller sought to combine the high technology of his day, motorized
vehicles and airplanes, with mysticism to create a new military science.[41]
For Stephen Biddle, the twentieth century saw the emergence of a distinct,
modern system of force employment (i.e., combined-arms maneuver) as
different actors adapted to the increasing lethality of modern firepower
and emulated one another.[42]

After the Cold War, scholars and practitioners highlighted an incipient
change in the character of war that shifted from material to human
concerns. Chief of Staff of the Army, General Gordon Sullivan, envisioned a new era of "post-industrial warfare" defined by a "new warrior
class," consisting of transnational criminals, terrorists, and ethnic groups
challenging the sovereign state and international order.[43] Similarly,
Mary Kaldor hypothesized a new mode of warfare defined by interna-
tionalized intrastate identity conflicts, illicit economic networks, and
guerilla tactics.[44] Robert Kaplan predicted a new anarchy and a new era
of struggles defined by resource competition, pandemics, urbanization,
demographic shifts, and state failure.[45] Martin van Creveld showed how
a new era of religious and ethnic conflict challenged the very foundation of Western military thought.[46] John Arquilla and David Ronfeldt
hypothesized the emergence of netwar as non-state actors structured as
networks engaged in transnational competition.[47]

Sir Rupert Anthony Smith, a former British Army General and veteran
of post–Cold War conflicts, proposed that a new paradigm defined the
character of war.[48] For Smith, the utility of force changed as industrial
warfare between organized nation-states gave way to war amongst the

people. In industrial war, states competed to mobilize their societies and generate sufficient combat power to defeat their opponent's military. After the Cold War, clear battlefields and uniformed combatants disappeared as social groups within rival populations competed in a test of wills. Military force was no longer decisive. Rather, the utility of force was establishing conditions for long-term conflict resolution, a concept you see enshrined in current US Army doctrine.[49]

Building on Smith's insights, in addition to the utility of force, the predominant forms of force and coercion are changing. There appears to be a cycle of competitive learning in contact reminiscent of J.F.C. Fuller's concept of a constant tactical factor, the process of counter-adaption to the introduction of new weapons and tactics.[50]

In the emergent character of war, these adaptions often take place in the human domain. Small groups challenge larger militaries through hiding amongst civilians and using modern, low-cost communication channels to mobilize support. Power is not fixed, but relational as actors compete to bring their network to bear against the enemy. These propositions lead to two important insights.

First, *mass, superior combat power and technology do not appear to be necessary conditions for victory in modern warfare.* Rather, war is a contest of wills, one in which the materially weaker side can emerge victorious. As Colin Gray noted, "the human dimension of war and strategy has a way of triumphing over technology."[51] This doesn't mean that military power, as traditionally defined, is obsolete. Rather, in the twenty-first century, bringing military power to bear is producing diminishing marginal returns. The United States is spending massive amounts of national treasure for increasingly limited outcomes.

The weak appear increasingly able to resist the strong. American political scientists have been interested in how the weaker side, the actor with fewer and less advanced capabilities, prevails dating back to the Vietnam War. Andrew Mack argued that there was an asymmetric relationship between major powers and minor opponents, owing to resolve and domestic politics.[52] Powerful actors tended to be politically vulnerable at home, with political factions subverting preferred government strategies whereas weak actors tended to be more unitary. Similarly, Gil Merom highlighted how domestic-level constraints in democracies tend to result in the wrong force mix and strategy.[53] Furthermore, from autonomous systems to land mines, transnational advocacy groups mobilize to limit the tactical choices available to modern military actors.

For Stephen Rosen, weak actors increase their bargaining power when they exhibit a willingness to suffer.[54] In an analysis of more than 200 conflicts between 1800 and 2003, Ivan Arreguin-Toft found a periodic break. Whereas in the early nineteenth century stronger actors emerged victorious in warfare, in the twentieth century the figure drops to less than 50%.[55] Through twelve comparative case studies, T.V. Paul found that weaker powers, which believe they have external support and can make rapid gains that present a fait accompli, will assume significant risk and attack larger actors.[56] For Patricia Sullivan, war outcomes pivot less on strength then on objectives. [57] Stronger powers find victory elusive when they seek to alter the behavior of a weaker adversary.

Second, *in contemporary warfare and strategic competition actors appear to engage in crisis politics beneath the level of major theater war.* Russia finds it cheap, less risky, and deniable to undermine American political institutions and magnify social cleavages through botnets and propaganda optimized for cyberspace. These covert actions, such as the 2016 US presidential-election hack,[58] are amplified by strategic signaling through large military exercises and nuclear modernization programs. There is a new stability-instability paradox. The sheer risks and costs of major theater war shift competition to Gray Zone conflicts.[59] In this arena, there is an increasing incidence of American adversaries pursuing their strategic ends in a manner that remains below the threshold for military intervention. Gray Zone conflicts elude US mental models and legal frameworks on the conflict spectrum between peace and war. These coercive efforts short of war extend to cyberspace and political warfare.

In contemporary strategy, access and influence are as important as firepower.

The idea of an emergent, interactive character to war can be contrasted with work on enduring national *ways of war*. A way of war is a tran-shistorical approach to the conflict by a political community. In Russell Weigley's original treatment, the American way of war refers to the preferred strategy of attrition and overwhelming force. In this reading, Ulysses S. Grant's emphasis on destroying the Army of Northern Virginia and the application of US airpower in the strategic bombing of Axis cities in World War II embody an enduring American way of war.[60] Max Boot later claimed that the American way of industrial-based warfare shifted after the introduction of widespread precision targeting.[61] With respect to Germany, Robert Citino argued for a distinctly German way of war that was organized around offensive solutions to defensive vulnerabilities between the Thirty Years' War and the fall of the Third Reich.[62] Liddell Hart claimed that there was a distinct British way of war based on economic pressure exercised through sea control, mobility, and surprise.[63] In contrast to these arguments, we focus less on enduring national approaches and more on how interactions between political communities at a particular historical juncture creates an emergent character to warfare.[64]

This book approaches the changing character of war as an evolutionary (as opposed to revolutionary) phenomenon. How groups interact will determine the types of wars they plan for and fight. Our understanding of war as evolutionary builds on the tradition established by Knox MacGregor and Williamson Murray in which they differentiate between military revolutions, as epoch-defining changes, and lesser revolutions in military affairs. Revolutions in military affairs deal with "devising new ways" of countering an adversary.[65] For Knox and Murray, these smaller revolutions required "the assembly of a complete mix of tactical, organizational, doctrinal and technological innovations in order to implement a new conceptual approach to warfare."[66]

Larger military revolutions, connected to the defining features of specific historical periods, are beyond the scope of this book. Closely associated with these epochs and their respective interplay of economic, social, political, and technological forces are larger questions about the operative character of strategy in a given period. Like military revolutions, defining the changing character of grand strategy is beyond the scope of the current book. We simply want to pause, reflect on the changing character of war, and propose possible ways to adapt current force structure and operational concepts to reflect the human domain.

APPROACH: NETWORK POWER

We propose that the pathway to success in future population-centric conflicts lies in understanding the human domain as a network and mobilizing local populations through civil society, economic and political relationships, and the security sector to achieve a position of advantage often before the first shot is fired. Understanding and empowering local actors is a key objective in modern conflict. As Sun Tzu states in his first principles, "win all without fighting, achieving the objective without destroying it."[67]

These local actors exist within a broader web of networks constituting the human domain. Just as hilltops and restricted terrain define the land domain in a given area, the networks through which humans interact in a social system define the human domain. Just as important as the hilltops are the road networks, patterns of trade and social conventions regulating the circulation of goods and services in a population. How people connect defines the human domain.

This human domain is a meso-level configuration in any conflict zone.[68] It connects local and global networks. For example, during the Cold War, multiple conflicts saw political entrepreneurs connect local grievances with great powers seeking peripheral proxies. Literature on the political economy of conflict zones illustrates how local predatory politics connect with transnational illicit markets.[69]

The central idea is that networks define the human domain. These networks are concatenations of 1) actors (i.e., from individuals to kinship groups and organizations 2) their relational ties (e.g., economic activity, social patterns, migration, etc.), and 3) patterns of previous interactions as both formal and tacit rules (i.e., how history codifies meaning). [70] Understanding the human domain requires first mapping the emergent, complex system that results from how networks connect actors, generate incentives, and shape interests.

Networks shape the character of war. An increasingly connected, densely populated planet implies that the human domain is where limited wars and indirect conflicts will be won or lost. Social theorist Manual Castells observed that

> while networks are an old form of organization in the human experience, digital networking technologies, characteristic of the Information Age, powered social and organizational networks in ways that allowed their endless expansion and reconfiguration, overcoming the traditional limitations of networking forms of organization to manage complexity beyond a certain size of the network.[71]

As seen in the Arab Spring, Ukrainian Maidan uprising, and previous Color Revolutions in Georgia and Ukraine, local resistance movements can form rapidly and challenge even powerful, coercive states. For example, Maria Stephan and Erica Chenoweth found that nonviolent campaigns were successful 53 percent of time owing in part to their ability to connect a broad array of actors to "enhance [their] domestic and international legitimacy and encourage more broad-based participation in the resistance."[72]

The idea of thinking about warfare as being waged between competing networks has its roots in earlier efforts to conceptualize conflict after the

Cold War. John Arquilla and David Ronfeldt introduced the concept of netwar to examine how non-traditional actors from terrorists, criminals, and activists challenged nation-states. [73] According to Arquilla and Ronfeldt:

> The term we coined was netwar, largely because it resonated with the surety that the information revolution favored the rise of network forms of organization, doctrine, and strategy. Through netwar, numerous dispersed small groups using the latest communications technologies could act conjointly across great distances. We had in mind actors as diverse as transnational terrorists, criminals, and even radical activists.[74]

Power, force, coercion, and persuasion take on different meanings when viewed through the lens of networks. Whereas the object of conflict is still to impose your will on the adversary, how you approach this task is a function of the networks connecting actors. These sets of relationships offer different opportunities for leverage and influence. According to Manual Castells, "in a world of networks, the ability to exercise control over others depends on ... the ability to constitute networks ... and the ability to connect and ensure the cooperation of different networks ... while fending off competition from other networks."[75]

The density of network connections in the modern world enables individuals and small groups to engage in strategic competition. These new, diffused powers usurp conventional state control and institutions.[76] Consider megacities. [77] While global cities in the North coordinate complex global economic activity, many megacities in the South—with few global functions and less controls—are experiencing an accelerated growth of informal settlements (commonly known as slums). In these under governed areas, community-based organizations and civil society organizations rise to build communal resilience in the absence of the state.[78] These self-organizing groups are threatened by malign organizations competing to mobilize the population. Military practitioners must gain a better understanding of these interactions and civil society to prevent, or if necessary, prevail in future conflicts.

Seeing the human domain as networks changes how one understands military operations and the use of power. Rather than viewing military operations singularly as the application of force against a discrete, physical object, we propose focusing on enabling friendly and disrupting adversary networks of influence in the human domain. To use Robert Dahl's conceptualization, power—to include military power—is a relation among people.[79] Drawing on Manuel Castells work on networks, we propose developing an operational concept for the human domain based on two types of network power:[80]

- *Networking power:* the capacity for influence that flows from connections between actors, to include influencing which connections form and disrupting other relationships.
- *Network-making power:* the capacity for influence that results from generating rules and standards (i.e., protocols) governing which actors connect and how they interact.

The goal is to understand the population and catalyze the formation of emergent networks that promote stability and provide access for future operations. The military, alongside other interagency actors, should create focal points for coordination that preface local relationships and local solutions.[81] The military becomes a coordinating agent more than an imposing force. From persuasion and positive inducements to more traditional threats of violence (i.e., coercion) and the use of force,[82] military actors generate a broad menu of options but seek to apply their influence indirectly and with a careful eye on how their actions affect relationships within the human domain.

Actors can employ networking and network-making power indirectly. This idea of taking an indirect approach to mobilizing local actors is consistent with the writings of Sun Tzu and Liddell Hart.[83] In seeking to mobilize these networks in support of strategic competition and warfighting, the proposed concept fits within the larger idea of Unified

Land Operations espoused by the US Army and its emphasis presenting the adversary with multiple dilemmas.[84] Our proposed concept also provides a framework for globally integrated operations as envisioned by the 2012 Capstone Concept for Joint Operations (CCJO). An operational design that prefaces network power in the human domain offers a focal point for integrating capabilities across "domains, echelons, geographic boundaries and organizational affiliations."[85]

NOTES

1. Secretary of Defense Robert M. Gates, "Militarization of Foreign Policy," (speech), July 15, 2008, U.S. Global Leadership Campaign, Washington, DC, http://www.africom.mil/newsroom/transcript/6258/transcript-us-defense-secretary-gates-warns-agains.

2. Alfred von Schlieffen, *Cannae* (Fort Leavenworth, KS: Command and General Staff School Press, 1931), vii, http://usacac.army.mil/cac2/cgsc/carl/download/csipubs/cannae.pdf.

3. For a discussion on Boyd's use of ancient history, see Major Richard M. Fournier, *Boyd and the Past: A look at the Utility of Ancient History in the Development of Modern Theories of Warfare* (Fort Leavenworth: KS: School of Advanced Military Studies, 2013), http://www.dtic.mil/dtic/tr/fulltext/u2/a583870.pdf. For Boyd's papers, including the referenced "Patterns of Conflict" brief, see http://www.dnipogo.org/boyd/patterns_ppt.pdf.

4. We thank Brigadier General William Bowers (USMC) for highlighting the importance of this example.

5. Titus Livius Livy, *The War with Hannibal* (New York: Penguin Books, 1965), 98.

6. Vanda Felbab-Brown, "Blood and hope in Afghanistan: A June 2015 update," Brookings Institute, May 26, 2015, http://www.brookings.edu/research/papers/2015/05/26-isis-taliban-afghanistan-felbabbrown.

7. Brandon Valeriano, Benjamin Jensen, and Ryan Maness, *Cyber Strategy: The Evolving Character of Power and Coercion* (New York: Oxford University, 2018).

8. On the concept of war amongst the people, see Rupert Smith, *The Utility of Force: The Art of War in the Modern Age* (New York: Vintage Press, 2008). On how global integration shapes patterns of competition and conflict, see Parag Khanna, *Connectography: Mapping the Future of Global Civilization* (New York: Random House, 2016); Thomas P.M. Barnett, *The Pentagon's New Map: War and Peace in the Twenty-First Century* (New York: Penguin, 2005); and Immanuel Wallerstein, *The Modern World-System: Capitalist Agriculture and the Origins of the European World-Economy in the Sixteenth Century* (New York: Academic Press, 1974).

9. JP 1-02, *Department of Defense Dictionary of Military and Associated Terms* (Arlington: Joint Chiefs of Staff, November 8, 2010 (as amended

through November 15, 2015). Note that while space is commonly referred to as a domain, Joint Doctrine technically defines it as an "environment" (JP 1-02, p. 224, JP 3-59).

10. For an account of the emergence of the air domain and its relationship with military innovation, see Williamson Murray and Alan Millet, *Military Innovation in the Interwar Period* (New York: Cambridge University Press, 1998).

11. JP 1-02, 98.

12. Department of Defense, *Joint Operational Access Concept (JOAC)* (Arlington: Department of Defense, January 2012), ii.

13. Smith, *The Utility of Force.*

14. Valery Gerasimov, "The Value of Science in Prediction," *Military-Industrial Kurier*, February 27, 2013, trans. Mark Galeotti, https://inmoscowsshadows.wordpress.com/2014/07/06/the-gerasimov-doctrine-and-russian-non-linear-war/.

15. Nadia Schadlow, "Peace and War: The Space Between," *War on the Rocks*, August 18, 2014, https://warontherocks.com/2014/08/peace-and-war-the-space-between/.

16. On the concept of an indirect approach, see Liddell Hart, Basil Henry, and Basil Henry, Strategy (New York: Meridian, 1991). Of note, our usage here reflects a broader conceptualization and applies the concept of an indirect approach to competition beyond conventional military operations.

17. There is an extensive, evolving literature that explores how local dynamics fuel intrastate conflict. See Lars-Erik Cederman and Manuel Vogt, "Dynamics and Logics of Civil War," *Journal of Conflict Resolution* 61 no. 9 (2017): 1992–2016; Stathis N. Kalyvas "The Ontology of 'Political Violence': Action and Identity in Civil Wars," *Perspectives on Politics* 1, no. 3 (September 2003): 475–494; James D. Fearon and David D. Laitin, "Ethnicity, Insurgency and Civil War," *American Political Science Review* 97, no. 1 (February 2003): 75–90; Scott Gates, "Recruitment and Allegiance : The Microfoundations of Rebellion," *Journal of Conflict Resolution* 20 (2002): 111–130; Macartan Humphreys and Jeremy M Weinstein "Who Fights? The Determinants of Participation in Civil War," *American Journal of Political Science* 52, no. 2 (April 2008): 436–455; Lars-Erik Cederman, Andreas Wimmer, and Brian Min "Why Do Ethnic Groups Rebel?: New Data and Analysis," *World Politics* 62, no. 1 (January 2010): 87–11; Paul Staniland "Organizing Insurgency: Networks, Resources and Rebellion in South Asia," *International Security* 37, no. 1 (Summer 2012): 142–

177; Séverine Autesserre, *The Trouble with the Congo: Local Violence and the Failure of International Peacebuilding* (New York: Cambridge University Press, 2010): Fotini Christia, *Alliance Formation in Civil Wars* (New York: Cambridge University Press, 2013); Jeremy Weinstein, *Inside Rebellion: The Politics of Insurgent Violence* (New York: Cambridge University Press, 2006); Ana Arjona, Nelson Kasfir, and Zachariah Mampilly, eds., *Rebel Governance in Civil War* (New York: Cambridge University Press, 2015); Kristin Bakke, Kathleen Gallagher Cunningham, and Lee J.M. Seymour, "A Plague of Initials: Fragmentation, Cohesion, and Infighting in Civil Wars," *Perspectives on Politics* 10, no. 2 (June 2012): 265–284; Francisco Gutierrez Sanin, "Telling the Difference: Guerillas and Paramilitaries in the Colombian Civil War," *Politics & Society* 36, no. 1 (March 2008): 3–34.

18. Mary Ellen Connell and Ryan Evans, "Russia's 'Ambiguous Warfare' and Implications for the U.S. Marine Corps," Center for Naval Analysis, May 2015, https://www.cna.org/CNA_files/PDF/DOP-2015-U-010447-Final.pdf.

19. Frank Hoffman and Michael C. Davies "Joint Force 2020 and the Human Domain: Time for a New Conceptual Framework?" *Small Wars Journal* (June 10, 2013), http://smallwarsjournal.com/jrnl/art/joint-force-2020-and-the-human-domain-time-for-a-new-conceptual-framework.

20. Dorothy Denning, "Rethinking the Cyber Domain and Deterrence," *Joint Forces Quarterly* 77 (2nd Quarter 2015): 9.

21. Richard Hooker and Joseph Collins, eds., *Lessons Encountered: Learning from the Long War* (Washington: National Defense University Press, 2015), 11.

22. Linda Robinson, Paul D. Miller, John Gordon IV, Jeffrey Decker, Michael Schwille, and Raphael S. Cohen, *Improving Strategic Competence: Lessons from Thirteen Years of War* (Santa Monica: RAND Arroyo Center, 2014).

23. Ibid., ix.

24. The Joint Staff J7, *Decade of War, Volume 1: Enduring Lessons from the Past Decade of Operations* (Suffolk: Joint and Coalition Operational Analysis, 2012), 3.

25. Defense Science Board, *Understanding Human Dynamics* (Washington: Office of the Secretary of Defense for Acquisitions, Technology and Logistics, 2009), 4.

26. Raymond T. Odierno, James F. Amos, and William H. McCraven, *Strategic Landpower: Winning the Clash of Wills*, Army Capabilities

and Integration Center, May 6, 2013, http://www.arcic.army.mil/app_
Documents/Strategic-Landpower-White-Paper-28OCT2013.pdf.

27. Robert Brown, quoted in J.M. Simpson, "Lt. Gen. Brown's Unique
Perspective on War: Lunch with Sun Tzu," Northwest Military.com,
November 26, 2013, http://www.northwestmilitary.com/news/military-
policy/2013/11/lieutenant-general-browns-unique-perspective-on-war/.

28. Odierno, Amos, and McCraven, *Strategic Landpower.*

29. John Schmidt, "A Practical Guide for Developing and Writing Military
Concepts," *Defense Adaptive Red Team Working Paper #02-4* (McClean,
VA: Hicks and Associates, December 2002), 7.

30. General Donn Starry, *Commander's Notes No. 3 – Operational Concepts
and Doctrine* (Fort Monroe, VA: Army Training and Doctrine Command,
1979), 1–2.

31. For an example of concept development and doctrinal change as catalysts of doctrinal development, see Benjamin Jensen, *Forging the Sword:
Doctrinal Change in the U.S. Army* (Palo Alto: Stanford University Press,
2016).

32. Carl von Clausewitz, *On War*, ed. and trans. by Michael Howard and
Peter Paret (Princeton: Princeton University Press, 1989).

33. Stephen Peter Rosen, "Net Assessment as an Analytical Concept,'" in
On Not Confusing Ourselves edited by Andrew W. Marshall, J.J. Martin,
and Henry Rowen (Boulder: Westview Press, 1991), 290. For an overview
of net assessment as a practice, see Thomas Mahnken, ed., *Competitive
Strategies in the 21st Century: Theory, History, and Practice* (Palo Alto:
Stanford University Press, 2012); Andrew Krepinevich and Barry Watts,
*The Last Warrior: Andrew Marshall and the Shaping of Modern American
Defense Strategy* (New York: Basic Books, 2015); Andrew Marshall, "The
Problems of Estimating Military Power," RAND Corporation, August
1966, https://www.rand.org/content/dam/rand/pubs/papers/2005/P341
7.pdf; Elliot Cohen, "Net Assessment: An American Approach," *JCSS
Memorandum No. 29* (Tel Aviv: Jaffee Center, April 1990): 1–25; Thomas
M. Skypek, "Evaluating Military Balances Through the Lens of Net
Assessment: History and Application," *Journal of Military and Strategic
Studies* 12, issue 2 (Winter 2010): 1–25; and Paul Bracken "Net Assessment:
A Practical Guide," *Parameters* (Spring 2006): 90–100.

34. Elliot Cohen, "Net Assessment: An American Approach," *JCSS Memorandum No. 29* (Tel Aviv: Jaffee Center, April 1990): 1–25, esp. 7.
This concept originally derives from Andrew Marshall's seminal study

on military power. See Marshall, "Problems with Estimating Military Power."

35. Emergence is a concept from complex systems. For the relationship between modern research into complexity science and Clausewitz's treatment of war, see Alan Beyerchen, "Clausewitz, Nonlinearity and the Unpredictability of War," *International Security* 17, no. 3 (Winter 1992): 59–90. For the implications of complex systems for international relations, see Robert Jervis, *System Effects: Complexity in Political and Social Life* (Princeton: Princeton University Press, 1999) and Randall Schweller, *Maxwell's Demon and the Golden Apple: Global Discord in the New Millennium* (Baltimore: John Hopkins University Press, 2014).

36. William H. McNeill, *The Pursuit of Power* (Chicago: University of Chicago, 1982).

37. T.X. Hammes, *The Sling and the Stone: On War in the 21st Century* (New York: Zenith Press, 2006), i.

38. Antoine J. Bousquet, *The Scientific Way of Warfare: Order and Chaos on the Battlefields of Modernity* (New York: Columbia University Press, 2009); Antoine Bousquet "Chaoplexic Warfare or the Future of Military Organization," *International Affairs* 84, no. 5 (September 2008): 915–929.

39. For an overview of Moltke's major ideas in English, see Antulio EJ. Echevarria II "Moltke and the German Military Tradition: His Theories and Legacies," *Parameters* (Spring 1996): 91–99.

40. Jacob W. Kipp, "The Origins of Soviet Operational Art, 1917–1936" in *Historical Perspectives of the Operational Art*, edited by Michael D. Krause and R. Cody Phillips (Washington: Center of Military History, 2007).

41. J.F.C. Fuller, *The Foundations of the Science of War* (London: Hutchinson and Company, 1926).

42. Stephen Biddle, *Military Power: Explaining Victory and Defeat in Modern War* (Princeton: Princeton University Press, 2010).

43. General Gordon Sullivan first used the term in a 1992 speech at the Land Warfare Forum.

44. Mary Kaldor, *Old and New Wars: Organized Violence in a Global World* (Stanford University Press, 1999). For an overview of the "new wars" literature see Martin Shaw, "The Contemporary Mode of Warfare? Mary Kaldor's Theory of New Wars," *Review of International Political Economy* 7, issue 1 (Spring 2000): 171–180, and Mary Kaldor, "In Defence of New Wars," *Stability: International Journal of Security and Development* 2, issue 1 (2013): 4.

45. Robert D. Kaplan "The Coming Anarchy: How Scarcity, Crime, Over-population, Tribalism, and Disease Are Rapidly Destroying the Social Fabric of Our Planet," *The Atlantic*, February 1, 1994; Robert D. Kaplan *The Coming Anarchy: Shattering the Dreams of the Post-Cold War* (New York: Vintage Press, 2001).

46. Martin van Creveld, *The Transformation of War: The Most Radical Reinterpretation of Armed Conflict Since Clausewitz* (New York: Free Press, 1991).

47. John Arquilla and David Ronfeldt, *The Advent of Netwar* (Santa Monica: RAND Corporation, 1996) and *Networks and Netwars: The Future of Terror, Crime and Militancy* (Santa Monica: RAND Corporation, 2001).

48. Smith, *The Utility of Force.*

49. Unified Land Operations calls for enabling conflict resolution. Department of the Army, *ADRP 3-0, Unified Land Operations* (Washington: Department of the Army, May 2014).

50. The concept of competitive learning through contact is reminiscent of J.F.C. Fuller's concept of a constant tactical factor. The constant tactical factor is Fuller's term for the process of counteradaption to the introduction of new weapons and tactics. For a discussion see J.F.C. Fuller, *Armament and History: The Influence Of Armament On History From The Dawn Of Classical Warfare To The End Of The Second World War*, revised ed. (New York: De Capo Press, 1998) and Azar Gat, *A History of Military Thought: From the Enlightenment to the Cold War* (New York: Oxford University Press, 2002).

51. Colin S. Gray, *Modern Strategy* (New York: Oxford University Press, 1999), 97.

52. Andrew Mack, "Why Big Nations Lose Small Wars: The Politics of Asymmetric Conflict" *World Politics* 27 no. 2 (1975): 175–200

53. Gil Merom, *How Democracies Lose Small Wars* (New York: Cambridge University, 2003).

54. Stephen Rosen, "War Power and the Willingness to Suffer" in *Peace, War and Numbers*, edited by Bruce M. Russett (Beverly Hills: Sage Publications, 1972).

55. Ivan Arreguín-Toft "How the Weak Win Wars: A Theory of Asymmetric Conflict," *International Security* 26, no. 1 (Summer 2001): 93–128.

56. T.V. Paul, *Asymmetric Conflicts: War Initiation by Weaker Powers* (New York: Cambridge University Press, 1994).

57. Patricia Sullivan, *Who Wins: Predicting Strategic Success and Failure in Armed Conflict* (New York: Oxford University Press, 2012).

58. For an overview and how cyber is a form of political warfare, see Benjamin Jensen, "The Cyber Character of Political Warfare," *Brown Journal of International Affairs* 24, no. 1 (2017): 151–179.

59. The first usage of the term "gray zone" was National Defense Program Guidelines by the Japanese Ministry of Defense, December 17, 2013, http://www.mod.go.jp/j/approach/agenda/guideline/2014/pdf/20131217 _e2.pdf. The term was later adopted in U.S. defense circles to describe competition through proxies, cyber, and special forces beneath the threshold of interstate war. For a discussion of the gray zone as a strategic framework, see David Barno and Nora Bensahel, "Fighting and Winning in the Gray Zone," *War on the Rocks*, May 19, 2015, http://warontherocks.com/2015/05/fighting-and-winning-in-the-gray-zone/; Michael Mazarr, "Struggle in the Gray Zone and World Order," *War on the Rocks* December 22, 2015, http://warontherocks.com/2015/12/struggle-in-the-gray-zone-and-world-order/; Adam Elkus "50 Shades of Gray: Why the Gray Zone Concept Lacks Strategic Sense," *War on the Rocks*, December 15, 2015, http://warontherocks.com/2015/12/50-shades-of-gray-why-the-gray-wars-concept-lacks-strategic-sense/; and Nadia Schadlow "Peace and War: The Space Between" *War on the Rocks*, August 18, 2014, http://warontherocks.com/2014/08/peace-and-war-the-space-between/; and Antulio Echevarria "How Should We Think about "Gray-Zone" Wars?" *Infinity Journal* 5 issue 1 (Fall 2015): 16–20.

60. Russell Weigley, *The American Way of War* (Bloomington: Indiana University Press, 1977). For a description of an earlier, pre-industrial American way of war, see John Grenier, *The First Way of War: American War Making on the Frontier, 1607–1814* (New York: Cambridge University Press, 2005). For an analysis of a new American way of war brought on by the proliferation of precision targeting, see Max Boot, *War Made New: Weapons, Warriors, and the Making of the Modern* World (New York: Gotham Press, 2007).

61. Max Boot, "The New American Way of War," *Foreign Affairs* (July/August 2003).

62. Robert Citino, *The German Way of War: From the Thirty Years' War to the Third Reich* (Lawrence: University of Kansas Press, 2005).

63. Basil Henry Liddell Hart, *The British Way of Warfare* (London: Faber and Faber, 1932).

64. For an interesting contrast to both Max Boot and Russell Weigley, see Antulio Echeverria, *Reconsidering the American Way of War* (Washing-

ton: Georgetown University Press, 2014). In the work, Echeverria also challenges the idea of enduring national ways of war.

65. MacGregor Knox and Williamson Murray, eds., *The Dynamics of Military Revolutions 1300-2050* (New York: Cambridge University Press, 2001), 12.

66. Ibid.

67. We use the translation in Victor's H. Mair's *The Art of War: Sun Zu's Military Method* (New York: Columbia University Press, 2009). The standard translation in use by most military practitioners are Samuel Griffith's translation, *Art of War* (New York: Oxford University Press, 1971) and Ralph Sawyer's translation, *Art of War* (New York: Westview, 1971). Along with Mair's treatment, the best overview of Sun Tzu's military theory is Derrick Yuen, *Deciphering Sun Tzu: How to Read The Art of War* (New York: Oxford University Press, 2014).

68. This observation is consistent with Stathis Kalyvas's work on master cleavages in civil wars. See "The Ontology of 'Political Violence': Action and Identity in Civil Wars," *Perspectives on Politics* 1, no. 3 (September 2003): 475–494.

69. For examples of work in this area, see Michael Pugh and Neil Cooper, *War Economies in a Regional Context: The Challenge of Transformation* (Boulder: Lynne Reinner, 2004).

70. This definition of a network is based on work in network sociology. For an overview, see Barry Wellman and S.D. Berkowitz, *Social Structures: A Network Approach* (New York: Cambridge University Press, 1988); Harrison White, *Identity and Control: A Structural Theory of Social Action* (Princeton: Princeton University Press, 1992); and Stanley Wasserman and Katherine Faust, *Social Network Analysis: Methods and Applications* (New York: Cambridge University Press, 1994).

71. Manuel Castells, *The Rise of Network Society: The Information Age: Economy, Society, and Culture* (New York: Wiley Blackman, 2009), xviii.

72. Maria J. Stephan and Erica Chenoweth "Why Civil Resistance Works: The Strategic Logic of Nonviolent Conflict," *International Security* 33, no. 1 (Summer 2008): 8.

73. Arquilla and Ronfeldt, *The Advent of Netwar*.

74. John Arquilla and David Ronfeldt, *Networks and Netwars: The Future of Terror, Crime, and Militancy* (Santa Monica: Rand Corporation, 2001), 2.

75. Manuel Castells, *Communication Power* (New York: Oxford University Press, 2009), 43. For an analysis of modern warfare through Castells' social theory, see David Blair, "Any Time, Every Place: The Networked

Societies of Warfighters in a Battlespace of Flows" (unpublished working paper, 2014).

76. Moses Naim, *The End of Power: From Boardrooms to Battlefields and Churches to States, Why Being in Charge Isn't What It Used to Be* (New York: Basic Books, 2013).

77. David Kilcullen, *Out of the Mountains: The Coming Age of the Urban Guerrilla* (New York: Oxford University Press, 2015); U.S. Army Strategic Studies Group, *Megacities and the United States Army: Preparing for a Complex and Uncertain Future* (Arlington: Headquarters, Department of the Army, 2014); and Douglas E. Batson "A First Look: Disaster Management Challenges in Lagos, Nigeria," *Homeland Defense & Security Information Analysis Center Journal* 2, no. 3 (Fall 2015): 9–16.

78. For an overview of the relationship between local resiliency and information technology, see Steven Livingston and Gregor Walter-Drop, *Bits and Atoms: Information and Communication Technology in Areas of Limited Statehood* (New York: Oxford University Press, 2014).

79. Robert A. Dahl, "The Concept of Power," *Behavioral Science* 2, no. 3 (July 1957): 202.

80. Manual Castells, "A Network Theory of Power," *International Journal of Communication* 5 (2011): 773–787. The definitions here merge Castells larger taxonomy.

81. The concept of focal points was first introduced by Thomas Schelling. See *Strategy of Conflict* (repr., Cambridge: Harvard University Press, 1981) and *Micromotives and Macrobehavior* (New York: W.W. Norton & Company, 2006 revised reprint). Robert Axelrod also demonstrates how even competitive interactions can develop cooperative equilibrium points; see *The Evolution of Cooperation* (New York: Basic Books, 1984) and *The Complexity of Cooperation: Agent-Based Models of Competition and Collaboration* (Princeton: Princeton University Press, 1997).

82. The concept of rational persuasion, manipulative persuasion, inducement, power, coercion, and physical force is derived from Robert Dahl's work. Other key works on power that inform the study are Anthony Giddens, *The Constitution of Society. Outline of the Theory of Structuration* (Cambridge: Cambridge University Press, 1982); Michel Foucault, *Discipline & Punish: The Birth of the Prison*, 2nd ed. (New York: Vintage Books, 1995); James Scott, *Weapons of the Weak: Everyday Forms of Peasant* (New Haven: Yale University Press, 1987); and Antonio Gramsci and Joseph A. Buttigieg, trans., *The Prison Notebooks* (New York: Columbia University Press, 2011).

83. B.H. Liddell Hart, *Strategy*, revised ed. (New York: Plume, 1991). For an overview of Sun Tzu's theory of war, see *Deciphering Sun Tzu* by Yuen and *The Art of War* by Mair.

84. ADRP 3-0, *Operations* (Arlington: Headquarters, Department of the Army, 2012), http://armypubs.army.mil/doctrine/DR_pubs/dr_a/pdf/adrp3_0. pdf; on the idea of presenting multiple dilemmas, see TRADOC Pamp 525-3.1, *The Army Operating Concept: Winning in a Complex World* (Fort Eustis: TRADOC, 2014), http://www.tradoc.army.mil/tpubs/pams/TP5 25-3-1.pdf.

85. Chairman of the Joint Chiefs of Staff, *Capstone Concept for Joint Operations* (Arlington: Department of Defense, 2012), iii.

CHAPTER 2

THE LAST WAR

Military practitioners use the phrase "lessons learned" to describe the process of synthesizing disparate experiences of wars into a theory of victory. Individuals learn from experience. As they interact with their environment, it produces signals that either confirm or deny existing organizational practices. The process is noisy, messy, and prone to conflicting discourses as competing voices seek to define what the military should learn, and through these arguments, recommend concepts and capabilities for shaping the future force.

The US military is currently in a complex process of distilling what happened, or should have happened, in the continuous war that followed September 11, 2001. This process of discovery and proclamation is captured in the lessons-learned literature, a corpus that encompasses thousands of books and articles and a myriad of voices, from senior military leadership to the heart of an army, its rank and file soldiers.

While some of the lessons of the long war have been quickly learned and assimilated in contemporary military doctrine, others have challenged prevailing norms and prompted a reexamination of the foundations of American military culture, American civil-military relations, and the character of contemporary conflict itself. This chapter explores this search for meaning in the profession of arms and uses it to map the changing character of war. The intent is not to assess the accuracy of individual accounts. Rather, the goal is to take stock of the range of perspectives on how US forces performed in Iraq and Afghanistan and also how the institution reacted—or learned organizationally—from these performances and to extract major cross-cutting themes from the work. This provides insights into the importance of mapping human geography and constructing a global security architecture built around networks. In this, the chapter is limited to lessons from intrastate conflict, the most likely threat, as opposed to great-power conflict, the most dangerous threat and primary driver of defense spending.

Exploring the lessons-learned literature reveals that while there was constant learning and adaptions to changing conditions at the tactical level, the military, if not its political masters, faced difficulty translating these lessons into strategic outcomes. This difficulty tended to involve, among other things, a failure to understand the human domain and transform these insights into clear political objectives.

CHANGE IS EASY, LEARNING IS HARD

Over the last forty years, it has become conventional wisdom that organizations can and do learn.[1] This learning is overwhelmingly driven by the recognized need for change. Within the military profession, practitioners search for ways to generate organizational change that balance current experience and historical lessons. To change, organizations assess these insights to adapt culture, routines, and processes to thrive in dynamic environments.[2] Organizational learning, which begins with individuals inside the organization, becomes incorporated into the organization through a variety of mechanisms, such as doctrine, processes, and education. Through this process of organizational learning, entities survive shock and adapt to new and different circumstances. Those organizations, especially military organizations, that do not learn are subject to battlefield, if not strategic, defeat.

However, organizational learning is not a given. It occurs unevenly, if at all, and is dependent on multiple factors and characteristics to succeed. Research into military learning constitutes a significant subset of the organizational learning scholarship. Scholars have considered multiple cases of military innovation and adaptation in both peace and war, attempting to find the principal drivers of success and failure.[3] Although individual authors emphasize different variables, their conclusions overlap. Put simply, the condition of war will produce incentives for adaption (i.e., single-loop learning) but organizations face difficulty translating these accumulated lessons into new theories of victory (i.e., double-loop learning). Change is fleeting without deeper introspection, which is the purpose of this book and our call for developing strategies to achieve a position of advantage in the human domain.

There are important questions about the factors that act as catalysts for change and whether these engines of adaption are internal or external to the military. In *Learning to Eat Soup With a Knife,* John Nagl contrasts the British military experience in Malaya with that of the US military during the Vietnam War. He emphasizes the importance of institutional memory, arguing that it constitutes the "conventional wisdom" of the organization about how to perform its tasks missions and functions.[4] These ideas find parallels in Benjamin Jensen's study on military innovation in the US Army after Vietnam. Changes in operational doctrine required institutional mechanisms that allowed soldiers to reimagine war removed from the iron cage of bureaucracy (i.e., incubators) and disseminate the ideas throughout the ranks (i.e., advocacy networks).[5]

Where these accounts chart the internal struggle of military professionals seeking to adapt, other authors see external failures as the catalyst for change. In *The Sources of Military Doctrine,* Barry Posen argues that military organizations are inherently conservative and thus will seldom "innovate autonomously."[6] As a result, he argues that military innovation occurs when the organization has endured a significant failure and an external civilian authority exerts pressure on the organization.[7] In *Winning the Next War,* Stephen Rosen differentiates between the drivers of learning in peacetime versus wartime. He argues that military innovation only occurs in wartime, as a result of "an inappropriate strategic goal being pursued or because the relationship between military operations and that goal have been misunderstood."[8] This insight echoes the seminal claim by earlier organizational theorists that "the rate of innovation is likely to increase when change in the environment make the existing organizational procedures unsatisfactory."[9] Thus, for Rosen, innovation in wartime is a direct result of initial failure often connected to a misalignment of ends-ways-means beyond the military.[10]

In addition to institutions, professional experience, and external threats, scholars locate the source of change in culture. Dima Adamsky finds cultural antecedents as the determining factor for how different countries responded to the "Revolution in Military Affairs."[11] Elizabeth Kier sees organizational culture as shaping French and British military doctrine in the interwar period.[12] Williamson Murray emphasizes the importance of culture in his large corpus of work on military learning and innovation. In "Military Culture Does Matter," Murray observes that "it may be the most important factor not only in military effectiveness on the battlefield, but in the processes of innovation during times of peace."[13]

In *Mars Adapting: Winning the War You're In,* Frank Hoffman argues that a military's ability to learn is contingent on four factors: leadership, organizational culture, learning mechanisms, and dissemination mechanisms. Specifically, Hoffman believes that to adapt, military leadership must be decentralized, operate using a "mission command" approach and be open-minded. Further, he maintains that the organizational culture must be neither hierarchically dominated nor doctrinally rigid, and must support lower-level (tactical) learning within it, as well as analysis and experimentation. Finally, according to Hoffman, to truly learn, a military must have both formal and informal information channels, as well as horizontal and vertical dissemination of learning.[14] For Hoffman, each of these factors must be present to some degree for military adaptation and learning to occur.

From these works, one can derive three broad catalysts for military learning. These are: 1) an internal reaction to a large shock or failure, 2) external pressure that overcomes the inherent conservatism of military culture, and finally 3) change driven internally by a "maverick" or visionary military leader. Each of these drivers can be found within the lessons-learned literature in Iraq and Afghanistan, yet we are left with only tactical adaptions and not significant military change.

The question then is what explains the absence of change despite the necessary catalysts? There certainly were localized changes, from human-terrain teams and key leader-engagement plans, and operational-level adaptions, such as the counterinsurgency manual. Yet, these initiatives have faded into the background as the military shifts back to focusing on conventional combat against near-peer competitors and the global pursuit mission associated with high-value individual targeting and counterterrorism.

The absence of enduring change appears to be partially explained by double-loop learning. The organizational learning literature differentiates between single-loop and double-loop learning. These concepts, developed in the 1970s by Chris Argyris and Donald Schon, are critical to understanding the nuances of the lessons-learned literature. Single-loop learning describes incremental learning where the objective is to fix problems within the current organizational structure.[15] Double-loop learning, in contrast, involves "changes in values and frames and calls for reflective inquiry that cuts across incongruent frames."[16] As a result, double-loop learning alters the system itself. It can result in changes in values and norms, as well as fundamental assumptions and preferred strategies.

Both types of learning are present within the military innovation literature. However, double-loop learning, which often entails significant change in organizational structure and culture, tends to be rare. In his study of learning within the German Army, Max Visser concludes that in war single-loop learning is common provided the chain of command is open-minded while double-loop learning is extremely uncommon, if not impossible, in combat units.[17] In *Mars Adapting,* Hoffman investigates what he calls the "institutional dialectic" of military adaptation. He explores case studies that show while single-loop learning is relatively common within the military, for double-loop learning to occur, top-down support, from either the highest levels of the military or from outside the military, is a necessary precondition.[18]

Furthermore, these lessons often require historical roots to resonate within a conservative military profession bound by tradition and rituals, as well as prone to accept historical claims over other sources of knowledge. This reliance, while justifiable, is often abused as leaders cherry pick different cases to justify their preferred institutional change. In "Lessons of History and Lessons of Vietnam," David Petraeus cautions, "it is important to recognize that history can mislead and obfuscate as well as guide and illuminate."[19] In "Military History: Is it Still Practicable?" Jay Luvaas observes that the military has a penchant for "scan[ning] the past for the magical formula that may ensure success in war."[20]

Despite this, neither Luvaas nor Petraeus dismiss the utility of history as a vehicle for military organizational learning. Rather, they argue that the best way to make history practicable is to understand what individuals were thinking when faced with particular situations.[21] Further, Murray observes that "few military organizations study the past with any rigor, although the success of those that do so has demonstrated its vital importance."[22] In his seminal lecture "The Use and Abuse of Military History," Sir Michael Howard warns against the use of history for "myth-making" and crafting historical accounts deliberately to underpin belief systems.[23] That said, Howard ultimately decides in favor of the use of history as a tool for military learning, believing that finding out *what really happened* outweighs the associated risks of incorrectly learning from history. The study of history, when done correctly, allows the military profession to understand continuity and change in context, and as a result, better understand their assigned missions.[24]

Historical accounts therefore tend to be fluid as the military profession searches for meaning. This dynamic is heightened by the stress and uncertainty of combat. Therefore, military organizations in war will likely see constant adaptions, what J.F.C. Fuller called the constant tactical factor, that fail to produce enduring institutional change (i.e., double-loop learning). They will speculate and experiment but fail to learn. Military professionals will mobilize competing historical claims as they articulate competing visions of warfare. Unless the institution is able to find a way to reconcile these competing claims and synthesize a new theory of victory, the myriad adaptions will fade away as the profession returns to its core missions. This observation is evident in the lessons-learned literature on Iraq and Afghanistan.

WHAT WE LEARNED IN THE LONG WAR: PEOPLE AND NETWORKS

Reading across the lessons-learned literature from Iraq and Afghanistan shows a profession, and larger ecosystem of observers, changing its understanding of the inherent challenges in military operations. Finding the enemy proved more difficult than finishing the fight. The friction of battle paled in comparison to the friction of local politics and the intersecting and ever-changing web of interests that motivated opposition to US interests. Key terrain was not just a hill with good fields of fire. It was often a relationship brokered between the military and a network of influencers, revealing social, economic, and political interests that were causing unrest.

Accounts of these wars fall broadly into three categories of lessons that overlap the ideal-typical levels of war: strategic, operational, and tactical. Strategic lessons reside at the highest levels of the government and military. At the strategic level, "policy planning and coordination happens, dominated by the dynamics of the national capital."[25] Strategic lessons involve decision-making about policy and political objectives shaping the conduct of the military operations as well as how bureaucracy distorts the process. Strategic lessons actually learned and institutionalized are likely to be the product of double-loop learning and involve substantial change in the national security enterprise and its culture. By connecting multiple constituencies, from policymakers to diplomats and senior military leaders, these lessons produce foundational assumptions about the military instrument of power and, under what circumstances a state can use military forces to achieve political objectives.

The other levels are more organic to the military. Operational lessons learned occur in theater, often within warfighting headquarters. These lessons and accounts generally concern the conduct of campaigns and military operations and form the intellectual bridge between top-down and the bottom-up learning. They can entail either single- or double-loop learning. Tactical lessons are those that occur on the ground, at the lowest levels. These constitute the individual accounts of soldiers, junior officers, and reporters embedded with units in the field.

Many of the accounts considered in this chapter are cross-cutting in nature. Further, many of them consider the interplay of one or more organizations during wartime. The intertwining of strategic and tactical lessons learned stands out in the accounts to follow. The long war appears to highlight a trend towards strategic compression, as the strategic and tactical collide. This compression is a result of the particularly localized political character of contemporary campaigns involving states, non-state actors, proxies, and other interlocutors. While all war is a continuation of politics by other means, wars amongst the people involve a larger number of political interests and therefore tend to have more complex relationships across the levels of war. A large number of the lessons learned in the current wars also involve intergovernmental exchanges with partners and allies, as well as interagency and interservice exchanges. That is, the lessons involve building a network that allows you to navigate and understand local, as well as coalitional, politics and maneuver accordingly. As a result, binning them cleanly is sometimes difficult. Nevertheless, the method is useful for extracting and analyzing major themes.

In his work, *Harsh Lessons: Iraq, Afghanistan and the Changing Character of War*, Benjamin Barry sorts the major lessons of the past wars using the same three level methodology. He argues that in both Iraq and Afghanistan, senior leaders came "extremely close to strategic defeat" due to multiple factors including, "inadequate leadership, reconstruction efforts, political strategy, military strategy and operational concepts, tactics and equipment."[26] For Barry, the fact that the US and its allies did not suffer strategic defeat in both cases demonstrates that learning was occurring at all levels, although perhaps not quickly enough to prevent near catastrophic setbacks.

Throughout the work, several major themes emerge. First, Barry highlights the increasingly political character of modern war, even at the tactical level.[27] Second, he emphasizes the need for influence in addition to kinetic war fighting. He states that "achieving influence is likely to be an increasingly important part of operations-in some cases as much or more than destroying enemies and seizing terrain."[28] Despite this admonition, he also observes that there was more "dismounted close combat" occurring than anyone was originally prepared for.[29] Finally, he comments repeatedly on the lack of unity of command and unity of effort throughout both theaters and at all levels from the alliance/national level to tactical units on the ground. Although he does acknowledge that it improved over time, Barry points to this lack of unity as an ongoing problem for coalition forces.[30]

In 2014, The RAND Corporation published, "Improving Strategic Competence: Lessons From 13 Years of War." In it the authors identified seven key lessons learned at the strategic level:

- US national security strategy suffers from a lack of understanding in the application of strategic art;
- An integrated civil-military process is a necessary but not a sufficient condition of effective national security strategy;
- Because military operations take place in the political environment of the state in which the intervention takes place, military campaigns must be based on a political strategy;
- Because of the inherently human and uncertain nature of war, technology cannot substitute for sociocultural, political, and historical knowledge and understanding;
- Interventions should not be conducted without a plan to execute stability operations, capacity-building, transition, and, if necessary, counterinsurgency;
- Shaping, influence and unconventional operations may be cost-effective ways of addressing the conflict that obviate the need for larger, costlier interventions; and,
- The joint force requires nonmilitary and multinational partners, as well as coordinated implementation among agencies, allies and international organizations.[31]

From these lessons, the RAND investigators develop two key conclusions. First, they argue that warfare has evolved beyond traditional high-intensity state versus state combat towards irregular conflicts involving non-state actors. Second, they assert that while the US Army learns both tactically and operationally, it struggles with larger, strategic implications and has difficulty adapting as a result.[32] In other words, the military struggles to turn battlefield adaptations (i.e., single-loop learning) into a larger theory of victory (i.e., double-loop learning).

Lessons that emphasize understanding local politics, building better partnerships, and engaging in difficult-to-measure influence campaigns (versus easy-to-measure targeted killing) tend to get stalled in the bureaucracy. Large budgets built around weapons systems designed for major theater war pull programs and budgets away from the human domain, a process accelerated by a mix of industry and congressional interests in big-ticket items. Training and education defaults to institutional memory and embedded preferences for joint combined arms and major contingencies against states, which in the case of China are some of the United States' largest trading partners. These reflections are speculation at this point as the causes of a failure of double-loop learning are outside the scope of the book. Yet, one can see a range of interests likely to limit the institutionalization of lessons learned that emphasize mapping human domain and local political interests and building the right networks required to achieve a position of relative advantage.

The failure to understand local political interests and how to translate these insights into influence operations and building partnership networks is echoed in other studies. In 2012, The Joint Coalition and Operational Analysis Center (JCOA), an entity of the US Joint Staff, published "Decade of War: Enduring Lessons From The Past Decade of Operations." This study is particularly noteworthy as it constitutes an amalgamation of forty-six studies conducted by JCOA during the first decade of combat after 9/11. The report outlined eleven strategic themes that emerged during the decade including:

- A failure to recognize, acknowledge, and accurately define the operational environment;
- Conventional warfare approaches often were ineffective when applied to operations other than major combat, forcing leaders to realign their ways and means of achieving effects;
- The US was slow to recognize the importance of information and the battle for the narrative in achieving objectives at all level; it was often ineffective in applying and aligning the narrative to goals and desired end-states;
- Failure to plan adequately and resource strategic and operational transitions endangered the accomplishment of the overall mission;
- Department of Defense (DOD) policies, doctrine, training, and equipment were often poorly suited to operations other than major combat, forcing widespread and costly adaptation;

- Multiple, simultaneous, large-scale operations executed in dynamic environments required the integration of general-purpose and special-operations forces, creating a force-multiplying effect for both;

- Interagency coordination was uneven due to inconsistent participation in planning, training, and operations, in addition to policy gaps, resource allocation, and differences in organizational cultures;

- Establishing and sustaining coalition unity of effort was a challenge due to competing national interests, cultures, resources, and policies;

- Partnering was a key enabler and force multiplier, and aided host-nation capacity building that was not always effectively executed nor adequately prioritized and resourced;

- States sponsored and exploited surrogates and proxies produced asymmetric challenges;

- Individuals and small groups exploited globalized technology and information to expand influence and approach state-like disruptive capacity. [33]

In 2015, National Defense University's in-house think tank, the Institute for National Strategic Studies (INSS), published its own compilation of the major lessons of fifteen years of war entitled *Lessons Encountered: Learning From The Long War.* As with the works already discussed, this effort also concluded that strategic lessons were the hardest for the US national security community to learn.[34] The work broke the lessons encountered out thematically, examining national-level decision-making, unity of effort/command, intelligence and information, security force assistance, and legal issues.

The conclusions largely echo those in previously discussed works. Specifically, the authors conclude that at the national level, politicians must better appreciate the complexities of military planning, while military leaders must be more willing to discuss the political linkages and implications of their military advice.[35] With regard to unity of effort and unity of command, the authors observed that both were continuing problems throughout the wars. They considered unity-of-effort challenges between the US military and the interagency, as well as between US and coalition partners and even within different US military units.[36] The authors were also particularly scathing about the overall quality of the intelligence effort in both theaters, stating that "neither national nor military intelligence in Iraq and Afghanistan was successful in supporting decision makers."[37]

Our effort here continues to build a comprehensive picture of the difficulty the US government and US military encountered in recognizing and inculcating strategic lessons learned in both wars. More importantly for this study, one starts to see the outline of the fundamental problem in war amongst the people: understanding local interests in terms of political objectives and building the right types of partnerships to influence key stakeholders in a manner that limits your adversaries' ability to mobilize support.

The importance of understanding human relationships and interests extends to other accounts as well. Anand Gopal's 2015 account of the war in Afghanistan, *No Good Men Among the Living: America, the Taliban, and the War Through Afghan Eyes,* offers a portrait of the war through the eyes of three Pashtuns. The book highlights how US policymakers and military officers failed to appreciate the complexity of local alliances prone to shift. [38] In particular, this lack of knowledge led the United States to rely on corrupt local leaders and warlords. In Gopal's account, this failure to understand local dynamics also led US Forces to not appreciate the full extent of popular anger over civilian casualties and night raids. Similarly, a lack of contextual knowledge left US forces susceptible to manipulation. In Gopal's account, rival groups fed US forces false information in an effort to settle disputes and dispose of their opponents. The combined result was a popular backlash against US forces seen as backing a corrupt regime. Gopal's work demonstrates how these challenges produced a series of tactical and strategic failures.

In *The Endgame: The Inside Struggle for Iraq from George W. Bush to Barack Obama,* Michael Gordon and Bernard E. Trainor argue that the surge decision in Iraq was a strategic success.[39] They also discuss how tactical units were able to cut deals with local warlords in a manner that created the space for the troop surge and counterinsurgency campaigns to work. In addition, special operations targeted hostile groups unwilling to make deals with the US or Iraqi forces. Seen in this light, the surge was less about the increased number of troops on the ground and the corresponding troop density, a key ratio in counterinsurgency theory, than it was about dividing enemy factions through a combination of carrots and sticks. That is, campaign strategy requires an understanding of local politics, indicative of the human domain, and how to build the right types of relationships to maneuver therein.

In Stanley McChrystal's memoir, *My Share of the Task*, the retired general highlights the importance of local engagement to counterinsurgency.[40] For McChrystal, counterinsurgency requires forging local partnerships and finding mechanisms to separate insurgents from the population. In discussing the war in Afghanistan, he states in 2009 that he found an under-resourced campaign with poor morale.[41] In addition, he had to find a way to fight a counterinsurgency campaign in the open due to media coverage, as well as manage divergent goals of different coalition partners. There were also fundamental problems of language that belied larger discursive differences between military and civilian leadership. According to McChrystal, "different cultures—the civilian, military, whatnot—all have their own lexicon, which cause differences in communication."[42] These communication breakdowns can have strategic level impacts due to a lack of understanding on what was actually agreed upon among agencies, partners, and allies.

In his subsequent book *Team of Teams*, McChrystal asks a critical question, "[The United States] has a large, well-trained, superbly equipped force, while [Al-Qaeda in Iraq] had to recruit locals and smuggle in foreign fighters...so why were we unable to defeat an under-resourced insurgency?"[43] For McChrystal the answer lies partially in organizational structure and process. The key to fighting a network was to become a network that encourages information sharing and creates a shared consciousness enabling mission command.

Michael Flynn laments the failures of the US intelligence community in Afghanistan along similar lines. In *Fixing Intel in Afghanistan*, he writes:

> Eight years into the war in Afghanistan, the US intelligence community is only marginally relevant to the overall strategy. Having spent the overwhelming majority of their collection efforts and analytical brainpower on insurgent groups, the vast US intelligence efforts are unable to answer the fundamental questions about the environment in which US, its allies and the people they are trying to persuade operate. [44]

As a result, Flynn concludes that the focus on the enemy comes at the expense of understanding the cultural and political contexts. That is, in modern war you have to understand the emergent relationship between friendly forces, enemy forces, and the environment. In this, the environment is often what dictates how and why enemy forces mobilize support. Flynn and his coauthors propose that managing information more holistically and geographically will yield a far greater understanding of the area of operations. They also return to the principles of counterinsurgency by noting that in "guerilla warfare" tactical-level detail is much more likely to be strategically significant than in conventional conflicts. [45] These insights highlight the importance of mapping the human domain and understanding the context of adversary action.

In *Thieves of State,* Sarah Chayes similarly observes that,

> Despite the thousands of intelligence professionals spread throughout the country, not to speak of the hundreds of diplomats and intelligence practitioners, the international community knew almost nothing useful about the government officials or local contractors we were dealing with. [46]

She concludes, "in a dozen years...data collection has exploded. But it has all been terror target focused."[47] In other words, focusing on the enemy rather than the local political interests and their underlying social and economic logic often limits battlefield success. You collect the wrong data and lose the signal in the noise.

Emma Sky's memoir, *The Unraveling: High Hopes and Missed Opportunities in Iraq*, captures failures to appreciate local politics and build the right relationships at two levels: tactical and strategic.[48] First, her anecdotes highlight both the lack of local knowledge resident in the military forces, as well as their limited preparations to secure areas. Conducting stability operations and wide-area security proved to be a harder task for forces trained to fight high intensity conflicts. In her accounts of advising senior US officials, including Generals Odierno and Petraeus, strategic failures emerge from how senior US State Department officials mismanaged their relationships with the Maliki government, effectively giving the Iraqi leader free reign to consolidate power and create the space in which groups like Daesh emerged.[49]

The other major strategic failure Sky notes was the inability to stop Iranian influence. She details how Qassim Suleimani, the head of the Iranian organization responsible for covert operations in the Middle East, was able to manipulate both Shiite political groups and a wide range of militias in Iraq.[50] Sky's account of Iran's manipulative influence harks back to Roger Trinquier's and David Galula's warnings against allowing cross-border safe havens in guerilla warfare.[51] Furthermore, given that Iranian influence used a network of local, Iraqi interlocutors, this insight highlights the importance of understanding local politics and the human domain sufficiently to interdict foreign agents.

In *Fiasco*, Tom Ricks highlights how ill-prepared US forces were for occupying Iraq.[52] Strategic failure bred operational challenges. Misguided assumptions about how the Iraqi people would treat American forces led to poor planning. First, there was a shift in objectives. Removing the Iraqi regime transformed into nation building, which created a "troop-to-task" issue. For Ricks, bad strategy produced inadequate war plans. Where Chief of Staff of the Army Eric Shinseki argued for a large force able to secure terrain and stabilize the population, [53] General Tommy Franks and a network of Pentagon appointees led by Secretary of Defense Donald Rumsfeld argued that the key to victory was a smaller force focused on speed.[54] While this network accurately described the rapid collapse of Iraqi forces, they did not see the possibility of a descent into an insurgency and refused to acknowledge the worsening conditions in 2004.[55] Because of the small size of the invasion force and its focus on high-intensity conflict, there were insufficient units and capabilities to secure the borders, restore basic services, and deal with large armed caches. The hallmark was the disbanding of the Iraqi Army. In addition, Ricks, like Sky, argues that tactics used by the US forces, including mass roundups and scandals like Abu Ghraib turned locals increasingly against US and coalition forces.

In addition to stemming the use of cross-border safe havens, military theory also echoes the need for robust local intelligence networks in order to succeed in a counterinsurgency fight. In addition to Galula and Trinquier's work, T.E. Lawrence emphasizes the requirements to understand both the local culture and the local intelligence networks in order to prevail. Lawrence states, "learn all you can.... Get to know their families, clans, tribes, friends and enemies, wells, hills, roads.... Get to speak their dialect of Arabic, not yours."[56] Michael Eisenstadt further emphasizes the criticality of understanding local culture as a prerequisite for victory. He argues that more than "book knowledge" is necessary, and like Lawrence before him, argues that "it is essential to cultivate a cadre of 'native informants' who are intimately familiar with local history, personalities, and tribal politics."[57] The importance of understanding the human domain, the web of interests that produce the context of political violence, is neither new nor novel. Each generation of soldiers deployed to control foreign populations in pursuit of national political objectives seems to discover this enduring principle too late.

Local context is the means by which foreign elements maneuver in intrastate conflict and counterinsurgency. In *The Wrong Enemy: America In Afghanistan: 2001–2014,* Carlotta Gall highlights the problem of proxy support to insurgents by neighboring states. She categorically states, "Pakistan, not Afghanistan, has been the true enemy."[58] Gall details how ISI support for the Taliban, part of a strategy of strategic depth, undermined both US military operations in Afghanistan and its search for Al Qaeda leadership. At the strategic level, US policymakers underestimated how much the ISI invested in the Taliban and their desire to use the group as a proxy. In Gall's account, the ISI, then led by General Ashfaq Pervez Kayani, used the US counterinsurgency operations in Iraq as a window of opportunity to relaunch a sustained Taliban insurgency in Afghanistan.[59] Furthermore, the corruption of the Karzai regime created a permissive environment for these returning Taliban.

From these accounts, several familiar themes once again emerge. First is the idea that the US military was not prepared to counter an insurgency in Iraq or Afghanistan, much less defeat one. Further, Ricks' account once again reinforces the narrative that the United States was also insufficiently aware of the importance of cultural understanding in a fight among the people. In "Principles, Paradoxes, Imperatives of Counterinsurgency," Cohen, Crane, and Nagl argue that in a COIN fight "analyzing the effect of any operation is impossible without understanding the society and culture in which the ...operation occurs."[60] Further they argue without a good intelligence network a counterinsurgent, "is like a blind boxer wasting energy flailing at an unseen opponent."[61]

Rajiv Chandrasekaran details similar strategic level failures in framing the problems inherent in occupation and building the right civil functions and forces for the task. [62] The Coalition Provisional Authority (CPA) tended to prefer political appointees over seasoned civil officials. These Young Turks focused on liberalizing the economy through privatization and modernizing the stock exchange at the expense of projects integrated with the military campaign that would stabilize the country.

Further, Chandrasekaran argues that the CPA hamstrung its own efforts by maintaining increasingly strict physical separation from the Iraqi people they were purportedly there to help as the insurgency became worse. This privileging of force protection over mission accomplishment further demonstrated that the CPA did not understand the type of conflict in which they were embroiled, or at least did not understand how to win in a counterinsurgency fight if indeed they recognized they were in one at all.

In George Parker's account of the Iraq war, *Assassin's Gate: America in Iraq,* he illustrates the strategic failure at the heart of the subsequent failed campaign: an inability to frame the problem.[63] Parker highlights how officials in the Bush administration had different reasons for advocating the Iraq campaign, from defending Israel to a grand notion of using military force to transform a nation into a democracy. He also highlights how the ideological homogeneity of the neoconservative movement led them to groupthink and a reluctance to consider dissenting viewpoints. He decries the "uniform mindset that takes hold of any hermetic, hierarchical institution with strong leaders and sense of common mission."[64] Thus for Parker, the failure was at the strategic level, but underpinned by the fact that administration failed to recognize the need to learn and lacked the cultural openness required to do so.

In *The Good War: Why We Couldn't Win the War or Peace in Afghanistan,* Jack Fairweather provides a comprehensive look at US intervention from 2001 to 2014. The account considers all levels from decision-making in DC to Karzai's palace in Kabul, to the tactical level of military patrols in poppy fields. He concludes that at the strategic level there was a failure to explore political alternatives and make deals with some Taliban leaders. In addition, in the aftermath of the initial invasion, which relied on small numbers of troops, warlords regained power in urban areas and sustained a regime of patronage and corruption that undermined popular support for the coalition backed government. [65] His chronicle clearly demonstrates the limitations of third party ambitions to reconstruct government on behalf of the Afghan people. His account echoes T.E. Lawrence's admonition, "do not try to do too much with your own hands.... It is their war, and you are there to help them, not win it for them."[66]

Many of the failures in the lessons-learned literature deal with inability to understand the culture and society in which the United States and allies were working. That is, contemporary military operations require mapping the human geography and building the right type of partnership networks to maneuver therein. In the words, of Army General Benjamin Freakley,

> Our real, long term dilemma is defining the significant military aspects of culture as they might apply in any theater and further determining how these various aspects of culture manifest themselves and might influence tactical operations.[67]

Much of the organizational learning literature requires institutional change as evidence of "learning." To an extent, this institutional change did occur in 2006 with the introduction of the Human Terrain Teams (HTTs) in both Iraq and Afghanistan. The trajectory of this change is recounted by Montgomery McFate and Janice Laurence in *Social Science Goes to War: The Human Terrain System in Iraq and Afghanistan.* McFate and Laurence observe that more than five years into the war in Afghanistan "US forces lacked the capacity to perceive, monitor, manage, manipulate, understand, and employ sociocultural information to guide reasoning and action."[68]

This account also echoes those of Flynn, Chase, and the JCOA study, once again highlighting that the intelligence apparatus in both theaters was focused nearly exclusively on lethal targeting rather than developing a more holistic understanding of the conflict. Finally, McFate argues that the entire war effort was hamstrung by what she identifies as "the cult of major combat operations" focused on "firepower, technology and peer enemies, to the exclusion of small wars and irregular enemies."[69] Despite increasing cultural understanding during these wars, the HTTs were an ephemeral institutionalization of lessons learned. They have since been stood down by the US military.

Ideally, lessons learned equally treat all three levels of war. Yet, major accounts of the last decade and a half rarely explore major campaigns at the operational level. A notable exception to this is Kim Kagan's *The Surge*, which is devoted nearly exclusively to capturing the operational level lessons of the surge in Iraq in 2007. Focusing more on General Odierno than on General Petraeus, she considers the success of the surge to be more a product of good operational campaigning rather than the more regularly credited Anbar awakening. She states the awakening,

> really would not have been possible without the hard and skillful fighting and negotiating of the Army.... Combat operations did not by themselves transform Iraq in 2007, but they were an essential part of the overarching strategy that did. The role of combat operations in counterinsurgency has not received remotely enough attention in recent years, and the campaign of 2007 can and must serve as a departure point for serious theoretical and practical thought about this important question....[70]

Despite Kagan's belief in the criticality of the operational level in the last war, the lessons-learned literature reveals much greater concern over the connection between the strategic and tactical levels of war and the seeming rift between them as it relates to understanding local political interests. The lessons-learned literature shows a military profession struggling to translate national policy into a series of actions that allowed deployed units and their local partners to gain a position of advantage in a landscape defined by an ever shifting web of interests and intrigue. Without a sufficient understanding of the human domain, the military advanced blindfolded across a minefield of local interests.[71]

CONCLUSION

The long war left the military at a crossroads. Multiple studies highlight the importance of understanding local political interests and the human domain as well as the need to build the right types of relationships to maneuver therein. Although the literature reviewed here is not exhaustive, it is representative of the major strands of thought within the corpus of the lessons-learned literature. In the end, strategic art, campaigns, and even tactical engagements all suffered from an excessive focus on the enemy over the environment in which they operate and the inability to build the type of networked relationships that increase freedom of action.

The long war shows a military profession left adapting to critical knowledge deficits and misaligned resources and political objectives. Learning lessons in most cases requires institutionalizing change. Given this metric, there are small signs the military profession locked in key insights from both its failures and its successes. There are multiple indicators of this, from the publication of the updated counterinsurgency manual in 2006,[72] to the elevation of Stability Operations as a core mission for the Department of Defense in 2005 and the adoption of Security Force Assistance Brigades in 2017.[73] Finally, one can look to the incorporation of operational design methodology and intermediate level and senior level schooling as evidence of military learning. Operational design was introduced in 2005 explicitly to "address some of the conceptual contra-dictions that...were becoming apparent with regard to the war in Iraq."[74] The question is whether this learning has truly been institutionalized or is being replaced with more entrenched and culturally comfortable practices associated with conventional warfare.

NOTES

1. For an overview of the military profession as it relates to innovation, see Benjamin Jensen, *Forging the Sword: Doctrinal Change in the U.S. Army* (Palo Alto: Stanford University Press, 2016).
2. Chris Argyris and Donald Schon. *Organizational Learning II: Theory, Method, and Practice.* (Reading: Addison-Wesley Publishing, 1996), xvii.
3. For an overview, see Adam Grissom, "The Future of Military Innovation Studies," *Journal of Strategic Studies* 29, no. 5 (2006): 905–934.
4. John Nagl, *Learning to Eat Soup With a Knife: Counterinsurgency Lessons from Malaya and Vietnam* (Chicago: The University of Chicago Press, 2005), 190.
5. Jensen, *Forging the Sword.*
6. Barry Posen, *The Sources of Military Doctrine: France, Britain and Germany Between the World Wars* (Ithaca: Cornell University Press, 1991), 210.
7. Ibid., 210–212.
8. Stephen Rosen, *Winning the Next War: Innovation and the Modern Military* (Ithaca: Cornell University Press, 1994), 35.
9. James March and Herbert Simon, *Organizations* (New York: Wiley-Blackwell, 1958), 184.
10. Of note, Rosen takes a more internal view during peacetime and looks at how creating new missions and supporting career paths enables endogenous change.
11. Dima Adamsky, *The Culture of Military Innovation: The Impact of Cultural Factors on the Revolution in Military Affairs in Russia, the US, and Israel* (Palo Alto: Stanford University Press, 2010).
12. Elizabeth Kier, *Imagining War: French and British Military Doctrine between the Wars* (Princeton: Princeton University Press, 1999).
13. Williamson Murray, "Military Culture Does Matter," *Foreign Policy Research Institute Wire* (January 21, 1999), http://www.fpri.org/article/1999/01/military-culture-does-matter/.
14. Frank Hoffman, *Mars Adapting: Winning the War You're In* (Annapolis: Naval Institute Press, forthcoming).
15. Leslie Graybeal, "Single Loop Learning: Key Terms," Business.com, February 22, 2017, https://www.business.com/articles/single-loop-learning-key-terms/.

16. Argyris and Schon, *Organizational Learning II*, xxiii.
17. Max Visser, "Learning Under Conditions of Hierarchy and Discipline: The Case of German Army, 1939-1940," *Learning Inquiries* 2 (6 June 2008): 127–137, http://download.springer.com/static/pdf/999/art%253A10.100 7%252Fs11519-008-0031-7.pdf?originUrl=http%3A%2F%2Flink.springer. com%2Farticle%2F10.1007%2Fs11519-008-0031-7&token2=exp=14901227 62~acl=%2Fstatic%2Fpdf%2F999%2Fart%25253A10.
18. Hoffman, *Mars Adapting*.
19. David Petraeus, "Lessons of History and Lessons of Vietnam," *Parameters* (Autumn 1986): 1, http://strategicstudiesinstitute.army.mil/pubs/ parameters/articles/2010winter/petraeus.pdf.
20. Jay Luvaas, "Military History: Is It Still Practicable?," *Parameters* (1982): 82–96, http://ssi.armywarcollege.edu/pubs/parameters/Articles/1995/ luvaas.pdf.
21. Ibid.
22. Williamson Murray, "Military Culture Does Matter."
23. Michael Howard, "The Use and Abuse of Military History" (lecture, Royal United Service Institute, London, October 18, 1961), http://ssi. armywarcollege.edu/jakarta/isapi_redirect.dll.
24. Ibid.
25. Rishikof et al, *The National Security Enterprise: Navigating the Labyrinth* (Washington, DC: Georgetown University Press, 2010), 32.
26. Benjamin Barry, *Harsh Lessons: Iraq, Afghanistan and the Changing Character of War* (London: International Institute for Strategic Studies [IISS], forthcoming).
27. Ibid., 15.
28. Ibid., 39.
29. Ibid., 86.
30. Ibid. 87.
31. Linda Robinson et al., *Improving Strategic Competence: Lessons From 13 Years of War* (Santa Monica: RAND, 2014), http://www.rand.org/pubs/ research_reports/RR816.html.
32. Ibid.
33. Joint Coalition and Operational Analysis, Division of the Joint Staff J7, *Decade of War, Volume I: Enduring Lessons from the Past Decade of Operations* (Washington, DC: The Joint Staff, 2012), http://handle.dtic. mil/100.2/ADA570341.

34. Richard Hooker and Joseph Collins, eds., *Lessons Encountered: Learning from The Long War* (Washington, DC: National Defense University Press, 2015), 10.
35. Ibid.
36. Ibid.
37. Ibid., 11.
38. Arnand Gopal, *No Good Men Among the Living: America, The Taliban and the War Through Afghan Eyes* (New York: Metropolitan Books/Henry Holt and Company, 2015).
39. Michael Gordon and Bernard Trainor, *The Endgame: The Inside Story of the Struggle for Iraq from George W. Bush to Barack Obama* (New York: Random House, 2012).
40. Stanley McChrystal, *My Share of the Task: A Memoir* (New York: Penguin Books, 2013),
41. Ibid.
42. Ibid.
43. Stanley McChrystal, Tatum Collins, David Silverman, Chris Fussell, and Paul Michael, *Team of Teams: New Rules of Engagement for a Complex World* (New York: Penguin Group, 2015).
44. Michael Flynn, Matt Pottinger, and Paul Batchelor, *Fixing Intel: A Blueprint for Making Intelligence Relevant in Afghanistan* (Washington, DC: Center For A New American Security, 2010) 7, http://online.wsj.com/public/resources/documents/AfghanistanMGFlynn_Jan2010.pdf.
45. Ibid, 8.
46. Sarah Chayes, *Thieves of State: Why Corruption Threatens Global Security* (New York: W. W. Norton & Company, 2016), 45.
47. Ibid. 46.
48. Emma Sky, *The Unraveling: High Hopes and Missed Opportunities in Iraq* (New York: Public Affairs, 2015).
49. Ibid.
50. Ibid.
51. For a discussion of the importance of geography in COIN fights, please see David Galula, *Counterinsurgency Warfare: Theory and Practice* (London: Praeger Books, 2006), 23–28; and Roger Trinquier, *Modern Warfare: A French View of Counterinsurgency*, Kindle ed. (Fort Leavenworth, Command and General Staff College, 2012), 79–81.
52. Thomas Ricks, *Fiasco: The American Military Adventure in Iraq, 2003 to 2005* (New York: Penguin Group, 2006).

53. General Erik Shinseki, Testimony before the Senate Armed Services Committee, February 25, 2003, https://www.youtube.com/watch?v=a_xchyIeCQw.

54. Donald Rumsfeld, "Transforming the Military," *Foreign Affairs* (May/June 2002), www.foreignaffairs.com/articles/2002.

55. Associated Press, "Rumsfeld: Do not call Iraqi Enemy Insurgents," November,29, 2005, http://www.nbcnews.com/id/10255205/ns/world_news-mideast_n_africa/t/rumsfeld-dont-call-iraqi-enemy-insurgents/#.WN1YLBiZPdc.

56. T.E. Lawrence, "The Arab Bulletin: The 27 Articles" The World War I Document Archives, Brigham Young University, https://wwi.lib.byu.edu/index.php/The_27_Articles_of_T.E._Lawrence.

57. Michael Eisenstadt, "Tribal Engagement Lesson Learned," *Military Review* 87, no. 5 (Sep/Oct 2007): 27.

58. Carlotta Gall, *The Wrong Enemy: America in Afghanistan: 2001–2014*, Kindle ed. (New York: Mariner Books, 2014), location 81.

59. Ibid., 89.

60. Eliot Cohen, Conrad Crane, and John Nagl, "Principles, Imperatives and Paradoxes of Counterinsurgency," *Military Review* 86, no. 2 (Mar/Apr 2006): 50.

61. Ibid.

62. Rajiv Chandrasekaran, *Imperial Life in the Emerald City: Inside Iraq's Green Zone* (New York: Random House, 2006), 1.

63. George Packer, *The Assassins Gate: America in Iraq* (New York: Farrar, Strauss and Giroux, 2014), 1.

64. Ibid., 319.

65. Jack Fairweather, *The Good War: Why We Couldn't Win the War or Peace in Afghanistan* (New York: Hachette Book Group, 2014), 1.

66. T.E. Lawrence, "The 27 Articles."

67. Benjamin Freakley, "Cultural Awareness and Combat Power," *Infantry Magazine* 94, no. 2 (March/April 2005): 1.

68. Janice Laurence, "The Human Terrain System: Some Lessons Learned and The Way Forward," in *Social Science Goes to War: The Human Terrain System in Iraq and Afghanistan*, edited by Montgomery McFate and Janice Laurence (Oxford: Oxford University Press, 2015), 292.

69. Ibid. 55.

70. Kimberly Kagan, *The Surge*, Kindle ed. (New York: Encounter Books, 2009), 197–200.

71. For some scholars, the inability to understand local politics, much less translate strategic objectives into tactical tasks, is a function of how the US military incorporated the operational level of war into its doctrine in the 1980s. For an overview of this argument, see Justin Kelly and Mike Brennan, *Alien: How Operational Art Devoured Strategy* (Carlisle: Strategic Studies Institute, 2009), viii, 1, http://www.dtic.mil/dtic/tr/fulltext/u2/a5 06962.pdf; and Hew Strachan, "Making Strategy: Civil Military Relations after the Iraq War," *Survival* (Autumn 2006): 75.
72. Headquarters, Department of Army, *FM 3-24; Counterinsurgency* (Washington, DC: Headquarters Department of the Army, December 2006).
73. Department of Defense, *Directive Number 3000.05: Military Support for Stability, Security, Transition and Reconstruction (SSTR)* (Washington, DC: Department of Defense, 2005), 2.
74. School of Advanced Military Studies, *Art of Design* (Fort Leavenworth: Combined Arms Command, 2005), 1, http://www.au.af.mil/au/awc/awcgate/sam/art_of_design_v2.pdf.

CHAPTER 3

THE RUSTING SWORD

In 1910, Normal Angell published *The Great Illusion*. The book grew out of a 1908 pamphlet entitled *Europe's Optical Illusion* challenging the "universal assumption that a nation, in order to find outlets for expanding population and increasing industry, or simply to ensure the best conditions possible for its people, is necessarily pushed to territorial expansion and the exercise of political force against others." Angell sought to undermine the prevailing view that "a nation's relative prosperity is broadly determined by its political power; that nations being competing units, advantage, in the last resort, goes to the possessor of preponderant military force, the weaker going to the wall, as in the other forms of the struggle for life."[1] For Angell, these assumptions were a mist that prevented humans from seeing the reality of how the connectivity of modern economic life changed the traditional application of political power and military force.[2]

In 1898, railroad financier Jan Bloch argued that industrial scale and emergent technologies made war so costly that rational statesmen would avoid large-scale confrontations.[3] Nations would have to mobilize millions of soldiers only to find themselves locked into costly stalemates and subject to the risk of economic, if not social, breakdown and unrest amongst their domestic populations. The people might revolt before the great armies broke the attritional stalemate. Bloch predicted the way states would fight World War I while underestimating just how irrational national security elites could be.

Today, a new cohort of social scientists is again arguing that war is in decline. First, war has become increasingly costly. Nuclear weapons, precision-strike capabilities, and cyber operations appear to limit major theater war by casting a shadow of escalating costs and risks on strategic decision-making. Second, interdependent and connected states prefer soft power.[4] Even revisionists states like Russia see a utility in political warfare and proxy war versus direct confrontation. Whereas Angell and Bloch's predictions of the declining use of war to advance the national interest in European relations proved premature, Stephen Pinker's empirical account of the decline of violence at all levels of social organization appears, for the moment, to be more enduring. As the world becomes increasingly connected, increased information exchange leads to a "debunking of ignorance and superstition."[5] Since the end of the Cold War, armed conflict has declined. The steepest decline was between 1992 and 2003. Since 2003, the number of armed conflicts has varied between thirty and forty per year, with internal conflicts being the predominant modality of political violence.[6] States appear to gain fewer benefits from their often substantial military investments in the uncertain gamble of war. When states do seek to leverage military force for strategic objectives, it often comes in the form of special operations and limited precision strikes as opposed to large bomber wings, land armies, or naval flotillas. The sword of conventional military power appears to be rusting.

Despite the horrors of the Syrian Civil War and global spread of terrorist groups like Daesh, there is a general decline in the use of force to settle disputes. This proposition appears counterintuitive. From 24-hour news networks to the incessant barrage of social media, we see war everywhere despite its documented long-term decline. If war is in decline, a proposition that while empirically verifiable clashes with our news feeds and prevailing perceptions, the question is why?

This chapter assesses the changing patterns of political violence over the last two generations. There appears to be a marked decline in decisive battle between states alongside a corresponding increase in the number of intrastate conflicts. In this, the majority of states face increasing restraints on the use of force to achieve political objectives. At the same time, the cost of holding territory is high relative to the expected gains. Yet, states continue to invest in force packages optimized for decisive battle and deterrence. While the decline might be a function of these investments and the increased costs associated with war (i.e., successful deterrence), there does appear to be a mismatch between the investments states make and the types of wars they fight. Last, in these conflicts, military effectiveness appears to be less about conventional capabilities and more about gaining an information advantage.

As a result, we are left with costly stalemates, albeit of a different character than those envisioned in 1898 by Jan Bloch. These stalemates involve low-level violence and unstable ceasefires. Decisive outcomes become elusive as actors seek networks of influence advancing their interests short of costly campaigns to control restive populations. These campaigns will require a different approach to translating military power into political objectives.

THE DECLINE OF DECISIVE BATTLE

The concept of decisive battle sits at the core of the military profession. In military history and classics, scholarly efforts to define the Western way of war revolve around showing enduring features in something called the West, an often elusive if not problematic category. Victor Davis Hanson locates the Western way of war in individualism as a cultural value and the quest for decisive battle, features whose origins he locates in Greek Hoplite infantry.[7] Geoffrey Parker contends this unique way of war reflects five core features, one of which is a preference for decisive battle in military theory and the profession of arms.[8] Military leaders at the core of professional military education embody this preference. For example, Napoleon advocated pressing the offense and sought decisive battles that allowed his forces to face large opposing coalitions. His schemes of maneuver stressed attacking rear and flank areas and the strategy of the central position: attacking two armies at their hinge as a means of achieving a defeat in detail.[9]

Yet, the search for decisive battle often seems elusive. In a comparative historical treatment of major nineteenth- and twentieth-century battles, Cathal Nolan argues that decisive victory is often an illusion.[10] Nolan warns that "often, war results in something clouded, neither triumph nor defeat. It is an arena of grey outcomes, partial and ambiguous resolution of disputes and causes that led to the choice of force as an instrument of policy in the first place."[11] There are rarely decisive victories that emerge from any one battle.

There also appears to be a marked decline in the number of decisive outcomes that result from armed conflicts. Looking across all types of conflict since 1946, figure 1 shows a sharp decline in decisive outcomes. The figure shows the number of armed conflicts, whether interstate or intrastate, that result in a clear victory for one of the protagonists or a less than optimal outcome in the form of ceasefires, peace agreements, or low-level activity less than 25 battle deaths a year. During the Cold War, 89% of armed conflicts resulted in a clear decision. In the post–Cold War period, this number dropped to 19.5%. After 9/11, the number drops further to 17.6%. The data illustrates the clear decline in decisive outcomes. More conflicts end in low-level activity and ceasefires than they do a clear decision. Breaking down the data further shows important differences between interstate and intrastate conflict.

Figure 1. Outcomes in Armed Conflict.

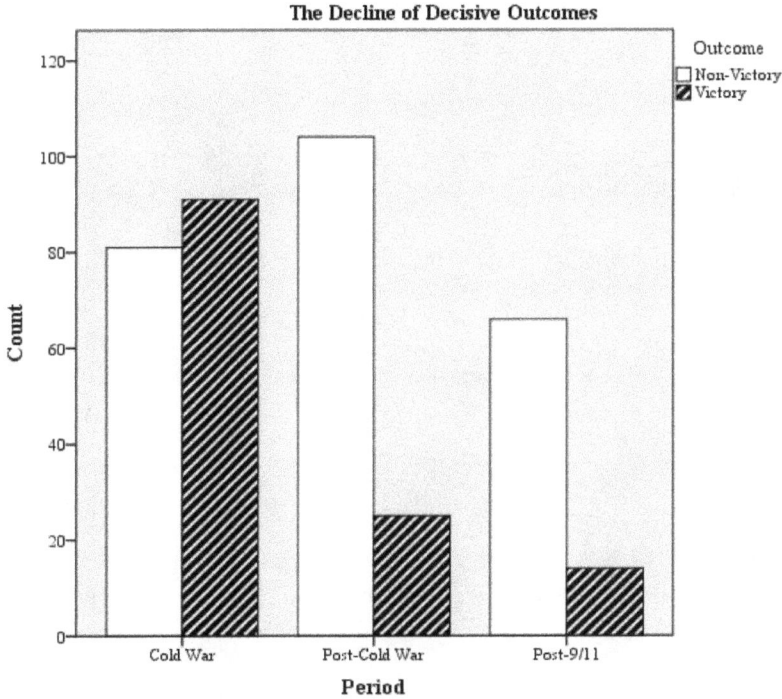

The Decline of Decisive Outcomes

Source. The figure is based on UCDP Conflict Termination Dataset.[12]

First, there are no statistically significant differences between interstate conflict outcomes across the three periods. Decisive outcomes shift from 31.6% of the total in the Cold War to 20% after 2001. The lack of a significant difference across periods is likely related to the low levels of interstate conflict since 1990 (only 9 in the dataset). Even those conflicts that did occur tended to be short and sharp, but often transitioned into more complex intrastate conflicts, to include proxy wars. For example, the rapid victory the United States achieved against the Taliban government in Afghanistan in 2002 and the Iraqi government in 2003 gave way to sustained insurgencies.

Table 3. Interstate Conflict.

Interstate Conflict Crosstabulation

Type Interstate	Period			Outcome		Total
				Non-Victory	Victory	
	Cold War	Count		39a	18a	57
		Expected Count		39.7	17.3	57.0
		% within Period		68.4%	31.6%	100.0%
		% within Outcome		84.8%	90.0%	86.4%
		% of Total		59.1%	27.3%	86.4%
		Standardized Residual		-.1	.2	
	Post-Cold War	Count		3a	1a	4
		Expected Count		2.8	1.2	4.0
		% within Period		75.0%	25.0%	100.0%
		% within Outcome		6.5%	5.0%	6.1%
		% of Total		4.5%	1.5%	6.1%
		Standardized Residual		.1	-.2	
	Post-9/11	Count		4a	1a	5
		Expected Count		3.5	1.5	5.0
		% within Period		80.0%	20.0%	100.0%
		% within Outcome		8.7%	5.0%	7.6%
		% of Total		6.1%	1.5%	7.6%
		Standardized Residual		.3	-.4	
Total		Count		46	20	66
		Expected Count		46.0	20.0	66.0
		% within Period		69.7%	30.3%	100.0%
		% within Outcome		100.0%	100.0%	100.0%
		% of Total		69.7%	30.3%	100.0%

Note. Each subscript letter denotes a subset of Outcome categories whose column proportions do not differ significantly from each other at the .05 level.

Table 4. Intrastate Conflict.

Intrastate Conflict Crosstabulation

Type	Period			Outcome		
				Non-Victory	Victory	Total
Intrastate	Cold War		Count	81_a	91_b	172
			Expected Count	113.3	58.7	172.0
			% within Period	47.1%	52.9%	100.0%
			% within Outcome	32.3%	70.0%	45.1%
			% of Total	21.3%	23.9%	45.1%
			Standardized Residual	-3.0	4.2	
	Post-Cold War		Count	104_a	25_b	129
			Expected Count	85.0	44.0	129.0
			% within Period	80.6%	19.4%	100.0%
			% within Outcome	41.4%	19.2%	33.9%
			% of Total	27.3%	6.6%	33.9%
			Standardized Residual	2.1	-2.9	
	Post-9/11		Count	66_a	14_b	80
			Expected Count	52.7	27.3	80.0
			% within Period	82.5%	17.5%	100.0%
			% within Outcome	26.3%	10.8%	21.0%
			% of Total	17.3%	3.7%	21.0%
			Standardized Residual	1.8	-2.5	
	Total		Count	251	130	381
			Expected Count	251.0	130.0	381.0
			% within Period	65.9%	34.1%	100.0%
			% within Outcome	100.0%	100.0%	100.0%
			% of Total	65.9%	34.1%	100.0%

Note. Each subscript letter denotes a subset of Outcome categories whose column proportions do not differ significantly from each other at the .05 level.

Russia pulled back its forces in 2008 in Georgia, returning to the frozen conflict status-quo prior as opposed to annexing its former republic. After using unconventional warfare to seize Crimea in 2014, Russia transitioned to wage a proxy struggle combining irregulars and non-declared conventional formations against Ukraine in the Donbass. States continue to use military force, but indirectly and often without decisive outcomes.[13]

With respect to intrastate conflict, there are statistically significant differences between the Cold War, post–Cold War, and post-9/11 periods. The expected counts of victory in the post-Cold War and post-9/11 periods are much larger than expected and distinct from the Cold War. That is, there are fewer decisive outcomes in the most frequently occurring form of political violence: *conflicts between people and their governments*. During the Cold War, intrastate victories occurred more than expected, while in the subsequent periods they occurred significantly less frequently. This reversal likely relates to shifting patterns of proxy support and the increased use of international and regional organizations to broker ceasefires.

These descriptive findings support the widely accepted conclusion that there are fundamental differences between intrastate conflict, including insurgency and counterinsurgency, and interstate conflict and competition, including conventional warfighting and deterrence. Empirical studies on conflict trends support this observation. The prevailing form of warfare since 1945 is between people and their government, called respectively either intrastate conflict or societal warfare. There was a "distinct rise in the number of civil conflicts, peaking in 1991, followed by a decline. 1991 witnessed 52 armed conflicts, in contrast to 2003 with 32. Since 2003 the number of armed conflicts has risen and fallen ranging between 30 and 40."[14] This type of conflict increased, throughout the Cold War period, often linked to decolonization, the resulting fragile states and transition periods, and proxy interventions.[15] This connection between state weakness, political transitions, and proxy intervention persists in contemporary conflict trends. As of mid-2014, there were twenty-three countries experiencing societal warfare in which state fragility and warfare were correlated.[16]

Contemporary societal wars tend to involve cross-border dimensions indicative of states unable or unwilling to control violent groups in their own territory. According to one study in 2015, "the several episodes of warfare plaguing the central and eastern Africa region involve ethnic militias and cross-border tensions. Militants from Uganda, Rwanda, and Burundi take refuge and continue to create havoc in the northeastern DRC and southern Sudan."[17] Similarly, criminal safe havens and illicit trafficking routes were explicitly associated with four of the twenty-three episodes of societal warfare.[18]

Fragile states and political transitions also change how groups compete for public goods and reconcile fundamental differences. Studies consistently find that regimes that are not purely democratic or authoritarian are the most prone to conflict. [19] Transitions tend to unsettle existing elite bargains and create opportunities for various interest groups to challenge the distribution of goods in a society. As a result, these transitions tend to increase societal warfare. According to one study, "societal warfare increased dramatically with the advent of the Arab Spring in January 2011; violent societal conflicts broke out in Egypt, Libya, Sudan, Syria, and Yemen in 2011."[20]

External actors also have interests in providing proxy support to these societal wars as a means of advancing their interests short of involving their conventional militaries directly in conflict. This incentive for proxy war parallels a renewed interest in Gray Zone competition. In contemporary warfare and strategic competition actors appear to engage in crisis politics beneath the level of major theater war.

What explains the decline of decisive outcomes in societal conflicts? First, the outcomes could be a function of strategy and how actors align their ends, ways, means, and risk. This alignment concerns the efficient allocation of resources. For Clausewitz, this alignment took the form of balancing means and ends. The political objective determines the level of effort and the allocation of resources. Patricia Sullivan's study of war outcomes echoes this logic. For Sullivan, neither the balance of capabilities nor resolve are sufficient to explain war outcomes. Rather, the nature of political objectives determines the outcome making strong states most likely to succeed when their objective is territorial annexation or regime change and less likely when states seek to coerce a weaker rival. That is, "strategic success in war requires that an actor's goals, available means, and strategic approach be aligned."[21] For Dan Reiter, combat acts as a feedback loop that reduces information asymmetries and uncertainty, allowing actors to determine the costs and benefits inherent in continuing to fight. [22] In this, the duration of conflict becomes tied to inherent commitment issues and determining whether or not agreements can be enforced.

Second, the emergent patterns of interaction in the international system could shape the character of war. This concept has roots in the English School and the concept of an anarchical society in which state interaction produces prevailing norms.[23] Extended to competition, confrontation and conflict, the idea finds resonance in Clausewitz and complex systems theory.[24] In these readings, conflict is an emergent phenomenon not reducible to any independent cost-benefit calculations or the actions of any one unit in a larger system.

Contemporary explorations of how the emergent character of the international system shapes intrastate conflict tend to pivot on more empirical findings and comparative studies of civil war than historically grounded assumptions about power and interest. The extent to which any one period sees decisive battles and certain types of conflict, such as intrastate political violence, hinges on how great powers, small states seeking to survive in their wake, and domestic actors interact. For Patrick Johnston and Brian Urlacher, "weak states and a decline in foreign conquest point to longer insurgencies after 1945, which in turn leads towards longer, less decisive intrastate conflicts."[25] For Stathis Kalyvas and

Laia Balcells, the international factor changing the prevailing technology of rebellion is great power sponsorship patterns.[26] During the Cold War, the United States and Soviet Union waged proxy struggles that increased the balance of military technology available to rebels and monetary resources available to client-states. This resource balance enabled more irregular conflicts, which tended to result in longer struggles and resulted in decisive wins for incumbents. After the Cold War, the decline of state sponsorship shifted conflicts toward symmetric nonconventional contests, a form distinct from the irregular insurgencies of the Cold War. These conflicts tended to end in a draw more frequently, helping to explain the decline in decisive outcomes.[27]

Reading across these two arguments a third possibility emerges. The decline in decisive outcomes hinges on both the misalignment of ends-way-means-risk and the shifting character of conflict. Localized political violence tends to take the form outlined by Laia Barcell and Stathis Kalyvas: symmetric nonconventional conflict in which weak states and weak rebel groups often use atrocities in place of military power to advance their interests. At the same time, great powers invest in material resources optimized for interstate warfare that does not necessarily help them in contemporary intrastate conflicts including countering state-sponsored proxies. There is a fundamental means mismatch.

THE DIMINISHING RETURNS OF CONVENTIONAL MILITARY POWER

Resource Mismatch

Though the national security strategies of multiple countries highlight the challenges of societal warfare and complex emergencies, the prevailing force structure and modernization paradigm for leading regional and global actors continues to be preparing for major episodes of armed conflict between states. In the United States, major procurement and modernization initiatives tend to focus on the low probability of interstate war with a major power. First, under the auspices of the Defense Innovation Initiative and Third Offset, the Department of Defense is looking for game-changing platforms to address a new era of strategic competition. This competition arises from a shrinking technological gap as countries like Russia and China invest in precision-strike capabilities and the enabling C4ISR infrastructure. As a result, the United States needs a new generation of offsetting capabilities—from autonomous systems to artificial intelligence—that reestablish the technological gap, and through it, enable a credible conventional deterrent.[28]

Second, existing service priorities are disproportionately oriented towards the high-end threat. The US Army is pursuing an Army Combat Vehicle Modernization Strategy that "calls for mobile protected firepower support for light infantry, improvements to Stryker mobility and lethality, upgrades to the Abrams tank and Bradley armored vehicles, and replacement of the obsolete M113 personnel carrier with the Armored Multi-Purpose Vehicle."[29] The US Navy is pursuing new carriers, estimated at over $12 billion per ship, destroyers, and frigates while looking for ways to fund a replacement to the Ohio-class ballistic missile submarines.[30] The Air Force faces "an uncomfortable period of attempting to support the acquisition of key future system while sustaining an aging fleet, against the backdrop of continued budget uncertainty."[31]

Russian military modernization initiatives illustrate a similar emphasis on equipment optimized for combat against a major power. The Cold War of 2030 will likely be "regionally rather than globally focused and primarily aimed at maintaining, and where possible increasing, Russian influence in Europe."[32] According to a RAND study:

> What is emerging is a "Cool War." This "Cool War" is quite different from the Cold War of the 1950s through the 1980s. It is regionally rather than globally focused and primarily aimed at maintaining, and where possible increasing, Russian influence in Europe, especially the post-Soviet space. However, while the "Cool War" is more limited than the Cold War, it could lead to a broad deterioration of political, economic, and military relations

between Russia and the Atlantic Alliance and spill over into other important areas, such as arms control. For example, Russia might decide to leave the Intermediate-Range Nuclear Forces (INF) Treaty to facilitate the deployment of a new generation of ground mobile long-range precision-guided land attack cruise missiles (LACMs).

In this Cool War, Russian elites continue to see a central role for nuclear weapons. Russia views its nuclear forces, to include tactical nuclear weapons, as a key counterweight to traditional US military advantages in precision strike and C4ISR. Whereas the United States sees nuclear weapons as a strategic deterrent, Russia sees its atomic arsenal as having both a political (i.e., deterrent) value and playing "a role in military planning that compensates for conventional weakness." [33]

To offset US and NATO capabilities, Russia is undergoing a significant military modernization program. These investments continue despite the fact that the majority of Russian subterfuge and intervention take place beneath the threshold of armed conflict. The 2008 conflict in Georgia was the exception. Crimea, Donbass, Chechnya, Transnistria, and Syria, as well as the active measures/political warfare campaign waged against the United States and European countries, are the norm. Yet, Russia, like the United States, focuses on the most dangerous course of action. The Russian State Armament Program (2011–2020) seeks to increase "the portion of advanced weapons in the inventory to 70–80% by 2020."[34] This modernization initiative includes: [35]

- 400 intercontinental ballistic missiles (ICBM) and submarine-launched ballistic missiles (SLBMs)
- 8 nuclear-powered ballistic missile submarines
- 100 military satellites
- 600 fixed wing aircraft
- 1,000 helicopters
- 2,300 tanks
- 2,000 self-propelled artillery systems

- 7,000 military vehicles
- 56 S-400 air-defense system battalions and
- 10 Iskander-M tactical ballistic missile brigades

The modernization portfolio also indicates a preference for selective military adaption designed to offset Western advantages. There is an ongoing Russian interest in "asymmetric technologies [that] 1) have a disruptive effect on Western technologies, 2) can be developed in areas where the domestic military industry has a particular advantage, and 3) are much cheaper to develop and produce than new Western technologies." [36]

Autonomous systems will likely play an increasingly prominent role in future Russian military modernization. The new Armata tank reflects this trend. The tank has an unmanned turret and auto-loader, and will come packaged with its own UAV.[37] The Russian Military Industrial Committee (MIC) estimates that by 2025, 30% of their combat formations will be partially autonomous.[38] To support this timeline, Russia established a new Military Robotics Laboratory in 2014. Through the software company, Unicum AI, the Russian government is also making investments in artificial intelligence that enable a military formation to "control up to ten robots at any one time, and independently organize task forces."[39]

The estimated $400-billion modernization initiative will almost certainly face budgetary pressures and fall short of the objective. Already in 2015, the roughly $60-billion defense budget was cut by five percent due to low oil prices and declining tax receipts.[40] According to a study by Moscow-based think tank Centre for Analysis of Strategies and Technologies (CAST), the modern Russian economy just does not generate enough resources to finance the current 2011–2020 rearmament program...[T]his seriously reduces the ability to efficiently renew the Russian armed forces' equipment."[41] Barring a return to high oil and gas prices, this generation of Russian leaders will face difficult choices about how to sustain a modernization designed to field a force capable of matching the United States despite allocating over five percent of their GDP on defense and still spending less than Saudi Arabia.

Like Russia, NATO countries are modernizing their forces. The Readiness Action Plan (RAP) agreed to at the 2014 Summit is the largest "reconfiguration of NATO capabilities since the end of the Cold War."[42] Since 2011, European defense acquisition priorities focus predominantly on conventional forces, "including combat aircraft, air-defence and surveillance systems, surface ships, submarines and maritime-patrol/anti-submarine warfare platforms; as well as armoured vehicles and air-mobility assets including transport aircraft and helicopters."[43]

Yet, multiple countries' security policy highlight the role of increasing irregular threats. The National Security Strategy for the United Kingdom envisioned a declining security situation predominantly linked to non-state actors and irregular threats, "from the rise of ISIL and greater instability in the Middle East, to the crisis in Ukraine, the threat of cyber-attacks and the risk of pandemics, the world is more dangerous and uncertain today than five years ago."[44] According to a 2016 German defense white paper, "the Bundeswehr needs the best possible equipment and sustainable funding in order to effectively meet challenges such as hybrid warfare, transnational terrorism, cyber-attacks, and pandemics and at the same time to fulfil the requirements of stronger national and collective defence."[45]

The trend is similar in Asia. Multiple Far East and Southeast Asian states, despite different security challenges, have increased their defense spending between 4–6% per year since 2012.[46] In 2015 South Korea released plans for defense expenditure increases of 7.2% per year between 2016 and 2020.[47] China has increased its nominal defense expenditures by double digits each year since 2001.[48] Many of these investments reflect an interest in denying US power projection (i.e., A2AD) while building Chinese power projection capabilities to protect economic interests like the One Belt One Road initiative. In this way, the investments resemble a nineteenth-century Mahanian strategy of securing lines of communication against rival states more than a twenty-first-century effort to protect overseas investments from internal unrest and instability.

Collectively, the balance of military investments, as means, reflects an orientation towards either preventing or "winning" interstate conflicts, as ends. The ends and means are aligned if the overarching objective is deterrence. The ends and means are not aligned if states also seek to address instability and localized political violence. That is, leading states are purchasing military capabilities that do not match the threats they are most likely to face.

Restraints on the Use of Military Force

Compounding this issue, there appear to be new restraints on the use of military force. Military organizations, at least those affected by the diffusion of human rights norms limiting how and where force can be applied, have a curtailed freedom of action that can impede their ability to achieve successful outcomes. Unlike the Russian or the Syrian government, most nations cannot engage in—nor would their populations or military leaders sanction—bombing campaigns targeting civilian targets they deem central to achieving military objectives.[49]

US Joint Doctrine differentiates between two limitations on military planning in the use of force to achieve political objectives: constraints and restraints.[50] A constraint is something that must be done, reflecting requirements placed on a military organization by their higher command. Constraints dictate actions, thereby restricting what a unit can do. The classic example is the 1944 campaign in France and the political requirement levied upon General Eisenhower to liberate Paris as opposed to bypass the city to focus on the German military.

A restraint is something that cannot be done, reflecting requirements placed on military organizations by higher command, and increasingly political authorities pressured by international organizations and networks of transnational advocacy networks, to prohibit action. The seminal example from the Korean War is the prohibition placed on

General MacArthur against striking Chinese targets north of the Yalu River.

In modern war, a wider range of actors can exert influence on the restraints placed on military organizations. Transnational advocacy groups and international agreements increasingly restrain ways and means in war. For some scholars, international agreements provide a focal point around which a range of actors, from transnational to domestic advocacy groups, can organize and lobby states and international organizations to change their behavior.[51] These groups often form transnational advocacy networks to pressure states by setting and enforcing standards through monitoring compliance, shaming violators through media campaigns, and pressuring domestic states and international organizations.[52]

Starting in 1973, a network of thousands of nongovernmental and international organizations began to organize around a campaign to ban landmines.[53] The campaign culminated in December 1997 when 122 countries signed a treaty banning landmines. At that time, and for many countries still, landmines were a key defensive capability that provided an obstacle to defend a key area or slow down an advancing enemy force. Yet, landmines are an indiscriminate killer that often cause more civilian than military causalities.

Even when these initiatives do not succeed in limiting the use of certain weapons, such as depleted uranium or thermobaric munitions, they add external pressure on military organizations. Multiple countries use armed unmanned systems, often called drones, for interdicting high value targets such as key personnel, supply networks, and weapons depots.[54] As of 2015, the United States, China, Russia, Iran, Nigeria, Turkey, and the United Kingdom all use armed drones. Two non-state actors, Hezbollah and the Islamic State, also field armed attack drones. Overall, eleven countries field over fifty-six types of drones in support of military operations.[55] Since 2001, these platforms have played a central role in US counterterrorism campaigns in Afghanistan, Pakistan, Yemen, and

Somalia.[56] In 2013, the United Nations Special Rapporteur for extrajudicial, summary, or arbitrary executions produced a report seeking to hold drone strikes to the standards of international law on the use of lethal force.[57] Nongovernmental groups like Amnesty International echoed these legal concerns, calling drone strikes extrajudicial killings.[58] In 2014, Pakistan sponsored a resolution through the United Nations Human Rights Council that called for ensuring "transparency in their records on the use of remotely piloted aircraft or armed drones and to conduct prompt, independent, and impartial investigations whenever there are indications of a violation to international law caused by their use."[59]

Even when these actions do not result in a formal agreement to prohibit the types of weapons or tactics used by military organizations, they create coordination challenges. Actors have to either hide their activities—and risk international condemnation—or ensure compliance. Extreme actors are willing to take this risk but do so at the expense of becoming peripheral actors. For example, Syria violated the prohibition and normative taboo against chemical weapons in its civil war.[60]

There are also systemic attributes that might be constraining the use of conventional military force. Beyond the spread of democracies and their documented pacifying effect,[61] international financial markets and global supply chains produce a capitalist peace that decreases the utility of conventional military force.[62] And though territorial disputes remain the most common catalyst for armed conflict,[63] there are reasons to believe that territory is not the primary driver of political interests amongst a web of connected trading states.[64]

The limited utility of taking territory is apparent in the disproportionately high costs of holding terrain. Real estate is getting expensive to maintain in a connected world. For example, Russian support to Abkhazia, the breakaway Georgia region, costs the Kremlin over $300 million per year in budget subsidies and pension payments.[65] The costs of maintaining and modernizing Crimea will likely exceed $3 billion dollars a year while leading to long-term economic decline as a result of

Western sanctions.[66] Shifting from annexation to temporary occupation, US deployments in Iraq and Afghanistan have cost between $1 and $3 trillion dollars depending on the estimate.[67] Even assuming the low estimate, $1 trillion, this cost is comparable to the projected cost of China's One Belt One Road network connecting Asia to Europe and Africa.[68] For the price of failed counterinsurgency campaigns, China is building an economic bridge to the world.

Declining Effectiveness

In addition to restraints on the use of force, the effectiveness of military organizations in achieving their desired political objectives is open to debate. First, even militaries that operate at a higher tactical level than then their adversaries do not always achieve strategic success. The effectiveness of military organizations is not the sole determinant of outcomes in modern warfare, regardless of whether it is interstate or intrastate. In their multivolume historical study on interstate war in the first half of the twentieth century, Alan Millet and Williamson Murray found that multiple military organizations (e.g., the German and Finnish militaries) were more effective than their enemies at the operational level but suffered strategic defeat.

The literature on military effectiveness offers insights into this dilemma. First, power does not equal success in modern war. Measuring the inputs of military power, such as the size of the economy and military age population, are only slightly better at predicting whether or not a military organization will be successful than flipping a coin.[69] According to Stephen Long, "political and territorial victories do not necessarily reflect military effectiveness, and states with greater levels of traditional power indicators (CINC scores, for instance) do not necessarily perform with high military effectiveness."[70]

Second, it is important to differentiate between tactical, operational, strategic, and political effectiveness. Battlefield success, the outcome of individual battles, rarely translates into winning the war. Yet, while observers can evaluate effectiveness at each level, the factors that determine outcomes at one level do not necessarily translate to another level.[71] For example, as of 2017 despite multiple successful raids (i.e., tactical level), the campaign (i.e., operational level) to support Afghan government efforts to maintain their territorial integrity and defeat the Taliban is stalled by a mismatch of ends and means and a fractured Afghan government.

The tension between varying outcomes at different levels of analysis is partly due to how military organizations generate and apply combat power. Military organizations generate combat power from an existing base of resources, given political and natural constraints. According to Millet, Murray, and Watman:

> Resources are assets important to military organizations: human and natural resources, money, technical prowess, industrial base, governmental structure, sociological characteristics, political capital, the intellectual qualities of military leaders, and morale. The constraints that military organizations must overcome are both natural and political. Natural constraints include such things as geography, natural resources, the economic system, population, time, and weather. Political constraints refer to national political and diplomatic objectives, popular attitudes towards the military, the conditions of engagement, and civilian morale.[72]

Those constraints that Allan R. Millet, Williamson Murray, and Kenneth H. Watman highlight reappear across multiple studies on military effectiveness. There are intervening, often non-material factors, that influence a state's ability to translate combat power into battlefield outcomes.[73] How a military fights—its doctrine and training—tends to change combat power.[74] Democratic regimes tended to have better logistics, greater initiative, and superior leadership leading to better battlefield outcomes, and through them, more success in war.[75] Cultural antecedents can determine how a state fights, as well as its overall effectiveness.[76] Civil-military relations can change the generation of combat power with fractured relations leading to purges of senior military leaders that undermine effectiveness.[77]

Most of the studies on military effectiveness tend to focus on conventional forces engaged in interstate struggles. Findings about what determines combat outcomes in intrastate conflict reflect concerns over regime type, insurgent goals, force structure, and how coercion is applied. First, whereas democracies tend to have better outcomes—defined as win, lose, or draw —in interstate conflict, there is no relationship between whether or not a country is a democracy and its success or failure in prosecuting a counterinsurgency campaign.[78]

Authoritarian regimes tend to produce more grievances through repression making it easier for insurgents to mobilize popular support.[79] Yet, these regimes also make it more difficult to organize and hence limit collective action.[80] The structure of authoritarian regimes—from politicized command structures to endemic corruption and a lack of popular support—tends to incentivize repression, lower the probability of reaching a peaceful settlement, and encourage future unrest.[81] The most dangerous regime type appears to be anocracies, polities that mix aspects of authoritarianism and democratic representation. These regimes tend to face difficulty in prosecuting counterinsurgent and counterterrorist campaigns.[82]

The character of the insurgent organization and its objectives play a role in determining outcomes. Insurgent movements can be thought of in two general categories based on their animating cause: ideology based and identity based.[83] As a consequence, identity-based conflicts tend to be harder to resolve.[84]

It is not just the animating cause of an insurgency that determines how it fights and its relative success in modern war, but the resource endowments insurgent leaders have when initiating resistance. According to Jeremy Weinstein, "rebel groups that emerge in environments rich in natural resources or with the external support of an outside patron tend to commit high levels of indiscriminate violence; movements that arise in resource-poor contexts perpetrate far fewer abuses and employ violence selectively and strategically."[85]

Just as resource endowments shape the character of insurgent violence, force structure decisions by states affect the outcome of counterinsurgency campaigns. In a study of the outcomes of counterinsurgency campaigns between 1800 and 2005, Jason Lyall and Isaiah Wilson III found that nineteenth-century military organizations, organized around mobile light-infantry organizations, achieved better outcomes than modern, mechanized formations. Mechanized forces led to a separation of the force from the population. Their "structural design inhibits information-gathering among conflict-zone populations. Faced with information starvation, mechanized forces often inadvertently fuel, rather than suppress, insurgencies."[86]

How counterinsurgents fight also plays a role in explaining outcomes. While traditional studies see the use of indiscriminate violence as counterproductive, select treatments finds the opposite. According to Kalyvas, "indiscriminate violence is likely to be effective when there is a steep imbalance of power between the two actors....as a conflict waxes on, we should observe a shift toward selective violence."[87] Jason Lyall finds that Russian artillery strikes against Chechen civilian areas, "led to a decrease in post-strike insurgent attacks."[88] Inversely, airpower in the Afghanistan conflict led to the opposite effect. In a separate study, Lyall found that "both airstrikes and shows of force are associated with increased insurgent attacks."[89] Either way, there is a declining utility to military force. The relative success of Russian artillery strikes at the tactical level, at best, led to only temporary periods of stability. Chechens continued to resist Russian forces. Airpower, according to Lyall, actually created "opportunities for insurgents to build and maintain reputations for cost tolerance and resiliency by quickly responding to counterinsurgent actions with their own violence."[90]

Similarly, the efficacy of targeting an insurgent or terrorist group's leadership is contested. From one perspective, leadership targeting either doesn't work or backfires, prolonging the group's survival.[91] From an alternative perspective, leadership targeting increases the probability of group collapse and reduces the magnitude and frequency of violence.[92] Either way, leadership targeting represents a declining utility of conventional military force. Rather than seeking decisive battles against enemy formations, military planners are searching for ways of employing assets ranging from drone strikes to raids conducted by special operations.

The declining effectiveness of conventional military organizations is likely linked to inherent information problems in warfare in general, and intrastate war in particular. Exploring the role of information in explaining the causes of war and the efficacy of force emerges from work on bargaining problems in interstate war.[93] Otherwise rational states assume the costs and risk of conflict due to private information, commitment problems, and issue indivisibility.[94] With respect to private information, two opposing actors in a conflict do not have perfect information about their opponent's capabilities or resolve. Furthermore, there are incentives to bluff, exaggerate capabilities, or conceal key systems. As a result, they cannot find a mutually beneficial alternative to the crucible of conflict. Second, each actor has difficulty trusting the other to abide by agreements reached in the present, which compounds problems with future commitments. Last, there are certain issues, usually associated with identity claims, which actors are unwilling to bargain over creating issue indivisibility challenges.

Intrastate conflicts, the most prevalent form of political violence today, tend to compound these information challenges.[95] Groups such as insurgents, terrorist cells, and civic activists all have incentives to conceal their true strength.[96] Information about these groups tends to be uncertain, fluid, and subject to change. As a conflict unfolds, battles provide a means for combatants to demonstrate their resolve and ability to impose costs on the party.[97] Second, power asymmetries accentuate commitment problems. While governments can offer reforms as alternative to violence, rebel groups often do not trust they will carry them out. Rebels tend to lose bargaining power in settlements more than states.[98] Last, intrastate conflict often involves "disputes over symbolically and strategically important territory" over which the combatants are unwilling or, owing to pressure from their constituencies, unable to bargain.[99]

Information challenges do not just function as catalysts for intrastate conflicts; they often shape the patterns of violence therein. The central information challenges in civil wars are determining levels of support and finding the enemy. Both the government and rebel groups compete for popular support.[100] According to Stathis Kalyvas, "in the civil war context information is produced exclusively or even primarily by civilian denunciations at the local level."[101] Both parties thus rely on local support to find the other combatant and sustain their struggle. According to Kalyvas:

> Armed groups must maximize the support they receive from that population and minimize the support that rival groups receive from the same population—put otherwise, they must minimize defection. To achieve this goal, armed groups deploy a variety of instruments, ranging from political persuasion and provision of public goods, all the way to coercion. Building on this foundation, the theory conceptualizes violence as an interaction between armed actors (be they rebel or state-allied actors) and the civilian population, one displaying characteristics associated with asymmetric information: political actors desire information that civilians possess. The important of information derives from the insight that coercion must be highly targeted (or selective) to be effective, i.e., it must target individuals on the basis of their actions, very much like law enforcement. In contrast, non-selective (or indiscriminate) violence, i.e., violence targeting individuals on the basis of collective profiling (such as their ethnic or religious identity or the place they live), will tend to be counterproductive, leading civilians to seek protection from the rival group, provided this option is available.[102]

Thus, the available information tends to produce distinct geographic variations in violence and alter the collective action problem. Indiscriminate violence often emerges from low information and hence low levels of control. [103] With respect to the collective action problem, nonparticipation in the struggle can carry significant risks. Whereas armed groups, be they government forces or insurgents, will provide intelligence to their members about possible attacks, nonparticipants lack such information and thus tend to be disproportionately targeted.[104] Furthermore, in war zones actors tend to manipulate information as a means of advancing personal agendas and narrow interests in the context of larger struggles.[105]

Information effects also tend to shape strategy selection by armed groups in intrastate conflict. Armed groups often use violence as a form of costly signaling. Studies on terrorist organizations highlight that:

> Terrorists are too weak to impose their will distinctly by force of arms. They are sometimes strong enough, however, to persuade audiences to do as they wish by altering the audience's beliefs about such matters as the terrorist's ability to impose costs and their degree of commitment to their cause. Given the conflict of interest between terrorists and their targets, ordinary communication or "cheap talk" is insufficient to change their minds or influence behavior. [106]

The central challenge in counterinsurgency is to find the enemy and target them, whether with lethal or non-lethal means, without alienating the population. By definition this is an information challenge. Counterinsurgents tend to rely on informing to identify combatants as a means of separating insurgents from the general population. This information often comes from local informants who transfer "sensitive and timely information from civilians and potentially disgruntled insurgents to counterinsurgent forces about the identities or activities of armed groups during wartime."[107] Informing produces tangible benefits. According to one study:

Information helps counterinsurgents offset insurgent informational advantages. Indeed, obtaining tips from locals can facilitate the selective targeting of insurgent leaders, the disruption of military operations (e.g., ambushes) and possible insurgent defections. Public knowledge that the counterinsurgent has penetrated the village may undermine the willingness of individuals to collaborate with insurgents for fear of discovery, further complicating insurgent recruitment and operations. In turn, the rise of informants can force insurgents to devote a greater share of their resources into hardening their organization against defection and information leaks, introducing new inefficiencies that may cripple their effectiveness. It is little wonder, then, that counterinsurgents typically build large and intrusive intelligence-gathering operations.[108]

If information is at a premium, the price of information should shape how armed groups and civilians act. A study of violence patterns in the Afghanistan, Iraq, and the Philippines found that,"as local economic conditions deteriorate, government forces and their allies are able to buy more intelligence on insurgents (i.e., the price of information falls)."[109] Multiple studies find that civilians withhold information as a means of punishing armed groups, whether government or insurgent, in intrastate conflict.[110] Force structure can also determine how much information a counterinsurgent or counterterror force gets about potential combatants. According to one study, lighter formations forced to forage and interact with locals tended to have "sufficient information about local populations to ensure their application of rewards and punishment was selective."[111]

CONCLUSION

Modern wars are predominantly intrastate and transnational struggles for political influence. These struggles are less decisive than war in previous epochs. In addition, there appears to be diminishing returns from the substantial investments states make in conventional military power. From emerging international restraints on the use of force and the increasing costs of holding territory to the importance of information in waging population-centric campaigns, the character of war is shifting. This shift highlights both a misalignment of strategic objectives and military resources and a new character of war. The question at the heart of this book is how to adapt to address this new world and ensure a more optimal allocation of resources and missions for military forces and civilian agencies in the twenty-first century.

NOTES

1. Norman Angell, *The Great Illusion: A Study on the Relation of Military Power to National Advantage* (New York: Putnam and Sons, 1913), x.
2. Christian Lous Lange, "Award Ceremony Speech,"" Nobel committee, December 10, 1934, http://www.nobelprize.org/nobel_prizes/peace/laureates/1933/press.html.
3. Jan Bloch, *The Future of War in its Technical, Economic and Political Relations* (Boston: Ginn Company, 1898), trans. R.C. Long, https://archive.org/details/futurewar00unkngoog. For a review of its influence, or more accurately lack thereof, amongst military professionals, see "The Centenary of the British Publication of Jean de Bloch's Is War Now Impossible? (1899–1999)," *War in History* 7, no. 3 (2000): 273–294.
4. Stephen Watts, Bryan Frederick, Jennifer Kavanagh, Anegla O'Mahony, Thomas S. Szayna, Matthew Lane, Alexander Stephenson, and Colin P. Clarke, *A More Peaceful World? Regional Conflict Trends and U.S. Defense Planning* (Santa Monica: RAND Corporation, 2017).
5. Stephen Pinker, *The Better Angels of Our Nature: Why Violence Has Declined* (New York: Penguin, 2011), 202.
6. Scott Gates, Håvard Mokleiv Nygård, Håvard Strand, and Henrik Urdal "Trends in Armed Conflict, 1946–2014," *Conflict Trends* 1 (2016), https://www.prio.org/Publications/Publication/?x=8937.
7. Victor Davis Hanson, *The Western Way of War: Infantry Battle in Classical Greece* (New York: Alfred Knopf, 1989); and Victor David Hanson, *Carnage and Culture: Landmark Battles in the Rise of Western Power* (New York: Doubleday, 2001).
8. Geoffrey Parker, "The Western Way of War" in *The Cambridge History of Warfare* edited by Geoffrey Parker (Cambridge: Cambridge University Press, 2005), 1–11.
9. Peter Paret, "Napoleon and the Revolution in War" in *Makers of Modern Strategy from Machiavelli to the Nuclear Age* edited by Peter Paret (Princeton: Princeton University Press, 1986), 123–142.
10. Cathal Nolan, *The Allure of Battle: A History of How Wars are Won and Lost* (New York: Oxford University Press, 2017).
11. Ibid., 2.
12. Non-victory is coded as any outcome that did not result in a Side A/government victory. These include ceasefires, peace agreements, and low-

level activity. This coding it meant to distinguish outcomes, not argue whether or not individual ceasefire or peace agreements are optimal for either side. The periods are 1946–1990 (Cold War), 1991–2001 (post–Cold War), and 2002–2013 (post-9/11). For more on the UCDP Conflict Termination Dataset, see Joakim Kreutz, "How and When Armed Conflicts End: Introducing the UCDP Conflict Termination Dataset," *Journal of Peace Research* 47, no. 2 (2010): 243–250.

13. These measurements do not factor threats and displays of force associated with militarized disputes. These actions are usually applied to measure deterrence and coercion short of war and outside the scope of the research.

14. Gates, Nygård, Strand, and Urdal, "Trends in Armed Conflict, 1946–2014."

15. Monty Marshall and Benjamin Cole, "Global Conflict Report 2014: Conflict, Governance, and State Fragility," Center for Systemic Peace (2015), 12–14, http://www.systemicpeace.org/vlibrary/GlobalReport20 14.pdf.

16. Ibid., 14.

17. Ibid., 31.

18. Ibid., 14.

19. For a discussion on the relationship between governance type and civil war, see James Fearon and David Laitin, "Ethnicity, Insurgency, and Civil War," *American Political Science Review* 97 (2003): 75–90; and Scott Gates, Havard Hegre, Mark P. Jones, and Havard Strand. "Institutional Inconsistency and Political Instability: Polity Duration 1800-2000," *American Journal of Political Science* 50, no. 4 (2006): 893–908.

20. Marshall and Cole, "Global Conflict Report 2014,", 30.

21. Patricia Sullivan, *Who Wins? Predicting Strategic Success and Failure in Armed Conflict* (New York: Oxford University Press, 2012), 5.

22. Dan Reiter, *How Wars End* (Princeton, NJ: Princeton University Press, 2009), 3.

23. On the English School and structural realism, see Hedley Bull, *The Anarchical Society* (Basingstoke: Palgrave, 1977); Barry Buzan, Charles Jones and Richard Little, *The Logic of Anarchy: Neorealism to Structural Realism* (New York: Columbia University Press, 1993), chapter 4; Barry Buzan and George Lawson, *The Global Transformation: History, Modernity and the Making of International Relations* (Cambridge: Cambridge University Press, 2015).

24. On systems theory and the study of conflict, see Alan Beyerchen, "Clausewitz, Nonlinearity and the Unpredictability of War," *International Security* 17, no. 3 (Winter 1992); Robert Jervis, *System Effects: Complexity in Political and Social* Life (Princeton: Princeton University Press, 1999); and Benjamin Jensen, "Emergence: the Changing Character of Competition and Conflict," *War on the Rocks* (February 6, 2017).
25. Patrick Johnson and Brian Urlacher, "Explaining the Duration of Counterinsurgency Campaigns" (unpublished manuscript, 2012), http://patrickjohnston.info/materials/duration.pdf.
26. Stathis N. Kalyvas, "International System and Technologies of Rebellion: How the End of the Cold War Shaped Internal Conflict," *American Political Science Review* 104, no. 3 (2010): 415–429.
27. Laia Balcells and Stathis N. Kalyvas, "Does Warfare Matter? Severity, Duration, and the Outcomes of Civil Wars," *Journal of Conflict Resolution* 58, no. 8 (2014): 1390–1418.
28. For an overview of the third offset, see Paul Norwood and Benjamin Jensen, "How the U.S. Army Remains the Master of Landpower," *War on the Rocks*, October 1, 2015, http://warontherocks.com/2015/10/how-the-u-s-army-remains-the-master-of-landpower/.
29. IISS, "Chapter Three: North America" *The Military Balance* 116, no. 1 (2016): 28, 55–162.
30. Ibid., 29.
31. Ibid., 30.
32. F. Stephen Larrabee, Peter A. Wilson, and John Gordon IV, *The Ukrainian Crisis and European Security: Implications for the United States and U.S. Army,* RAND Corporation, (Santa Monica, January 1, 2015), 17, http://www.rand.org/pubs/research_reports/RR903.html.
33. Roger N. Mcdermott, *Russia's Conventional Military Weakness and Strategic Nuclear Policy* (Fort Leavenworth: Foreign Military Studies Office, December 16, 2015), 4, http://fmso.leavenworth.army.mil/Collaboration/international/McDermott/Russia-NuclearPolicy.pdf.
34. IISS, "Chapter Five: Russia and Eurasia" *The Military Balance* 116, no.1 (2016): 55–162, 170.
35. Janis Berzins, "Russia's New Generational Warfare in Ukraine: Implications for Latvian Defense Policy" National Defence Academy of Latvia, Center for Security and Strategic Research, Policy Paper No. 2 (April 2014), 6. The bulleted list is taken directly from the text.

36. Tor Bukkvoll, "Iron Cannot Fight - The Role of Technology in Current Russian Military Theory," *Journal of Strategic Studies* 34, no. 5 (October 26, 2011), 681–706, esp. 699.

37. Michael Peck, "Russia's New Tank Comes with a Drone" C4ISR Network, April 25, 2016, http://www.c4isrnet.com/story/military-tech/uas/2016/0 4/25/armata-russian-tank-drone-uav/83502782/.

38. Tamir Eshel, "Russian Military to Test Combat Robots in 2016," *Defense Update*, December 31, 2015, http://defense-update.com/20151231_russian-combat-robots.html; David Hambling, "Russia Wants Autonomous Fighting Robots, and Lots of Them" *Popular Mechanics*, May 12, 2014, http://www.popularmechanics.com/military/a10511/russia-wants-autonomous-fighting-robots-and-lots-of-them-16787165/

39. Sara Malm, "Skynet has arrived: Russian military firm produces AI technology that enables robots to make decisions without human intervention, just like Terminator's killer machines" *Daily Mail*, October 25, 2015, http://www.dailymail.co.uk/news/article-3280685/Skynet-arrived-Russian-military-firm-produces-AI-technology-enables-robots-make-decisions-without-human-intervention-just-like-Terminator-s-killer-machines.html

40. Franz-Stefan Gady, "Putin to Press on With Russia's Military Modernization," *The Diplomat*, June 27, 2015.

41. Thomas Grove, "Economic Crisis Slows Putin's Plans to Modernize Russian Military," *The Wall Street Journal*, May 6, 2015.

42. IISS, "Chapter Four: Europe" *The Military Balance* 116, no. 1 (2016): 55–162.

43. Ibid., 63.

44. HM Government, *National Security Strategy and Strategic Defence and Security Review 2015*, November 2015, https://www.gov.uk/government/uploads/system/uploads/attachment_data/file/478936/52309_Cm_9161_NSS_SD_Review_PRINT_only.pdf, p. 5.

45. The German Federal Government, *White Paper: On German Security Policy and the Future of the Bundeswehr*, 13 July 2016, http://www.new-york-un.diplo.de/contentblob/4847754/Daten/6718448/160713weibuchEN.pdf, p. 8.

46. IISS, "Chapter Six: Asia" *The Military Balance* 116, no. 1 (2016): 55–162, 215.

47. Ibid.

48. Ibid., 214.

49. Though immoral and of questionable utility, counter value targeting (i.e., targeting civilian populations) is a technique for either reducing civilian support for the targeted actor (i.e., a punishment or risk strategy) or seeking to clear terrain for follow on military force. On punishment and risk strategies in coercive air campaigns, see Robert Pape, *Bombing to Win* (Ithaca: Cornell University Press, 2014).
50. JP 5-0, IV-8.
51. Beth A. Simmons, *Mobilizing for Human Rights: International Law in Domestic Politics* (Cambridge: Cambridge University Press, 2009).
52. Margaret E. Keck and Kathryn Sikkink, *Activist Beyond Borders* (Ithaca: Cornell University Press, 1998); Khagram Sanjeev, James Rikker, and Kathryn Sikkink, eds., *Restructuring World Politics: Transnational Social Movements, Networks and Norms* (Minneapolis: University of Minnesota Press, 2002). For an overview of the literature on transnational advocacy networks, see Richard Price, "Transnational Civil Society and Advocacy in World Politics," *World Politics* 55, no. 4 (2003): 579–606.
53. For an overview of the issue, see Mark Gwozdecky and Jill Sinclair, "Landmines and Human Security," in *Human Security and the New Diplomacy*, edited by Rob McRae and Don Hubert (Montreal: McGill-Queen's University Press, 2001), 28–40. According to R. Charli Carpenter, The International Committee of the Red Cross mentioned prohibiting the use of mines in a 1973 report and the weapons were also a topic in the 1977 Additional Protocols to the Geneva Convention and the 1980 Conventional on Conventional Weapons, which limited their use against civilian targets, see "Vetting the Advocacy Agenda: Network Centrality and the Paradox of Weapon Norms," *International Organization* 65, no. 1 (2011): 69–102.
54. Words matter. The United States Air Force calls these systems remotely piloted vehicles (RPV). Most other defense actors refer to unmanned systems as drones, remote autonomous system (RAS), or simply unmanned systems.
55. Datablog, "Drones by country: who has all the UAVs?" *The Guardian*, 2012, https://www.theguardian.com/news/datablog/2012/aug/03/drone-stocks-by-country.
56. According to Bureau of Investigative Journalism, since 2001 the United States has conducted more than 500 non-battlefield strikes killing more than 4,000 individuals; see http://www.thebureauinvestigates.com/category/projects/drones/ drones-yemen/ as it appears in Sarah E. Krebs

and Geoffrey P.R. Wallace, "International law, military effectiveness, and public support for drone strikes," *Journal of Peace Research* (2016): 1–16.

57. United Nations, "Drone attacks: UN rights experts express concern about the potential illegal use of armed drones," October 25, 2013, http://www.ohchr.org/en/NewsE vents/Pages/DisplayNews.aspx?NewsID¼13905.

58. Amnesty International, "Will I be next? US drone strikes in Pakistan," October 21, 2013, https://www.amnestyusa.org/reports/will-i-be-next-us-drone-strikes-in-pakistan/.

59. United Nations Human Rights Council, "Ensuring use of remotely piloted aircraft or armed drones in counter-terrorism and military operations in accordance with international law, including international human rights and humanitarian law," Twenty-Fifth Session, Agenda Item 3, A/HRC/25/L.3, March 24, 2014, http://www.un.org/ga/search/view_doc.asp?symbol=A/HRC/25/L.32.

60. For an overview of the campaigns against chemical weapons, see Richard Price, *The Chemical Weapons Taboo* (Ithaca: Cornell University Press, 2007).

61. Bruce Russett and John Oneal, *Triangulating the Democratic Peace: Democracy, Interdependence, and International Organizations* (New York: W.W. Norton, 2001).

62. Eric Gartzke, "The Capitalist Peace" *American Journal of Political Science* 51, no. 9 (2007): 166–191.

63. John Vasquez, *The War Puzzle* (New York: Cambridge University Press, 1993).

64. Richard Rosencrance, *The Rise of the Trading State: Commerce and Conquest in the Modern World* (New York: Basic Books, 1986); for a discussion on these effects as they relate to China, see M. Taylor Fravel, "International Relations Theory and China's Rise: Assessing China's Potential for Territorial Expansion," *International Studies Review* 12, no. 4 (2010): 505–532.

65. William Schreiber, "The Hidden Costs of a Russian Statelet in Ukraine," *The Atlantic*, March 4, 2014, https://www.theatlantic.com/international/archive/2014/03/the-hidden-costs-of-a-russian-statelet-in-ukraine/2841 97/. The cost calculation is based on figures from X page 9. Report No. 224, "Abkhazia: The Long Road to Reconciliation," International Crisic Group, 10 April 10, 2013, https://www.crisisgroup.org/europe-central-asia/caucasus/abkhazia-georgia/abkhazia-long-road-reconciliation.

66. Ilan Berman, "Paradise Lost in Crimea," *Foreign Affairs*, September 8, 2015, https://www.foreignaffairs.com/articles/ukraine/2015-09-08/paradise-lost-crimea.

67. Amy Belasco, *The Cost of Iraq, Afghanistan, and Other Global War on Terror Operations Since 9/11* (Washington: Congressional Research Services, 2014).

68. Jane Perlez and Yufan Huang, "Behind China's $1 Trillion Plan to Shake Up the Economic Order," *New York Times*, May 13, 2017.

69. Biddle, *Military Power*, 20–21.

70. Stephen B. Long, "A Winning Proposition? States' military effectiveness and the reliability of their allies," *International Politics* 52, no. 3 (2015): 341.

71. Allan R. Millet, Williamson Murray, and Kenneth H. Watman, "The Effectiveness of Military Organizations," *International Security* 11, no. 1 (1986): 38

72. Millet, Murray, and Watman, "The Effectiveness of Military Organizations," 37.

73. For an overview of these factors, see Risa A. Brooks, "The Impact of Culture, Society, Institutions, and International Forces on Military Effectiveness," in *Creating Military Power: The Sources of Military Effectiveness*, edited by Risa Brooks and Elizabeth A. Stanley (Stanford: Stanford University Press, 2007). For an alternative perspective that the level of economic development determines military effectiveness, see Michael Beckley, "Economic Development and Military Effectiveness," *Journal of Strategic Studies* 33, no. 1 (2010): 43–79.

74. Stephen Biddle, *Military Power: Explaining Victory and Defeat in Modern Battle* (Princeton, Princeton University Press, 2010); and Trevor N. Dupuy, *Numbers, Predictions, and War*, revised ed. (Fairfax, VA: Hero Books, 1985).

75. Dan Reiter and Alan Stam, "Democracy and Battlefield Military Effectiveness," *Journal of Conflict Resolution* 42, no. 3 (1998): 259.

76. Ruth Benedict, *The Chrysanthenum and the Sword: Patterns of Japanese Culture* (Boston, MA: Houghton Mifflin, 1946); Kenneth Pollack, *Arabs at War: Military Effectiveness, 1948–1991* (Omaha: University of Nebraska Press, 2002); and Stephen Rosen, "Military Effectiveness: Why Society Matters," *International Security* 19, no. 4 (1995), 5–31.

77. Risa A. Brooks, *Political-Military Relations and the Stability of Arab Regimes* (London: International Institute for Strategic Studies, 1998).

78. Jason Lyall, "Do Democracies Make Inferior Counterinsurgents? Reassessing Democracy's Impact on War Outcomes and Duration," *International Organization* 64 (2010): 167–192.

79. Jeff Goodwin, *No Other Way Out: States and Revolutionary Movements, 1945–1991* (New York: Cambridge University Press, 2001).

80. Doug McAdam, *Political process and the development of Black insurgency* (Chicago: University of Chicago Press, 1982). For an overview of the effects of regime type on civil wars, see James Raymond Vreeland, "The Effect of Regime on Civil War: Unpacking Anocracy," *Journal of Conflict Resolution* 52, no. 3 (2008): 401–425.

81. Daniel Byman, "Death Solves All Problems: The Authoritarian Model of Counterinsurgency," *Journal of Strategic Studies* 39, no. 1 (2016): 62–93.

82. On anocracies and counterinsurgency, see Ben Connable and Martin C. Libicki, *How Insurgencies End* (Santa Monica: RAND, 2010). For a discussion of anocracy and terrorism, see Erica Chenoweth, "Terrorism and Democracy," *Annual Review of Political Science* 16 (May 2013): 355–378.

83. Chaim Kaufmann, "Possible and Impossible Solutions to Ethnic Civil Wars," *International Security* 20, no. 4 (Spring 1996): 136–175. On how identity-based groups complicate conflict resolution, see Monica Duffy Toft, *The Geography of Ethnic Violence: Identity, Interests, and the Indivisibility of Territory* (Princeton, NJ: Princeton University Press, 2003); and Stacie E. Goddard, "Uncommon Ground: Indivisible Territory and the Politics of Legitimacy," *International Organization* 60, no. 1 (Winter 2006): 35–68.

84. Alexander B. Downes, "The Problem with Negotiated Settlements to Ethnic Civil Wars," *Security Studies* 13, no. 4 (Summer 2004): 230–279

85. Jeremy Weinstein, *Inside Rebellion: The Politics of Insurgent Violence* (New York: Cambridge University Press, 2007), 7.

86. Jason Lyall and Isaiah Wilson III, "Rage Against the Machines: Explaining Outcomes in Counterinsurgency Wars," *International Organization* 63 (2009): 67–106, esp. 70.

87. Stathis Kalyvas, *The Logic of Violence in Civil War* (New York: Cambridge University Press, 2006), 167.

88. Jason Lyall, "Does Indiscriminate Violence Incite Insurgent Attacks? Evidence from Chechnya," *Journal of Conflict Resolution* 53 (2009): 357.

89. Jason Lyall, "Airpower and Coercion in Counterinsurgency Wars: Evidence from Afghanistan" (working paper, 2013), www.jasonlyall.com.

90. Ibid.

91. Studies highlighting the limits of leadership targeting include Daniel Byman, *A High Price: The Triumphs and Failures of Israeli Counterterrorism* (New York: Oxford University Press, 2011); Jenna Jordan, "When Heads Roll: Assessing the Effectiveness of Leadership Decapitation," *Security Studies* 18, no. 4 (December 2009): 719–755; Pape, *Bombing to Win*; Robert A. Pape, "The Strategic Logic of Suicide Terrorism," *American Political Science* 97, no. 3 (August 2003): 1–19.

92. Studies highlighting the benefits of leadership targeting include Patrick J. Johnston, "Does Decapitation Work? Assessing the Effectiveness of Leadership Targeting in Counterinsurgency Campaigns," *International Security* 36, no. 4 (2012): 47–79; and Brian Price, "Targeting Top Terrorists: How Leadership Decapitation Contributes to Counterterrorism," *International Security* 36, no. 4 (2012): 9–46.

93. Thomas Schelling, *Strategy of Conflict* (Cambridge: Harvard University Press, 1966); James Fearon, "Rationalist Explanations for War," *International Organization* 49 (1995): 379–414; Robert Powell, *In the Shadow of Power: States and Strategies in International Politics* (Princeton: Princeton University Press, 1999); Dan Reiter, "Exploring the Bargaining Model of War," *Perspectives on Politics* 1 (2003): 27–43; and Alan Smith and Alan Stam, "Bargaining the Nature of War," *Journal of Conflict Resolution* 6 (2004): 783–813.

94. Fearon, "Rationalist Explanation for War."

95. Barbara Walters, "Bargaining Failures and Civil Wars," *Annual Review of Political Science* 12 (2009): 243–361.

96. Ibid., 245.

97. James Fearon, "Why Do Some Civil Wars Last So Much Longer than Others?" *Journal of Peace Research* 41, no. 3 (2004): 275–301; David Cunningham, "Blocking Resolution: How External States Can Prolong Civil Wars," *Journal of Peace Research* 47 no. 2 (2010): 875–892; and J. Michael Grieg, "Rebels at the Gates: Civil War Battle Locations, Movement, and the Openings for Diplomacy," *International Studies Quarterly* 59 (2015): 680–693.

98. Walters, "Bargaining Failures and Civil Wars," 243–361, esp. 245; Barbara Walters, "The Critical Barrier to Civil War Settlement" *International Organization* 51, no. 3 (1997): 335–364; and *Committing to Peace: The Successful Settlement of Civil Wars* (Princeton: Princeton University Press, 2002).

99. Walters, "Bargaining Failures and Civil Wars," 243–361, esp. 247; Stacie Goddard, "Uncommon Ground: Individual Territory and the Politics of Legitimacy," *International Organization* 1 (2006): 35–68.
100. Stathis Kalyvas, *The Logic of Violence in Civil War* (Cambridge: Cambridge University Press, 2006).
101. Stathis Kalyvas, "Micro-Level Studies of Violence in Civil War: Refining and Extending the Control-Collaboration Model," *Terrorism and Political Violence* 24 (2012): 658–668.
102. Ibid., 660.
103. Ibid., 661.
104. Stathis Kalyvas and Matthew Kocher, "How Free is Free Riding in Civil Wars? Violence, Insurgency, and the Collective Action Problem," *World Politics* 59, no. 2 (2007): 177–216.
105. Stathis Kalyvas, "The Ontology of Political Violence: Action and Identity in Civil Wars" *Perspectives on Politics* 1, no. 3 (2003): 475–494.
106. Andrew Kydd and Barbara Walters, "The Strategies of Terrorism," *International Security* 31, no. 1 (2006): 49–80, esp. 50.
107. Jason Lyall, Yuki Shirato, and Kosuke Imai, "Co-Ethnic Bias and Wartime Informing," *The Journal of Politics* 77, no. 3 (2015): 833–848, esp. 834.
108. Ibid., 834.
109. Eli Berman, Michael Callen, Joseph H. Felter, and Jacob N. Shapiro, "Do Working Men Rebel? Insurgency and Unemployment in Afghanistan, Iraq, and the Philippines," *Journal of Conflict Resolution* 55, no. 4 (2011): 496–528, esp. 498.
110. Luke Condra and Jake Shapiro, "Who Takes the Blame? The Strategic Effecs of Collateral Damage," *American Journal of Political Science* 56 (2012): 167–187; Matthew Kocher, Thomas Pepinsky, and Stathis Kalvyas, "Aerial Bombing and Counterinsurgency in the Vietnam War," *American Journal of Political Science* 55 (2011): 201–218.
111. Jason Lyall and Isaiah Wilson III, "Rage Against the Machines: Explaining Outcomes in Counterinsurgency Wars," *International Organization* 63 (2009): 67–107, esp. 73.

CHAPTER 4

INFORMATION WARFARE

On July 22, 2016 Russia revived an old tactic for a new era. Guccifer 2.0, a known front for Kremlin hackers, passed stolen correspondence from the Democratic National Committee (DNC) to Wikileaks. Thousands of e-mails ignited a media frenzy reinforced by Russian propagandists seeking to show a corrupt, decaying democratic order in the United States. Russian operatives bought social media ads on major outlets such as Facebook, Twitter, and Google amplifying this image of America in decline. Facebook ads and posts alone are estimated to have reached 126 million Americans.[1] The unique combination of cyberattacks with social and traditional media reflects a twenty-first-century version of political warfare: a mix of nonmilitary measures, propaganda, and psychological warfare designed to influence an adversary. The world witnessed an information warfare campaign optimized for our new connectivity.[2]

Information warfare is not new. In addition to propaganda and deception, competitors have long sought to target decision-making through attacking connectivity and the flow of information. During the Spanish-American War (1898), the US Navy destroyed undersea cables connecting Cuba with the rest of the Spanish Empire as a means of isolating the island and limiting the ability of the Spanish to coordinate their forces.

[3] During the late nineteenth century, the British developed extensive plans to defend communications across the empire as well as attack undersea cables linking competitors during a crisis.[4] These efforts to protect and attack information pathways as a means of altering combat power continued into World War I. Both sides of the conflict attacked connectivity, often through undersea cables, in an effort to "manipulate the flow of government and business information related to the management of the war effort."[5] These information warfare campaigns also included propaganda designed to subvert the adversary from within. The Ottomans unsuccessfully called for a Holy War against the Allied powers in 1914 while the German Half Moon Camp sought to radicalize Muslim soldiers in the British and French forces as means of undermining unit cohesion.

More than singling out military targets, these information warfare efforts involved strategic objectives such as isolating the enemy and limiting their ability to access neutral countries for supplies or finances. In a protracted war, the great powers "grasped that information was important because it served as a force multiplier, and that because of this importance the conduits and key nodes for the movement of that information needed to be targeted. Moreover, they did not limit their focus to the military applications of information to battle but expanded it to the wider role of information as a commercial, financial, or diplomatic tool in the larger geostrategic environment." [6]

In a hyperconnected world, it is not just great powers that engage in information warfare. Activists, extremists, and revisionist states—from North Korea to Iran—actively manipulate the flow of information as a form of coercion designed to alter decision-making. They launch cyber intrusions to destabilize adversaries and threaten strategic escalation, combining at every step propaganda and coercion to influence rivals and their domestic audiences. A connected world presents new opportunities. Just as the increased commercial, financial, and communications connectivity of pre–World War I Europe made it possible for planners to compel their adversary beyond the battlefield, today's hyperconnected world raises the prospects of using information warfare to shape strategic competition.[7] These struggles will take place more in the realm of propaganda and coercive threats in cyberspace than direct physical attacks. The struggle for the flanks in the twenty-first century are efforts to access and undermine the integrity of information networks while influencing populations through media feeds.

While conventional military power appears to be generating diminishing returns, there seems to be a new premium on influence. Information warfare appears to be a low-cost, low-risk form of coercion and manipulation with few barriers to entry. It is an optional counter to US military capabilities. Actors can limit the effectiveness of precision-strike capabilities through corrupting command networks while using tailored propaganda to target the political will and legitimacy of rivals and threaten civilian populations with punishing attacks against critical infrastructure, like the financial system, or mass identity theft. This is a world defined by threat and influence, not decisive battles.

To place the argument in context, there is a long, historical chain that connects practitioners seeking to conceal their strengths, gain insights into their competitors, and achieve a position of relative advantage. For Chinese strategist Sun Tzu, information was a way of achieving decisive advantage; "all warfare is based on deception" and "what enables the wise sovereign and the good general to strike and conquer, and achieve things beyond the reach of ordinary men, is foreknowledge."[8] To win without fighting, the highest art of war, required attacking by stratagem and undermining the enemy's plan. For the Indian strategist and political theorist Kautilya, the ruler collected and manipulated information as a form of internal control in which, "there is a dense network of stationary and mobile secret agents and informants collecting information about treasonous activities, corruption, serious crime and the popular mood."[9]

In Book I, Chapter 6, "Information in War," Clausewitz defined information as "all the knowledge which we have of the enemy and his country;

therefore, in fact the foundation of all our ideas and actions."[10] The original German term was *nachrichten* or messages. While information was a foundation, it is unstable. For Clausewitz, "most reports are false, and the timidity of men acts as a multiplier of lies and untruths," and the "difficulty of seeing things correctly, which is one of the greatest frictions in war makes things appear quite different to what was expected."[11] The only respites to these tendencies were experience and an understanding of the "law of probability"—methods for separating the signal from the noise.[12]

Similarly, winning the fight for information is a recurrent theme in military theory across the ages. In Sun Tzu, sound strategy requires concealing intentions and deception, "when able to attack, we must seem unable; when using our forces, we must seem inactive; when we are near, we must make the enemy believe we are far away; when far away, we must make him believe we are near." Mongolian hordes conducted extensive reconnaissance, used psychological warfare, and applied deception (including feigned retreats).[13] Napoleon used intelligence to reduce uncertainty at multiple levels. The famed strategist, "used embassies at the strategic level. He used cavalry and spies at the operational level. He sought to use cavalry not only to gather intelligence but also to deceive an opponent as to his own strength and intentions."[14] In the American Civil War, telegraph tapping and cutting played an important role. In the early stages of World War I, Germany and Great Britain tried to cut undersea cables as a means of limiting each other's ability to coordinate their globally arrayed forces.[15] In the modern era, mass propaganda—whether delivered by radio, television, or agitprop and the arts—played an important role in great power competition.

What is new is the sheer volume of information available in war and the relative costs of manipulating it. Major military actors are developing new concepts for employing information warfare combining traditional propaganda with cyber operations as a means of offsetting conventional military capabilities. For many political actors, the problem in modern warfare is a capabilities gap. Confronted either by the significant power projection capabilities of the United States and its ability to wage global war, actors increasingly respond by manipulating information.

To examine this trend, this chapter is organized as follows. First, contemporary information warfare is defined based on the evolution of US security perspectives that see information as a form of military power. Second, the discussion shifts to a review of contemporary Chinese and Russian approaches to information warfare. The chapter then concludes by considering how non-state actors, seen through the lens of social movement theory, engage in contentious politics and a larger war of narratives that offsets US military advantages.

LEARNING TO FORGET INFLUENCE: THE EVOLUTION OF INFORMATION WARFARE IN THE UNITED STATES

The irony of the 2016 election hack is that the United States pioneered the tactic. In 1948, the United States launched a covert political warfare campaign to manipulate the Italian elections.[16] The effort involved a sophisticated approach to manipulating the media, blackmailing the opposition, and waging a propaganda campaign that limited Communist freedom of action. From 1948 to 1956, the United States waged similar campaigns under an emerging theory of influence short of war against the Soviets called political warfare. This form of influence and coercion at its core often involved manipulating public opinion and perception to achieve a position of advantage. Yet, after the Cold War, US strategists seem to have forgotten these age-old dark arts and narrowed the scope of information warfare to precision strikes against rival networks and protecting friendly information.

In a classified 1948 Policy and Planning Staff Memorandum, George Kennan defined political warfare as operations that "range from such covert actions as political alliances, economic measures, and white propaganda to such covert operations as clandestine support to friendly foreign elements, black psychological warfare and even encouragement of underground resistance in hostile states."[17] Whereas "white propaganda" reveals its origin, "black psychological warfare" hides its origin and can denote false statements attributed to other groups in order to undermine them. For Kennan, political warfare was, "the logical application of Clausewitz's doctrine in time of peace. In broadest definition, political warfare [was] the employment of all means at a nation's command, short of war, to achieve its national objectives."[18]

Political warfare is, from a theoretical perspective, an example of coercion. In international relations, coercion is the use of threats and limited action to alter behavior.[19] It is more potential than actual force; taking minimal, often indirect, action to alter the cost-benefit calculation of an adversary short of using such brute force as would result in a major military campaign.[20] Avoiding brute force is the key to coercion. Force is threatened, even used at a lower threshold short of open battle, to achieve a concession short of war. Hence, for Nobel Laureate Thomas Schelling, coercion is the exploitation of potential force.[21]

Given its clandestine nature and indirect approach, political warfare works in the background to increase the credibility of other threats and to undermine the adversary's ability to resist.[22] The central task of any coercive strategy is "to create in the opponent the expectation of costs of sufficient magnitude to erode his motivation to continue what he is doing."[23] In this, success depends "on whether the initial coercive action or threat stands alone or is part of a broader credible threat to escalate pressure further if necessary."[24] Political warfare shapes the environment, animating this "broader credible threat" by creating risk and uncertainty for the target. It is not a clear signal, but rather a wave of background noise that limits the target's freedom of action. The task is thus more about increasing the cost of making choices that are unfavorable to the initiator than it is about forcing a concession.[25]

Political warfare was a key vector of competition during the Cold War. Before the missile gap, there was an influence gap. And, for many leading thinkers of the time, the Soviets were masters of political warfare. According to Kennan, "Lenin so synthesized the teachings of Marx and Clausewitz that the Kremlin's conduct of political warfare has become the most refined and effective of any in history."[26] A declassified 1951 CIA memorandum echoed this perspective, asserting that "in the Soviet concept, a state of political and psychological warfare is the normal relationship between Communist and capitalist states. Armed conflict is merely the employment of additional means in the conduct of this continuing struggle."[27] Officials also assumed that political warfare would be a key component of any larger military attack by the Soviet Union. According to a May 9, 1950, CIA memorandum, "the USSR regards political and psychological warfare as an integral rather than incidental in the waging of war."[28] Political warfare was a means of coercing an adversary before hostilities, and once the fighting began, a means of undermining its cohesion.

To respond to such coercion, the United States needed its own means to undermine the Soviets from within while pursuing a strategy of containment. [29] Contrary to the view of containment as a defensive posture, thinkers like Kennan "advocated an aggressive program of clandestine warfare against communism, involving propaganda, sabotage, subversion, and paramilitary engagement."[30] Visions of early political warfare efforts included low-cost, low-risk, plausibly deniable methods for undermining Soviet resolve and cohesion while limiting communist expansion.

These activities built on Allied efforts in World War II. In 1939, British Colonel Lawrence Grand, head of the War Office GS(R), circulated a paper advocating an irregular warfare approach to challenging the Axis powers.[31] Hugh Dalton, the British Minister of Economic Warfare, picked up these ideas and helped lay the groundwork for the Special Operations Executive (SOE). Dalton served as a member of the executive committee of the Political Warfare Executive.[32] The organization helped create an infrastructure for resistance in neutral and Axis-occupied countries through activities ranging from setting up wireless communication networks to supporting resistance groups.

On the other side of the Atlantic, the US Office of Strategic Services (OSS) also ventured into the world of political warfare. According to unclassified doctrinal manuals, "strategic services" were "all measures taken to enforce our will upon the enemy by means other than military action."[33] These actions included activities designed "to aid and give direct support to the furtherance of protected or actual military operations; to destroy the will and ability of the enemy to resist; and to deprive the enemy of the support of his allies and of neutrals and strengthen resistance within occupied countries."[34]

For example, the Political Warfare Plan for Operation Overlord, the 1944 Normandy invasion, called for undermining German morale through various activities including appealing to over six million foreign workers in Germany to slow down production and supporting resistance movements in the Balkans as a means of tying down German military units.[35] The plan stated that political warfare "must, at the proper time, exploit and canalize political ferments existing behind enemy lines" in support of larger objectives including bombing campaigns, deception operations, and major ground campaigns.[36]

As such, the concept of political warfare and strategic services was a logical referent for strategists seeking to counter the Soviet Union in 1947.[37] In December of that year, the Truman administration published NSC 4-A, which tasked the CIA with taking the lead on covert psychological warfare operations that reflected elements of earlier efforts in World War II. The declassified directive opened by stating:

> the National Security Council, taking cognizance of the vicious psychological efforts of the USSR, its satellite countries, and Communist groups to discredit and defeat the aims and activities of the United States and other Western powers, has determined that, in the interests of world peace and US national security,

the foreign information activities of the US Government must be supplemented by covert psychological operations.[38]

By the summer of 1948, the renewed focus on psychological warfare broadened to include covert action operations when the Truman administration published NSC 10/2. The document advocated political warfare and called for a new organization, the Office of Policy Coordination (OPC), to coordinate

> propaganda, economic warfare; preventive direct action, including sabotage, anti-sabotage, demolition and evacuation measures; subversion against hostile states, including assistance to underground resistance movements, guerrillas and refugee liberation groups, and support of indigenous anti-communist elements in threatened countries of the free world.[39]

Table 5 lists the OPC's lines of effort, referred to in the document as lines of clandestine activity, based on an October 1948 declassified memorandum.

PSYCHOLOGICAL WARFARE

One of the predominant forms of political warfare in the early Cold War was psychological warfare. Poison pens—false letters sent to undermine an enemy—and rumors were techniques used by the OSS during World War II and subsequently adopted by the new OPC. During the World War II Operation Hemlock, anonymous letters were sent to Gestapo officers spreading rumors that officials were engaged in activity in support of the Allies.[40] In a separate operation, OSS operatives created a fake holiday greeting from a German mayor and sent it to frontline troops. The letter outlined sacrifices on the home front designed to undermine German military confidence in the Nazi regime.[41]

Table 5. 1948 Organization for Political Warfare.

Functional Group I – Psychological Warfare
Program A – press (periodical and non-periodical)
Program B – radio
Program C – miscellaneous (direct mail, poison pen, rumors, etc.)
Function Group II – Political Warfare
Program A – Support of Resistance (Underground)
Program B – Support of Displaced Persons and Refugees
Program C – Support of Anti-Communists in Free Countries
Program D – Encouragement of Defection
Functional Group III – Economic Warfare
Program A – Commodity operations (clandestine preclusive buying, market manipulation and black market operation)
Program B – Fiscal operations (currency speculation, counterfeiting, etc.)
Functional Group IV – Preventive Direct Action
Program A – Support of Guerillas
Program B – Sabotage, Countersabotage and Demolition
Program C – Evacuation
Program D – Stay-behind
Functional Group V – Miscellaneous
Program A – Front Operations
Program B – War Plans
Program C – Administration
Program D – Miscellaneous

Source. Memorandum from Assistant Director for Policy Coordination (Wisner) to Director of Central Intelligence Hillenkoetter, October 48, 1968, Emergence of the Intelligence Establishment, document 306, https://history.state.gov/historicaldocuments/frus1945-50Intel.

False flags—making it seem as if an act was carried out under another nation's flag—were a form of covert action designed to manipulate perception and undermine morale and cohesion. A group attempts to conceal its involvement by creating the perception that a separate group made an inflammatory statement, carried out some act of sabotage, subversion, or physical attack. For example, during the September 1931 Mukden incident, Japan covertly blew up a section of railway in Manchuria and shifted the blame onto China as a pretext for seizing the territory and installing a puppet government.[42]

Much of the earlier psychological warfare efforts focused not only on these rumors and false flags but also on building an infrastructure for disseminating ideas that countered Soviet propaganda. For example, the CIA covertly established Radio Free Europe/Radio Liberty under the veil of a private broadcaster to "contribute to the liberation of the nations imprisoned by the Iron Curtain by sustaining their morale and stimulating in them a spirit of non-cooperation with Soviet-dominated regimes."[43] The agency also established state-private networks that used private groups—ranging from foundations and action committees to arts organizations—to undermine Soviet messaging and shape the occupied areas for liberation.[44] These efforts included the Crusade for Freedom fundraising drives, which sponsored exile programming on Radio Free Europe/Radio Liberty.[45]

Sabotage

Another key attribute of political warfare was sabotage and preventive action that undermined an adversary's critical capabilities and cohesion short of armed conflict. As seen figure 2, this logic extended beyond the CIA to the military services. By 1950, the US Army published a series of classified manuals to support unconventional military activity in support of political warfare. As the figure illustrates, indirect action could limit the connection between political leaders and the economic sector, as well as between the economic sector and the security services.

Figure 2. How to Undermine a State from Within.

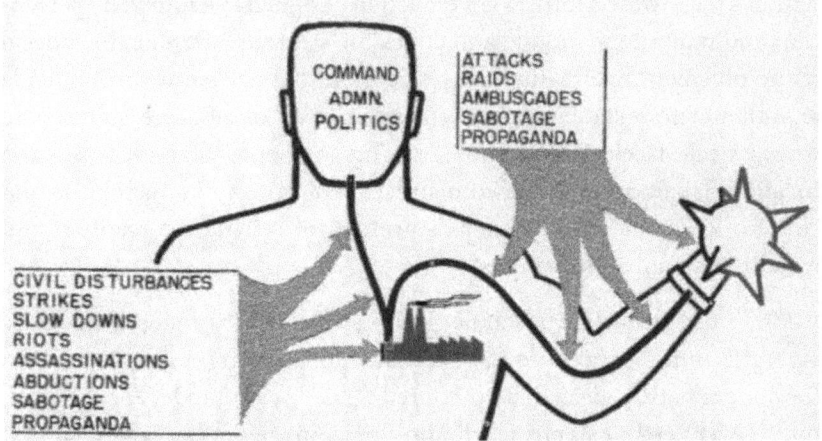

Source. ST 31-20-1, 1950, *Operations against Guerilla Forces* (Fort Benning: The Infantry School), 10, http://cgsc.contentdm.oclc.org/cdm/ref/collection/p4013coll9/id/908.

POLITICAL WARFARE COMES OF AGE IN CYBERSPACE

Cyber operations offer a new vector of covert political warfare. Cyber coercion involves digitally exploiting "the power to hurt."[46] Intrusions, logic bombs, website defacements, viruses, and Distributed Denial of Service (DDoS) operations indirectly compel an adversary without physical attack. Through these measures, an actor's power to hurt becomes "the power to hurt online."[47] Martin Libicki situates cyber operations on an escalation ladder between economic coercion and the use of physical force short of nuclear exchange.[48]

In peacetime competition, cyber coercion is an indirect and additive form of *compellence*. Compellence refers to using coercive action to change a state's existing behavior.[49] The concept can be differentiated from deterrence, which seeks to stop a state from taking aggressive action. Cyber coercion is indirect in that it signals in the covert sphere—like early forms of political warfare—and achieves success by enhancing perceptions of resolve and managing escalation, rather than by employing direct, overt threats.[50] Even when cyber operations fail to achieve a concession, they signal the risk of escalation and demonstrate resolve.[51] Cyber coercion is additive in that, like coercive diplomacy, success depends "on whether the initial coercive action or threat stands alone or is part of a broader credible threat to escalate pressure further if necessary."[52] The extension of classical political warfare operations such as psychological warfare and sabotage to the digital domain demonstrates this logic. What is interesting is that techniques the United States helped pioneer fell by the wayside as the superpower became addicted to precision strike after the Cold War. From Stuxnet to Edward Snowden's leaks about precision counterespionage campaigns against China, sabotage prevails more than propaganda for US strategists in the twenty-first century.

In the 1990s, scholars started to focus more on the role of information in warfare than as a vector for influence in political warfare. This early body of scholarship and practitioner reflections stressed how the ability to accumulate and to process information faster than your adversary changed warfare.[53] Information warfare represented "actions intended to protect, exploit, corrupt, deny, or destroy information or information resources in order to achieve a significant advantage, objective or victory over the adversary."[54] These actions pivoted on capabilities "to know, to deny knowledge, and to manipulate information." [55] Information warfare thus implied collecting and processing information about the enemy, denying them access to critical information about your own forces, and deceiving them through manipulating information. Influence operations faded into the background.

The strategy of information warfare conceived along these lines was, "based upon the defense and attack of information and information systems."[56] While military forces have always tried to defend and attack information systems, especially in the form of the enemy's commanders understanding of the situation, "the importance of this form of conflict has been magnified many times over with the computer and Internet revolutions."[57]

According to Air Force Doctrine Department 2-5, Information Operations (1998),

> The Air Force believes that to fully understand and achieve information superiority, our understanding of information operations must explicitly include two conceptually distinct but extremely interrelated pillars: information-in-warfare—the "gain" and "exploit" aspects or other information-based processes—and information warfare—the "attack" and "defend" aspects. Information warfare involves such diverse activities as psychological operations, military deception, electronic warfare, both physical and information ("cyber") attack, and a variety of defensive activities and programs. It is important to stress that information warfare is a construct that operates across the spectrum, from peace to war, to allow the effective execution of Air Force responsibilities.

The connectivity of the information age changed the ways and means associated with the objective (i.e., end) of attacking an adversary's information system and their internal cohesion:

> a typical goal of conventional warfare is to destroy or degrade the enemy's physical resources, whereas the aim of IW [information warfare] is to target information assets and infrastructure, such that the resultant damage may not be immediately visible or detectable to the untrained eye: These strikes are called soft kills. In practical terms, cyberwarfare means infiltrating, degrading, or subverting the target's information systems using logic bombs or computer viruses.[58]

The interest in information warfare paralleled after action reviews of the Gulf War and the emergence of the internet. The dotcom boom of the 1990s occurred while military theorists were analyzing how the US-led Coalition achieved victory against Iraq in Desert Storm. Though the Coalition used few precision weapons, the dramatic television footage of laser-guided bombs heading to their target reflected for some the first shots of a new form of warfare. According to Peter Feaver, in these optimistic accounts:

> Desert Storm was a preview of a new era, with prototypes and first-generation systems hinting at the likely course of conflict in the next century. Under the new form of warfare, called information warfare (IW), information-processing ability becomes each side's center of gravity and therefore the focus of military effort, both offensive and defensive. Conflicts will turn on whether one side can control the other side's ability to process information while protecting its own information processing from the efforts of the enemy to control it. The side that can conquer its opponent's information while preserving its own information from enemy attacks will prevail. The side that loses control over its information will lose.[59]

This view of information warfare as the "manipulation or disruption of information distribution networks" along offensive and defensive lines found its way into military doctrine.[60] The US Army Information Operations manual stated, "Information operations (IO) encompass attacking adversary command and control (C2) systems (offensive IO) while protecting friendly C2 systems from adversary disruption (defensive IO). Effective IO combines the effects of offensive and defensive IO to produce information superiority at decisive points."[61] The US Air Force drew a direct connection between information superiority and gaining air and space superiority.[62] In Joint Doctrine, employing instruments of power in the information environment "requires the ability to securely transmit, receive, store, and process information in near real time. The nation's state and non-state adversaries are equally aware of the significance of this new technology, and will use information-related capabilities (IRCs) to gain advantages in the information environment, just as they would use more traditional military technologies to gain advantages in other operational environments."[63] In this reading, information operations became the employment of these IRCs to "influence, disrupt, corrupt, or usurp the decision-making of adversaries and potential adversaries while protecting [your] own."[64] The focus was on commanders not their populations and precision as opposed to coercion. The logic of political warfare shifted to the logic of precision strike.

In cyberspace, targeting decision making meant seeking a means to manipulate and control information.[65] Pre-Stuxnet, cyber thinkers focused on syntactic and semantic targets. Syntactic targets were the rules and processes governing the flow of information. If you change those rules or process, you alter the flow of information and shape decision-making. Semantic targets were the content of messages themselves, or the underlying meaning. If you change the content of the message, you shape decision-making. In either case, the idea was to cause an actor to make a suboptimal decision. Seen in this light, cyberspace was a form of achieving virtual attrition, a "forced decrease in operational effectiveness."[66]

Thinkers began to see more conventional uses for cyber manipulation in the early 1990s. Paralleling the Revolution in Military Affairs (RMA), advocates argued that cyber created new battlefield dynamics and expanded the space-time boundaries of conflict.[67] Specifically, the cyber dimension had unique spatial and temporal characteristics. [68] First, it led to a spatial expansion by enabling, through computer networks, attackers to extend the depth of battlefield. Second, in relation to civilian audiences, it expanded the battlefield. Communications networks connected domestic audiences to war in a new way, allowing adversaries to manipulate the media and deny civilian support for military action. Third, cyber warfare led to temporal acceleration. The speed of attack became the speed it took to circulate images or send malicious code through computer networks. Cyber warfare removed distance and connected populations in a new way that would change how wars were fought.

Precision killed influence. By 2006, *Joint Publication 3-13 Information Operations* no longer spoke of information warfare. Information operations became a much narrower task of "affecting enemy decisions and decision-making processes" and defending friendly command networks.[69]

The net result was an approach to cyberspace and contemporary information operations that was largely limited in scope when compared to the Cold War legacy of psychological warfare, propaganda, and other political warfare efforts. According to a Center for Strategic and Budgetary Assessment report, "the American approach to information operations and warfare is largely tactical, bottom-up, and stove-piped into a series of disparate communities and organizations."[70]

LEARNING TO MANIPULATE: THE EVOLUTION OF INFORMATION WARFARE IN CHINA

In contrast to the United States, China takes a much broader view of the role of information manipulation as a form of power. Chinese perspectives on information warfare emerge from Chinese strategic theory, including the concepts of *shih* and People's War, adapted to modern conditions and defeating a technologically superior adversary (i.e., the United States). The connectivity of the modern world changes the character of war and enables China to focus, beyond traditional military targets, on a broader range of social, political, and economic objectives designed to undermine US resolve and capabilities. [71] Information warfare in this reading is inherently coercive and designed to change the balance of information, and through it, the balance of power over time. Combining subjective and objective factors, psychological warfare and cyber intrusions, gives China a strategic advantage for the twenty-first century.

In 1985, a young PLA officer proposed a new form of warfare, "take home battle," in which networks across society mobilize to wage information warfare on behalf of the nation. [72] The officer, Shen Weiguang, stated that "those who take part in information war are not all soldiers... rapid mobilization will not just be directed to young people; information-related industries and domains will be the first to be mobilized and enter the war."[73] The concept bridged Mao's concept of People's War with emerging capabilities.

People's War, best articulated in Mao Tse Tung's *On Protracted War*,[74] called for mobilizing popular support and waging a protracted guerilla struggle before transitioning to conventional operations. With respect to information warfare, Shen Weiguang saw networks of citizens and businesses mobilizing in cyberspace. He saw modern connectivity as increasing the mobilization potential and creating new attack surfaces for guerilla campaigns designed, whether through lethal or non-lethal means, to wear down an enemy over time. According to leading Chinese cyber thinkers writing ten years later, these guerilla attacks in cyberspace would target, "the enemy's weak parts and dead angles….[using] network special warfare detachments and finding some computer experts to form a shock brigade of network warriors who specialize in looking for critical nodes and controls centers on the enemy network and sabotaging them."[75]

In addition, Chinese thinkers drew on a deep body of strategic theory about attacking shih, which is best of thought of as similar to a center of gravity. Shih is strategic power. It is the source of one's strength. According to Tai-tsung, a Tang dynasty ruler, in war "cause the enemy's strategic power [shih] to constantly be vacuous, and my strategic power to always be substantial."[76] In the book of *Campaign Stratagems*, shih is the "combination of the friendly situation, enemy situation, and the environment; as the sum of all factors impacting the performance of the operational efficiency of both sides; and as the key factor determining the rise and fall of operational efficiency."[77]

Shih, defined variously as "momentum, potential energy, force, the strategic configuration of power, strategic advantage," is often inherent in the situation such that "the velocity of cascading water can send boulders bobbing about is due to its strategic advantage (shih)." [78] Shih is therefore interdependent as opposed to independent. Each situation has an inherent potential. The wise commander exploits that potential to gain an advantage. Looking back at Mao's *On Protracted War*, the inherent potential was the strategic depth of China (i.e., Japan could attack coasts but had trouble in the interior) and its sheer size (i.e., importance of unifying the population). As Sheng Weiguang pondered cyber warfare in 1985, shih was the ability to accelerate and decentralize mobilization for People's War in cyberspace.

With classical and Marxist thought as a foundation, the 1991 Gulf War became a catalyst for contemporary Chinese strategic thinking on information warfare.[79] Leading PLA thinkers saw the conflict as the harbinger of a new way of warfare.[80] Whereas US analysts tended to highlight this Revolution in Military Affairs focusing on how satellite constellations, command networks, and stealth aircraft enabled precision military strikes, Chinese thinkers took a broader view. According to James Mulvenon, PLA theorists believed that information warfare, "played a significant role in the US victory. A commonly held belief, for example, is that the US military used computer viruses to disrupt and destroy Iraqi information systems."[81] Chinese strategists held that information was the key to victory. According to Wang Pufeng:

> Information war is a product of the information age, which to a great extent utilizes information technology and information ordnance in battle. It constitutes a "networkization" [*wangluohua*] of the battlefield, and a new model for a complete contest of time and space. At its center is the fight to control the information battlefield, and thereby to influence or decide victory or defeat.[82]

Information as a theory of victory is a theme similarly captured in Wang Houqing and Zhang Xingye, *The Science of Campaigns*. For Houqing and Xingye, "integrated combat operations directed at the battlefield sources from which any enemy probes for information, his information channels, and his information processing and decision-making systems, so as to disrupt an enemy's ability to control information and seize and maintain battlefield information superiority." [83] In this new world, offense is easier than defense. The side that disrupts the other's information first gains a position of advantage.

This logic is on display in Chinese cyber strategy. According to Timothy Thomas, for Chinese thinkers, "a cyber strategy is the result of the creative use of subjective thought to manipulate or guide objective cyber conditions, which are the dynamic new aspects of the strategic environment."[84] Again, shih is interdependent with the environment; that is, strategic advantage arises based on how enemy, friendly, and environment factors interact. In this reading, the key is to apply classic stratagems in a new world to maximize shih. According to Thomas, for Chinese cyber thinkers "a packet of electrons can execute a stratagem such as 'rustle the grass to startle the snake,' that is, cause firewalls to alert and thus expose defense capabilities when probed."[85]

The relationship between objective and subjective factors is central to understanding how classical stratagems manifest as cyber strategy in Chinese military circles. For the PLA,

> Subjective refers to a person's thinking or understanding. Objective refers to the material world existing outside of a person's consciousness. The relationship between subjective and objective is a dialectical unity. Objective does not rely on subjective and exists independently, it is the source of subjective, it determines subjective; subjective reflects objective, and actively reacts with objective, under certain conditions it determines the effect of objective. The objective world is constantly developing and changing, and a person's understanding must also accordingly develop and change.[86]

Objective factors alter how we subjectively understand a situation. How we understand a situation determines the art of the possible in strategy. For Chinese thinkers, the modern objective factors in cyberspace relate to connectivity and how it alters options. Again, People's War and shih animate this emergent logic. First, the United States is highly connected and thus highly vulnerable in cyberspace. The lack of rules and regulations for cyberspace compared to traditional warfare and Chinese censorship alongside the ability to monitor its population relative to the United States' compound this vulnerability.

Second, long-term power depends on intellectual property. Innovation is the key to growth. In the information age intellectual property and trade secrets are central to innovation and increasing productivity. Thus, altering the balance of information will alter the balance of power over time.

Third, information warfare, especially as waged in cyberspace, offers the optimal conditions for traditional guerilla warfare. Attacks have higher degrees of anonymity than traditional sabotage. The number of attack vectors is large (i.e., the enemy has long supply lines susceptible to raids). The potential for propaganda and espionage are high. Hackers —whether state-based, state-sponsored, or indirectly state-inspired— can "use packets of electrons as stratagems to manipulate perceptions and actions."[87]

At its core, the objective factor driving strategy in the modern world is the relationship between information and power. The Chinese strategic community's "view of the relationship between information and power has crystalized in the past half century, as the world economy has global-ized, and as information has become even more integrated with develop-ment."[88] This objective factor underlies the concept of "informationized war" in the PLA textbook, *The Science of Military Strategy*. In the text, the authors maintain that informationized warfare is similar to earlier Soviet ideas of a reconnaissance-strike complex. It aims:

> to seize and maintain strategic information superiority and information superiority on the battlefield. One seeks to achieve strategic goals through information control and information attack, including conducting soft sabotage or hard destruction of the infrastructure, basic information sources or battlefield informa-tion systems, the armed forces of a country relies on for survival through information network in order to achieve its strategic goals. This is an all-new strategic concept and strategic model.[89]

Connectivity, the relationship between information and power, as an objective factor creates new strategic models. With respect to information warfare, the new model means attacking the enemy's decision cycle along multiple fronts. In 1995, Shen Weiguang, defined information warfare as "decision control warfare, where information is the main weapon designed to attack the enemy's cognitive and information systems and influence, contain or change the decisions of enemy policy makers and their consequent hostile actions. The main target of IW is the enemy's cognitive and trust systems, and the goal is to exert control over his actions."[90]

Decision control warfare is not limited to cyberattacks or propaganda in isolation. Rather, it is an organic whole that involves lethal and non-lethal attack surfaces designed to take advantage of shih in a connected world. According to Larry Wortzel:

> China's military doctrine depends on incorporating information technology and networked information operations. The PLA's warfighting concepts for employing signals intelligence and electronic warfare have expanded to include cyber warfare, attacks on satellites, and information confrontation operations (*xinxi duikang zuozhan*). Along with these more technical aspects of information operations, the PLA's combination of psychological warfare; the manipulation of public opinion, or media warfare; and the manipulation of legal arguments to strengthen China's diplomatic and security position, or what China calls "legal warfare," join together in a comprehensive information operations doctrine.[91]

Seen from this perspective, information warfare alters the application of shih. Rather than coerce through a show of objective force, "a cyber show of force can involve actually mapping and showing an opponent his strategic cyber geography, thereby deterring an opponent due to the exposure and exploitability of his key nodes and infrastructure."[92] The logic of cyber espionage is two-fold. It alters the long-term information balance as it relates to economic growth, political advantage, and military options. More importantly, it deters. It reminds an adversary that they are vulnerable without a significant escalation, an approach on display in the Operation of Personnel Management hack in 2015.[93]

Manipulation forms a key component of modern information warfare. According to Laurent Murawiec, "just as in Sun Zi's times, the aim of war —or the aim of China's regional strategy—is not to 'destroy the enemy' but to 'convince' him." China will play to its own strengths, of which its psycho-political manipulation, mind games, and actions at a distance are the most honed."[94] The connectivity of the modern world provides new vectors for influence and manipulation.[95]

The two leading superpowers appear to be taking different approaches with respect to the role of information in competition, confrontation, and conflict. This distinction is captured in a CSBA study:

> The US Joint Staff has banished "information warfare" from its official lexicon and largely relegated information operations to a combat support role that exploits cyber tools to influence enemy cognition and decision-making processes. While some theorists in the Chinese military once held similar views, Yuan Wenxian at the PLA's National Defense University argued in 2009 that information operations had progressed from a supporting role to that of an indispensable important measure in joint campaign operations under informationized conditions.[96]

LEARNING TO DISTORT: THE EVOLUTION OF INFORMATION WARFARE IN RUSSIA

> [The] method of conflict has altered in the direction of the broad use of political, economic, informational, humanitarian, and other nonmilitary measures—applied in coordination with the protest potential of the population. All this is supplemented by military means of a concealed character, including carrying out actions of informational conflict and the actions of special-operations forces.
> —General Valery Gerasimov,
> "The Value of Science in Prediction," *Military-Industrial Kurier*
> (February 27, 2013)

Russia's approach to using information as a form of coercion has a foundation in Soviet practices. From agitprop to psychological warfare and active measures, the Soviet Union invested significant time and resources in a sustained effort to manipulate domestic and international audiences. For Maria Snegovaya, "Russia's modern information warfare adapts Soviet reflective control to the contemporary geopoltical context."[97] The Kremlin uses information warfare as an asymmetric response to compensate for its weaker military position. Despite sustained military modernization, the Russian military spent less on defense in 2015 than Saudi Arabia. The military is getting better, but still has significant issues in logistics, the number of high-quality units, and affording sustained combat operations. According to Snegovaya, "the Russian military compensates for its relative weakness with indirect, subtle strategies that aim to confuse the enemy about its goals. Confusing the enemy is key to Russia's information war concept."[98]

This strategy of confusion and manipulation has antecedents in the Soviet concept of reflective control. According to Timothy Thomas, "reflective control is defined as a means of conveying to a partner or an opponent specially prepared information to incline him to voluntarily make the predetermined decision desired by the initiator of the action."[99] Reflective control is about influencing your enemy to make suboptimal decisions that benefit you. Rather than attack the enemy's decision cycle, it seeks to manipulate through misinformation and deception.

The concept first appeared in the Soviet military literature in the late Cold War. [100] In fact, Russian thinkers after the fall of the Soviet Union held that the Strategic Defense Initiative was a reflective control campaign designed to get the Soviets to spend money they didn't have on countering futuristic weapons that didn't exist. Reflective control operated at the strategic example, as seen in the SDI example, but also at the operational and tactical level. At lower echelons, reflective control aligned with Soviet ideas about the importance of *maskirovka* (deception) and the use of disinformation to confuse "the enemy's decision-making processes."[101]

Similar to reflexive control, the Soviet concept of Active Measures (*aktivnyye meropriyatiya*) used propaganda to target Western media outlets.[102] For example, in 1984 Soviet operatives planted a story in an Indian newspaper that the AIDS virus was the result of US genetic experiments. [103] Like the 2016 US Presidential Election hack, these campaigns sought to undermine a rival population's faith in political leaders and institutions and disrupt relations between allies. Under Putin, this strategy extends to increasing Russia's leverage in post-Soviet space as a counter to the Color Revolutions that swept through Georgia, Ukraine, and Kyrgyzstan.[104] Connectivity, the web of global networks, and the velocity of information in cyberspace amplify the benefits of using disinformation to undermine rivals.[105]

This emphasis on confusing an adversary, either for purposes of paralyzing their decision apparatus as part of a larger coercion effort or misleading them to make suboptimal decisions, takes center stage in Putin's approach to international relations. It shouldn't surprise the international community that a KGB officer who once worked in East Germany puts a premium on information. Reflecting on why he wanted to join the KGB as a teenager, Putin once said, "one man's effort could achieve what whole armies could not. One spy could decide the fate of thousands of people."[106] According to John Emerson, building on its Soviet legacy Russia takes a 4D approach:

> dismiss—as Putin did for over a month with the obvious fact that Russian soldiers had occupied Crimea in the Russian news; distort —as an actress did in playing the role of a pro-Russian Ukrainian; distract—as Russian media did with ludicrous theories about what happened to Malaysian Airlines Flight 17; dismay—as Russia's ambassador to Denmark did in March when he threatened to aim nuclear missiles at Danish warships if Denmark joined NATO's missile defense systems.[107]

This 4D approach, at both the strategic and the operational level, implies shifting lines of effort in competition, confrontation, and conflict. According to Rod Thorton, "Western military thinkers tend to look upon what they refer to as information operations merely an adjunct to their campaign plans. In contrast, for Russian military thinkers, information now has a decisive quality. For Russian thinkers, the center of gravity is perception, "the Russian view of modern warfare is based on the idea that main battlespace is in the mind, and, as a result, new-generation wars are to be dominated by information and psychological warfare with the main objective being to reduce the necessity for deploying hard military power to the minimum necessary, making the opponent's military and civilian population support the attacker to the detriment of the their own government and country."[108]

From a Russian perspective, an information-rich, connected world dominated by risk-averse Western populations will very likely continue to present new opportunities for the use of tailored military coercion in support of limited political objectives. The desired end-state will likely not be to seize new terrain as much as it is to deny adversary initiative. The logic of defensive geopolitics implies that Moscow, the besieged fortress, will likely continue to be under attack from the expansion of NATO and Western promotion of democracy and human rights. To counter these strategic offensive actions, Russian forces will match their strength (disinformation and propaganda campaigns backed by threats of military force) against the West's weakness (political will and a war-weary cosmopolitan population). The objective is to reestablish Moscow's traditional security buffer and provide Russia with increased bargaining power relative to other states in a multipolar international system. Russia survives by threatening to fight above its weight class and using influence campaigns to undermine Western resolve.

From a Russian perspective, the character of war started to change in 1991. First, Russian thinkers see the Gulf War, similar to PLA writings on informationized warfare, as "the first war of the new age."[109] In that conflict, Russian observers claim the United States used an "electronic knockdown" before the first shot was fired, which enabled them to launch a "massive attack" with EW assets and an accompanying "aerial offensive by the air force and sea-based cruise missiles, reinforced with reconnaissance strike aircraft, artillery barrages, and remote-controlled aerial vehicles."[110]

Second, senior Russian officials like the Chief of Staff of the Russian Military, General Gerasimov, believe the West is using democracy promotion, economic liberalization, and human rights propagated through nongovernment organizations, as means of inciting civil unrest in targeted countries. Specifically, military thinkers see an unbroken chain for events that started in the 2000 nonviolent protest against Milosevic, evolved during the 2004 and 2005 colored revolutions in Ukraine and Georgia, and reached their culmination in the 2009–2011 Arab Spring.[111] These two dynamics, unleashing a population against its government and information enabled deep strikes, are the central ideas in New-Generation Warfare.

Information operations and unconventional lines of effort take on new importance. Operatives conduct psychological operations through multiple media channels that target both their adversary's leadership and population, as well as Russia's own domestic audience. New Generation Warfare prefaces actions designed to turn foreign populations against their governments—subterfuge, insurrection, and protests—as logical and legitimate. The intent, to use Sun Tzu's phase, is to win without fighting. Backed by Russian conventional forces conducting snap exercises and nuclear blackmail, adversaries who are confronted with persistent, tailored propaganda and unconventional warfare within their own borders will offer concessions short of escalating to major theater war.

In addition to propaganda and unleashing the protest potential of the population, New-Generation Warfare theorists argue that the fight for information is the decisive battle. According to one source, "no goal will be achieved in future war unless one belligerent gains information superiority over the other."[112] The reconnaissance and counter-reconnaissance fight takes place across the entire electromagnetic spectrum and collapses information and intelligence into a single, seamless information campaign. The 2010 Russian military doctrine sees this information campaign as dominating the initial phases of future conflicts, blinding an adversary's command and control, disrupting their ISR, conducting a *maskirovka* (deception) operation, and, through propaganda, seizing the moral high ground in the international community.[113]

This fight for information will likely be coordinated by nontraditional military entities operating at the strategic, as opposed to operational or tactical, level. Representatives from the Federal Protection Service (FSO), Federal Security Service (FSB), the Foreign Intelligence Service (SVR), and Military Intelligence (GRU)—not traditional conventional military units or military districts—will likely play a leading role in the design and execution of the campaign. As seen in Estonia in 2007,[114] Georgia in 2008[115] and Ukraine in 2014,[116] the campaign will also include the use of proxies in the form of cyber criminals and so-called patriotic hacktivists.

Russian views of future war invert traditional military doctrine. Historically, Western military doctrine does not view the fight for information as the main effort. These treatises define reconnaissance, counter-reconnaissance, propaganda, cyberattacks, and deception—all elements of Russian information warfare campaigns—as shaping efforts that set up a decisive battle between maneuver forces. Further at the strategic level, New-Generation Warfare implies a fundamental shift from previous views of ends, ways, and means in Russian military thought. The ends shift from seizing and holding terrain to denying vital areas to the enemy or fixing the enemy as a prelude to compelling a desired political decision.

Cyber coercion is a central part of this strategy to manipulate perceptions and, in wartime, paralyze enemies. Russians use cyber warfare not for the decisive strikes envisioned by the United States but to signal the risk of escalation while distorting information through web sites defacements and denial of service attacks, efforts seen in Estonia, Georgia, and Ukraine.[117] Cyber intrusions offer a means of signaling potential competitors and undermining alliance integrity. For example, groups linked to Russia targeted German infrastructure during the Ukrainian conflict including the German Bundestag computer networks. According to observers, "There is wide consensus among cyber-security specialists that the malware used in the December 2015 [Ukrainian] attack was an upgraded version of BlackEnergy, linked to the Russia-backed group Sandworm known for zero-day attacks (vulnerabilities unknown to the software's vendor) against Ukrainian, EU, and NATO officials, and industrial control systems in the United States."[118] During the same time period, Ukraine had its airports and TV networks hacked as well.[119] According to another source, "German authorities are certain that a Trojan virus attack against the Bundestag's computer network in the first half of 2015 was carried out by a Russian-government-funded hacker group known by the names Sofacy and APT28."[120]

The fight for information extends to the public domain and distorting opinion consistent with the concept of active measures. According to Inkster, "a new feature of Russian information warfare has been the troll factory, in which Russian state employees masquerading as ordinary members of the public maintain a barrage of social-media posts supporting the Russian government, attacking foreign politicians and commentators, and spreading disinformation. Efforts have been made to automate some of these activities."[121] Russia practices a new style of information operations designed to confuse and paralyze. These operations rely "on the fact that Western governments simply lack resources that would be required systematically to refute or debunk the huge number of stories put out, and on the Western media's professional obligation to report both sides of the story, thereby giving a veneer of legitimacy to Russian fabrications."[122]

These information campaigns and limited cyber intrusions are reinforced with military exercises designed to signal escalation risk. At the operational level, Russian forces conduct snap exercises and partial nuclear mobilizations in order to compel the target while simultaneously deterring external intervention. In the Crimea operation, this involved noncontact warfare and escalation control. According to one source, the Russians left "responsibility for escalation to the enemy" and "manipulated risk to their advantage" as a means of deterring "Ukrainian armed resistance" and "achieving a peaceful annexation of the peninsula."[123]

At the tactical level, the New Generation War involves significant increases in the number of unmanned systems, use of proxies, and the employment of optimized combined arms units at lower echelons to increase the size of unit frontages. [124] Unlike US approaches that use UAS to queue precision fires, Russians use multilayered UAS networks, from quadcopters to medium-altitude ISR platforms, to queue mass artillery fires. Similar to UAS, electronic warfare (EW) assets exist at the strategic, operational, and tactical level and are employed in both offensive and defensive mission sets. Proxies, prisoners, criminal groups, and contractors offer cheap infantry sources that can temporarily hold terrain and, when dispersed across the battlefield, disrupt the ability of the adversary to mass. Last, the use of battalion tactical and company tactical groups pushes the combined arms fight down to lower echelons and increases the frontage units can control.[125]

As seen above, there are important differences between Russian, Chinese, and US approaches to information warfare. The US concept of information warfare, in the RMA paradigm, focused on precision strikes targeting C4ISR. The Chinese approaches focused on altering the balance of information to increase shih (situational power). The Russian approach to information warfare places a much greater emphasis on how uncertainty and confusion can paralyze decision-making and create opportunities for coercive leverage.

LEARNING TO WAGE A WAR OF NARRATIVES:
AN EXTREMIST PERSPECTIVE

States are not the only strategic actor developing new theories of victory for strategic competition predicated on information warfare. The evolution of how violent extremist networks use information to mobilize recruits and signal rivals illustrates the central role of information in contemporary warfare. The rise and, at the time of this writing, decline of Daesh tell this story.

Daesh has its roots in extremist movements in Iraq dating back to 2000, when Jordanian Abu Musab al-Zarqawi formed the Jamaat al-Tawhid wal Jihad.[126] Al-Zarqawi moved his operation from Afghanistan to Iraq after the 2001 invasion. By summer of 2003, al-Zarqawi's network took part in a larger Sunni insurgency in Iraq. The group had a troubled relationship with Al-Qaeda. Though maintaining ideologically similar goals, the groups differed with respect to tactics. Al-Zarqawi preferred extreme acts of violence, earning the nickname "the Sheikh of Slaughter" that core Al-Qaeda assessed as alienating the population. Unlike other Iraqi insurgent groups, al-Zarqawi's network relied more on suicide bombers than on traditional guerilla tactics such as ambushes and hit-and-run attacks. The group also "targeted a wide variety of groups: the Iraqi security forces, Iraqi Shia and Kurdish political and religious figures, Shia Muslim civilians, foreign civilian contractors, and UN and humanitarian workers."[127]

In 2006 the US military killed al-Zarqawi, and his network suffered a series of crucial defeats. In 2008 the Sunni Awakening limited the extent to which the extremist network could rely on support from Sunni tribal elements, who were now aligning with Coalition forces in exchange for positions in the Iraqi security forces. By June 2010, "80 percent of the group's 42 leaders, including recruiters and financers, had been killed or captured."[128]

The decapitation of al-Zarqawi's former network created a leadership vacuum filled by Abu Bakr al-Baghdadi. Al-Baghdadi took advantage of a politically weak Iraqi state and the departure of US forces to rebuild al-Zarqawi's former network. The group benefited from the Syrian Civil War. Al-Baghdadi changed the group's objective to, "the overthrow of illegitimate governments and the creation of an Islamic caliphate."[129] With this new objective, he rebranded the group the Islamic State of Iraq and Syria (ISIS) and subsequently into the Islamic State, referred to here as Daesh.

One of the defining features of al-Zarqawi's network that continued throughout its evolution into Daesh was the display of violence online. According to Ahmed Hashim, al-Zarqawi,

> was very adept at using the Internet to promote his message, recruit personnel and terrorize his enemies, posting his first communiqué on a jihadist website in April 2004. Through creating a worldwide network, Zarqawi's volunteers posted messages from their leader and videos of militant acts, like beheadings, on multiple servers. This avoided delays in downloading and made it difficult for the material to be removed from the World Wide Web.[130]

Daesh built on this tradition, continuing to post videos, creating multiple online platforms in venues ranging from Twitter to Instagram and producing films, such as *Flames of War*, and published a glossy magazine, *Dabiq*. The group used music videos, often playing rap in the background of the attack videos. According to a recent study, these efforts represented a new phenomenon of popjihadism:

> Jihadism has become a media phenomenon. Videos distributed by IS and other radical groups, with their own YouTube accounts, flourish on the Internet. The films appeal to Muslim youth with messages of martyrdom and loyalty packaged in rock and rap video formats.....What these popjihadists express in blogs is crucial and highly influential for their friends at home..... Through Twitter, Facebook, Instagram, and Tumblr, IS easily spreads its message to a Western audience. Yilmaz, a smiling Dutch jihadist with

Turkish roots, has become a social media sensation with his Tumblr account Chechclear.Tumblr.com glorifying his stint in Syria as the ultimate adventure by posting photos of warfare alongside children and kittens.[131]

Daesh and its sympathizers integrated this popjihadism with appeals by respected community figures. A recent German study on radicalization found that only "18 percent of jihadists were radicalized through online resources. By far the most important variable for the radicalization of German youth is contact with imams and mosques (23 percent) and with friends who have gone off to fight in the jihad before them (30 percent)."[132]

Daesh used multiple communication pathways to expose targeted recruits to an extremist master narrative, a "coherent system of inter-related and sequentially organised stories that share a common rhetorical desire to resolve a conflict by establishing audience expectations according to the known trajectories of its literary and rhetorical form."[133] These master narratives transcend a particular moment or culture and create new sites of meaning making, helping targeted audiences make sense of events in a way that legitimates the extremists and their cause.

The group used connectivity, in the form of proliferating information pathways, to wage a twenty-first-century propaganda campaign.[134] This campaign proved extremely successful in recruiting young Muslims, who often financed their own travel to join the group in Iraq and Syria. Though not definitive, some studies estimate that over 20,000 foreign fighters from over ninety countries traveled to Syria since 2011, including more than 3,000 Westerners.[135] Kurdish estimates go further, estimating over 200,000 foreign fighters.[136] Recruits were pursued through multiple media outlets. Daesh portrayed the creation of the Caliphate in romanticized terms that specifically linked their struggle with larger historical and political grievances that rationalized the targeted individual's personal grievances and sense of victimization.[137]

Social media presents the mutilated body as a map of a wider array of political and social memes. The connectivity of the modern world enables a rhizomatic approach to information warfare. Social media becomes a rhizome that "ceaselessly establishes connections between semiotic chains, organizations of power, and circumstances relative to the arts, sciences, and social struggles."[138] In the extreme versions, competition for the network becomes the focus of battle[139] and "geography, terrain, and logistics drop out of the calculus; the combat zone is, theoretically, anywhere on the network."[140]

Furthermore, Daesh integrated information warfare into its conventional operations. In the June 2014 attacks across Iraq, Daesh conducted a "shock-and-awe" campaign consisting of "lightning attacks" on Iraqi population centers.[141] Once in the city, Daesh would seize police, municipal offices, and critical infrastructure like water and electricity that allowed them to control the population. Parallel to these military actions:

> ISIS information operations conducted by Shura Council leaders convinced several military and local leaders to resign and flee their posts, eventually giving rise to "stab in the back" stories of betrayal. Remaining military units and civilian leaders were isolated and targeted by suicide bombers or assassination squads or murdered en masse when captured, to send a message to remaining government forces. Videos of massacres were distributed widely, reaching the remaining Iraqi troops on the front lines. Many Sunnis, in particular, had no reason to fight for the Maliki government and deserted in large numbers.[142]

Daesh demonstrates how small groups can leverage the connectivity of the modern world to achieve a position of relative advantage. Beyond using social media to mobilize a global network of fighters, Daesh integrated their influence operations with targeted acts of violence. Extreme violence took the form of spectacle designed to amplify propaganda themes and messages. Future extremist networks will likely emulate these tactics.

LEARNING TO WAGE INFORMATION WARFARE

Multiple actors are rediscovering the importance of waging influence campaigns alongside their investments in military capabilities and use of coercion to achieve their political objectives. Decision makers are turning to information warfare as a substitute for the diminishing returns of conventional military power. Yet, there are important differences in how different actors approach the definition and securitization of information.

Despite pioneering modern forms of political warfare that relied on a mix of propaganda, public diplomacy, and covert action, the United States uses information more as a precision weapon in a cyber domain than an influence vector. Psychological operations and military information operations remain unloved and unfunded areas. This approach can be contrasted with Russian use of cyberspace and traditional media outlets to wage a relentless assault of global public opinion. Russia focuses on amplifying societal fault lines and creating enough chaos and confusion to distort how segments of the population view critical issues. Regardless of these differences, there is a common thread across all major political actors, including non-state networks like Daesh: *altering how actors perceive the world around them and connect to one another is a critical form of strategic practice in the twenty-first century.* To do so requires not just media outlets or more covert cyber access but also a clear understanding of the fears, wants, and needs of local communities.

NOTES

1. David Ingram, "Facebook says 126 million Americans may have seen Russia-linked political posts," *Reuters*, October 30, 2017.
2. Sections from this chapter are drawn from Benjamin Jensen, "The Cyber Character of Political War," *Brown Journal of International Affairs* 24, no. 1 (2017): 159–171.
3. Jonathan Reed Winkler, "Information Warfare in World War I," *Journal of Military History* 73 no. 3 (2009): 845–867, esp. 847.
4. Daniel Headrick, *Invisible Weapon: Telecommunications and International Politics, 1851–1945* (New York: Oxford University Press, 1991).
5. Winkler, "Information Warfare in World War I."
6. Ibid., 846–847.
7. For an example, see work on economic warfare plans on the eve of World War I, Nicholas Lambert, Planning Armageddon: British Economic Warfare in the First World War (Cambridge: Harvard University Press, 2012).
8. Sun Tzu, *The Art of War*, trans. Lionel Giles, http://classics.mit.edu/Tzu/artwar.html
9. Michael Liebig, "Statecraft and Intelligence Analysis in the Kautilya-Arthashastra," *Journal of Defence Studies* 8, no. 4 (2014): 27–54.
10. Carl Von Clausewitz, *On War* (London: N. Trübner, 1873. Col James John Graham translation), http://www.clausewitz.com/readings/OnWar1873/BK1ch06.html#a. The translation of Carl von Clausewitz's *On War*, ed. and trans. Michael Howard and Peter Paret (Princeton: Princeton University Press, 1989), use intelligence instead of information. The original German was news or messages.
11. Ibid.
12. Ibid.
13. For an overview of Mongolian strategy and operational art, see Tim May, *The Mongol Art of War* (South Yorkshire: Pen and Sword, 2007).
14. David Chandler, "Napoleon, Operational Art, and the Jena Campaign" in *Historical Perspectives on Operational Art* edited by Michael Krause and R. Cody Phillips (Washington, DC: Center for Military History, 2005), 27–68.
15. For an overview of information warfare as it relates to early global communications networks, see Daniel Headrick, *Invisible Weapon: Telecom-*

munications and International Politics, 1851–1945 (New York: Oxford University Press, 1991).

16. For an overview of this case, see Kaeten Mistry, "The Case for Political Warfare: Strategy, Organization and US Involvement in the 1948 Italian Election," *Cold War History* 6, no. 3 (2006): 301–329.

17. Policy Planning Staff Memorandum, May 4, 1948, Foreign Relations of the United States, 1945–1950, Emergence of the Intelligence Establishment, document 269, https://history.state.gov/historicaldocuments/frus1945-50Intel.

18. Policy Planning Staff Memorandum, May 4, 1948, Foreign Relations of the United States, 1945–1950, Emergence of the Intelligence Establishment, document 269, https://history.state.gov/historicaldocuments/frus1945-50Intel.

19. Schelling, *Strategy of Conflict*; Daniel Byman and Matthew Waxman, *The Dynamics of Coercion: American Foreign Policy and the Limits of Military Might* (New York: Cambridge University Press, 2002); Philip Haun, *Coercion, Survival, and War: Why Weak States Resist the United States* (Palo Alto: Stanford University Press, 2015).

20. Schelling, *Strategy of Conflict*.

21. Ibid., 9.

22. On covert signaling, see Austin Carson and Keren Yarhi-Milo, "Covert Communications: The Intelligibility and Credibility of Signaling in Secret," *Security Studies* 26, no. 1 (2017): 124–156. On covert action and escalation management, see Austin Carson, "Facing Off and Saving Face: Covert Intervention and Escalation Management in the Korean War," *International Organization* 70, (2016): 103–131.

23. Alexander George, "Coercive Diplomacy" in *The Use of Force: Military Power and International Politics* edited by Robert J. Art and Kenneth N. Waltz (Lanham: Rowan and Littlefield, 2009), 77.

24. Ibid.

25. For work exploring how covert action works as an indirect form of coercion that enables escalation management, see Austin Carson, "Facing Off and Saving Face: Covert Intervention and Escalation Management in the Korean War," *International Organization* (2015): 1–29.

26. Policy Planning Staff Memorandum, May 4, 1948, Foreign Relations of the United States, 1945–1950, Emergence of the Intelligence Establishment, document 269, https://history.state.gov/historicaldocuments/frus1945-50Intel.

27. CIA, "Intelligence Memorandum No. 288, Subject: Political Alignments and Major Psychological Warfare Vulnerabilities in the Event of War before July 1951," May 9, 1950, https://www.cia.gov/library/readingroom/docs/CIA-RDP78-01617A000900190002-0.pdf.

28. Ibid.

29. For an overview of how containment and this policy of liberation emerged, and often collided, see Sarah-Jane Corke, "Bridging the Gap: Containment, Covert Action and the Search for the Missing Link in American Cold War Policy, 1948–1953," *Journal of Strategic Studies* 20, no. 4 (1997): 45–65.

30. Kenneth Osgood, "Hearts and Minds: The Unconventional Cold War," *Journal of Cold War Studies* 4, no. 7 (2002): 85–107. For an overview of containment as a defensive posture, see John Lewis Gaddis, *Strategies of Containment* (New York: Oxford University Press, 1982). For a look at political warfare as form of counterforce employed under the umbrella of containment seeking to rollback Soviet power, see Gregory Mitrovich, *Undermining the Kremlin: America's Strategy to Subvert the Soviet Bloc, 1947–1956* (Ithaca: Cornell University Press, 2000).

31. Paper by Colonel Grand dated March 2, 1939, cited in William Mackenzie, *The Secret History of SOE: The Special Operations Executive, 1940–1945* (London: Little Brown Book Group, 2002).

32. For an overview of the SOE and its contributions, see Neville Wylie, "Ungentlemanly Warriors or Unreliable Diplomats? Special Operations Executive and Irregular Political Activities in Europe," *Intelligence and National Security* 20, no. 1L (2005): 98–120.

33. Declassified Provisional Field Manual, 1943, Strategic Services (Washington: Joint Chiefs of Staff), 1, http://cgsc.contentdm.oclc.org/cdm/ref/collection/p4013coll9/id/930

34. Ibid.

35. OSS – Outline Plan for Political Warfare for Operational Overlord/Plan for Psychological Warfare Against Germany, Propaganda Objectives and Themes, May 22, 1944, https://www.cia.gov/library/readingroom/docs/CIA-RDP13X00001R000100370007-7.pdf.

36. OSS - Outline Plan for Political Warfare for Operation Overlord/Plan for Psychological Warfare Against Germany, Propaganda Objectives and Themes, 1944. May 22, 1944, https://www.cia.gov/library/readingroom/docs/CIA-RDP13X00001R000100370007-7.pdf

37. For an overview of the early Cold War, see Melvyn Leffler, *A Preponderance of Power: National Security, the Truman Administration, and the Cold*

War (Palo Alto: Stanford University Press, 1993); and John Lewis Gaddis, *The United States and the Origins of the Cold War, 1941–1947* (New York: Columbia University Press, 2000).

38. Memorandum from the Executive Secretary of the National Security Council (Souers) to Director of Central Intelligence Hillenkoetter. 1947. Emergence of the Intelligence Establishment, document 257, https://history.state.gov/historicaldocuments/frus1945-50Intel.

39. NSC 10/2 National Security Council Directive on Office of Special Projects, June 18, 1948, Emergence of the Intelligence Establishment, document 306, https://history.state.gov/historicaldocuments/frus1945-50Intel.

40. P.K. O'Donnell, *Operatives, Spies, and Saboteurs* (New York: Free Press, 2004)

41. C. Laurie, *The Propaganda Warriors: America's Crusade Against Nazi Germany* (Lawrence, KS: University Press of Kansas, 1996).

42. James Weland, "Misguided Intelligence: Japanese Military Intelligence Officers in the Manchurian Incident, September 1931," *Journal of Military History* 58, no. 3 (1994): 445–460.

43. Arch Puddington, *Broadcasting Freedom: The Cold War Triumph of Radio Free Europe/Radio Liberty* (Lexington, University of Kentucky Press, 1999), 43.

44. Scott Lucas, *Freedom's War: The American Crusade against the Soviet Union* (New York: NYU Press, 2000).

45. For examples of these networks, see Richard J. Aldrich. "OSS, CIA, and European Unity: The American Committee on United Europe, 1948–1960" Diplomacy and Statecraft 8, no. 1: 184–227; Giles Scott-Smith, "The Free Europe University in Strasbourg: U.S. State-Private Networks and Academic Rollback," *Journal of Cold War Studies* 16, no. 2 (2014): 77–107.

46. Thomas Schelling, *Arms and Influence* (New Haven: Yale University Press, 1966), 2.

47. Jon Lindsay and Eric Gartzke, "Cyber Coercion: The Stability-Instability Paradox Revisited" in *The Power to Hurt: Coercion in Theory and Practice*, edited by Kelly M. Greenhill and Peter J. P. Krause (New York: Oxford University Press, forthcoming). For an overview of cyber coercion, see Travis Sharp, "Theorizing Cyber Coercion: The 2014 North Korean Operation against Sony," *Journal of Strategic Studies* (2017): 898–926; and Erik Gartzke, "The Myth of Cyberwar: Bringing War in Cyberspace Back Down to Earth," *International Security* 38, no. 2 (2013): 41–73.

48. Martin Libicki, *Cyberwar and Cyber Deterrence* (Santa Monica: RAND, 2009), 26.

49. Schelling, *Arms and Influence*, 71–73.
50. On covert signaling, see Carson and Yarhi-Milo, "Covert Communications." On covert action and escalation management, see: Austin Carson, "Facing Off and Saving Face: Covert Intervention and Escalation Management in the Korean War," *International Organization* 70 (2016): 103–131.
51. For examples of how covert action between rivals can produce sunk costs and counter-escalation risks, see Carson and Yarhi-Milo, "Covert Communications."
52. George, "Coercive Diplomacy," 77.
53. James Adams, *The Next World War: Computers Are the Weapons and the Front Line is Everywhere* (New York: Simona and Schuster, 1998); Winn Schwartau, ed., *Information Warfare: Cyberterrorism: Protecting Your Personnel Security in the Electronic Age* (New York: Thunder's Mouth Press, 1996); John Arquila and David Ronfeldt, *The Advent of Netwar* (Santa Monica: RAND, 1996); A. Boulanger, "Catapults and Grappling Hooks: The Tools and technology of Information Warfare" *IBM Systems Journal* 37, no. 1 (2001): 106–114; D. E. Denning, *Information Warfare and Security* (Reading: Addison-Wesley, 1999); Martin Libicki, *What is Information Warfare?* (Washington, DC: National Defense University Press, 1995); Roger C. Molander, Andrew Riddile, and Peter A. Wilson, *Strategic Information Warfare: A New Face of War* (Santa Monica: RAND, 1996).
54. J.I. Alger, "Introduction" in Information Warfare: *Cyberterrorism: Protecting Your Personnel Security in the Electronic Age*, edited by Winn Schwartau (New York: Thunder's Mouth Press, 1996)
55. Bradley A. Thayer , "The Political Effects of Information Warfare: Why New Military Capabilities Cause Old Political Dangers," *Security Studies* 10, no. 1 (2000): 43–85, esp. 47.
56. Robert J. Bunker, "Battlespace Dynamics, Information Warfare to Network, and Bond-Relationship Targeting," *Small Wars and Insurgencies* 13, no. 2 (2002): 97–108, esp. 101.
57. Ibid.
58. Blaise Cronin and Holly Crawford, "Information Warfare: Its Application in Military and Civilian Contexts," *The Information Society* 15 (1999): 257–263, esp. 258.
59. Peter D. Feaver, "Blowback: Information Warfare and the Dynamics of Coercion," *Security Studies* 7, no. 4 (1998): 88–120, esp. 88.
60. Ibid., 90.

61. U.S. Army, FM 3-13, *Information Operations: Doctrine, Tactics, Techniques, and Procedures* (Arlington: Headquarters, Department of the Army, 2003), v.

62. U.S. Air Force, AFDD 2-5, *Information Operations* (Arlington: Secretary of the Air Force, 1998).

63. Joint Chiefs of Staff, *JP 3-13, Information Operations* (Arlington: Department of Defense, November 20, 2014), ix.

64. Ibid.

65. Martin Libicki, *Conquest in Cyberspace: National Security and Information Warfare* (New York: Cambridge University Press, 2007).

66. John Stillon and Bryan Clark, *What It Takes to Win: Succeeding in 21st Century Battle Network Competitions* (Washington: Center for Strategic and Budgetary Analysis, 2015), 3. Joshua Epstein also develops the concept of virtual attrition in his study of Soviet airpower; see Joshua Epstein, *Measuring Military Power: The Soviet Air Threat in Europe* (Princeton: Princeton University Press, 1984).

67. On battlefield dynamics in the 1990s, see Robert J. Bunker, *Five-dimensional (Cyber) Warfighting: Can the Army After Next be Defeated through Complex Concepts and Technologies?* (Carlisle Barracks: US Army War Collegel, Strategic Studies Institute, 1998).

68. Ibid., 98–99

69. See Center for Strategic and Budgetary Assessments (CSBA), *Countering Enemy "Informationized Operations" in War and Peace*, 2013, http://www.esd.whs.mil/Portals/54/Documents/FOID/Reading%20Room/Other/Litigation%20Release%20-%20Countering%20Enemy%20Informationized%20Operations%20in%20Peace%20and%20War.pdf.

70. CSBA, *Countering Enemy*, 41.

71. For a discussion on the similarities and differences between US and Chinese approaches to information warfare, see Paul J. Bolt and Carl N. Brenner, "Information warfare across the Taiwan Strait," *Journal of Contemporary China* 13 no. 38, (2004): 129–150.

72. For an overview of earlier Chinese cyber thinkers, see Mark A. Stokes, *China's Strategic Modernization: Implications for the United States* (Carlisle: Strategic Studies Institute, 1999); Bolt and Brenner, "Information warfare across the Taiwan Strait."

73. Wei Jincheng, "New Form of People's War," *Jiefangjun Bao*, June 25, 1996, p. 6 as downloaded in translated form from the FBIS webpage, as it appears in Timothy Thomas, *Behind the Great Firewall of China: A Look at*

RMA/IW Theory From 1996–1998 (Leavenworth: Foreign Military Studies Office, 1998), http://www.au.af.mil/au/awc/awcgate/fmso/chinarma.htm.

74. Mao Tse-tung, "On Protracted War," in *Selected Works of Mao Tse-tung*, vol. II (Peking: Foreign Languages Press: Peking, 1967), 113–194.

75. Li Yinnian, quoted in "New Subjects of Study Brought about by Information Warfare," by Huang Youfu, Zhang Bibo, and Zhang Song, *Jiefangjun Bao*, November 11, 1997, p. 6 as translated on the FBIS web page, December 23, 1997, as it appears in Timothy Thomas, *Behind the Great Firewall of China: A Look at RMA/IW Theory From 1996–1998* (Leavenworth: Foreign Military Studies Office, 1998), http://www.au.af. mil/au/awc/awcgate/fmso/chinarma.htm.

76. Yuen, *Deciphering Sun Tzu.*

77. Zhang Xing Ye and Zhang Zhan Li, eds., Campaign Stratagems, National Defense University, 2002, pp. 8–18 as quoted in Timothy Thomas, *China's Cyber Incursions: A Theoretical Look at When They See and Why They Do it Based on a Different Strategic Method of Thought* (Leavenworth: Foreign Military Studies Office, 2013), 5, http://indianstrategicknowledgeonline. com/web/Chinas-Cyber-Incursions.pdf .

78. Yuen, *Deciphering Sun Tzu*, 45

79. James Mulvenon, "The PLA and Information Warfare" in *The People's Liberation Army in the Information Age* edited by James Mulvenon and Richard Yang (Santa Monica: RAND, 1999), 177.

80. An example of this trend is the book *Xinxi zhanzheng yu junshi geming* [Information Warfare and the Revolution in Military Affairs] by Wang Pufeng (Beijing: Junshi kexueyuan, 1995).

81. "Army Paper on Information Warfare," *Jiefangjun bao* (June 25, 1996), 6, as quoted in Mulvenon, *The People's Liberation Army*, 178.

82. Wang, *Xinxi zhanzheng yu junshi geming*, 37, as quoted in Mulvenon, *The People's Liberation Army*, 180.

83. Bolt and Brenner, "Information warfare across the Taiwan Strait," 133–134; Wang Houqing and Zhang Xingye, eds., *Beijing Science of Campaigns* [in Chinese] (Beijing: National Defense University Publishing House, 2000).

84. Timothy Thomas, *China's Cyber Incursions: A Theoretical Look at What They See and Why They Do It Based on a Different Strategic Method of Thought* (Leavenworth: Foreign Military Studies Office, 2013), 2.

85. Ibid., 2.

86. Xinhua Cidian [Xinhua Dictionary; 1985], 1106, as quoted in Thomas, *China's Cyber Incursions*, 2.

87. Thomas, *China's Cyber Incursions*, 2.

88. Dean Cheng, *Cyber Dragon: Inside China's Information Warfare and Cyber Operations* (Westwood: Praeger Press, 2017), 1.

89. Peng Guangqian and Yao Youzhi, eds., *Science of Strategy* (Beijing: Department of StrategicResearch, Military Science Press, 2001), 21; Peng Guangqian and Yao Youzhi, eds., *TheScience of Military Strategy* (Beijing: Military Science Publishing House, 2005), 18, as quoted in CSBA, *Countering Enemy*, 34.

90. Timothy Thomas, "Human Attack Networks," *Military Review* (September-October 1999), http://www.au.af.mil/au/awc/awcgate/fmso/humannet.htm.

91. Larry Wortzel, *The Chinese People's Liberation Army and Information Warfare* (Carlisle: Strategic Studies Institute, 2014), 1.

92. Thomas, "Human Attack Networks," 5.

93. Brendan I. Koerner, "Inside the Cyberattack That Shocked the US Government," *Wired*, October 23, 2016, https://www.wired.com/2016/10/inside-cyberattack-shocked-us-government/.

94. Laurent Murawiec, *Vulnerabilities in the Chinese Way of War* (Washington, DC: Hudson Institute,2004), 187–188. Note that overall, Murawiec is skeptical of the PLA approach and assesses that there is a high probability of overextension and misjudging the efficacy of the approach.

95. The preceding review of Chinese literature and perspectives on it focused on international rivalry and not the extensive campaign China wages on its own citizens. For an overview of these activities, see Kaveh Waddell, "Why Google Quit China—and Why It's Heading Back," *The Atlantic*, January 19, 2016, https://www.theatlantic.com/technology/archive/2016/01/why-google-quit-china-and-why-its-heading-back/424482/ and Beina Xu and Eleanor Albert, "Media Censorship in China," Council on Foreign Relations, February 17, 2017, https://www.cfr.org/backgrounder/media-censorship-china.

96. Yuan, Lectures on Joint Campaign Information Operations, 18, as quoted in CSBA, *Countering Enemy*.

97. Maria Snegovaya. *Putin's Information Warfare in Ukraine: Soviet Origins of Russia's Hybrid Warfare* (Washington: Institute for the Study of War, 2015), 10.

98. Ibid., 11.

99. On reflective control, see Timothy L. Thomas, "Russia's Reflective Control Theory and the Military," *Journal of Slavic Military Studies* 15 (2004): 237–256.

100. Snegovaya, *Putin's Information Warfare*, 12.
101. Ibid.
102. Lothar Metzl, "Reflections on the Soviet Secret Police and Intelligence Services," *Orbis* 18, no. 3 (1974): 917–930, esp. 921.
103. Nigel Inkster, "Information Warfare and the US Presidential Election" Survival 58, no. 5 (2016): 23–32.
104. Sinnikukka Saari, "Russia's Post-Orange Revolution Strategies to Increase its Influence in Former Soviet Republics: Public Diplomacy" Europe-Asia Studies 66, no. 1 (2014): 50–66.
105. Valeriano, Jensen, and Maness, *Cyber Strategy*.
106. Chris Bowlby, "Vladimir Putin's formative German years," *BBC*, March 27, 2015, http://www.bbc.com/news/magazine-32066222
107. John B. Emerson, "Exposing Russian Disinformation" Atlantic Council, June 29, 2015, http://www.atlanticcouncil.org/blogs/ukrainealert/exposing-russian-disinformation.
108. Janis Berzin, Russia's New-Generation Warfare in Ukraine: Implications for Latvian Defense Policy (National Defense Academy of Latvia, Center for Security and Strategic Research, 2014, Policy Paper 2), 5.
109. Col. S.G. Chekionv and Lt. Gen. S.A. Bogdanov, "The Nature and Content of New-Generation Warfare," *Military Thought: A Russian Journal of Miltiary Theory and Strategy* 4 (2013), http://www.eastviewpress.com/Files/MT_FROM%20THE%20CURRENT%20ISSUE_No.4_2013.pdf.
110. Ibid., 15.
111. Rose McDermott, "Gerasimov Links Russian Military Modernization to the Arab Spring" *Eurasia Daily Monitor*, March 6, 2013; Rose McDermott, ed., *The Transformation of Russia's Armed Forces* (New York: Routledge, 2015).
112. Chekionv and Bogdanov, "New-Generation Warfare," 15
113. Roland Heickero, *Emerging Cyber Threats and Russian Views on Information Warfare and Information Operations* (Stockholm: Swedish Defense Research Agency, 2010), 4.
114. Stephen Herzog, "Revisiting the Estonian Cyber Attacks: Digital Threats and Multinational Responses" *Journal of Strategic Security* 4 no. 2 (Summer 2011), 49–60.
115. Paulo Shakarian, "The 2008 Russian Cyber Campaign Against Georgia," *Military Review* (November-December 2011), http://usacac.army.mil/CAC2/MilitaryReview/Archives/English/MilitaryReview_20111231_art013.pdf.

116. Tim Maurer and Scott Janz, "The Russia-Ukraine Conflict: Cyber and Information Warfare in a Regional Context," *The International Relations and Security Network*, October 17, 2014, https://www.files.ethz.ch/isn/187945/ISN_184345_en.pdf.

117. Valeriano, Jensen, and Maness, *Cyber Strategy*.

118. Lora Chakarova and Alex Kokcharov, "Critical European infrastructure increasingly likely to be targeted by Russian cyber groups in three-year outlook," IHS Jane's Intelligence Review (London, February 10, 2016).

119. Pavel Polityuk, "Exclusive: Hackers may have wider access to Ukrainian industrial facilities," Reuters, January 27, 2016, http://mobile.reuters.com/article/idUSKCN0V51H1.

120. Der Spiegel, "Report: Germany Blames Russia For Parliament Cyberattack, RFE/RL," February 1, 2016, http://www.rferl.org/content/russia-germany-blame-parliament-cyberattack/27520670.html.

121. Inkster, "Information Warfare and the US Presidential Election"; on automating tools, see Kier Giles. "Russia's New Tools for Confronting the West"Chatham House, March 21, 2016, https://www.chathamhouse.org/publication/russias-new-tools-confronting-west.

122. Inkster, "Information Warfare and the US Presidential Election," 30.

123. Kristin Ven Bruusgard, "Crimea and Russia's Strategic Overhaul," *Parameters* 44 no, 3 (2014): 84–85.

124. Interview with Dr. Philip Karber, December 10, 2015.

125. Rose McDermott, "Moscow Resurrects Battalion Tactical Groups," *Eurasian Daily Monitor* 9 no. 203 (2012); "Reversal of Fortune," *The Economist*, September 6, 2014. For a historical perspective on Russian military efforts to employ combined arms elements below the regimental and brigade level, see Lester Grau, *Restructuring the Tactical Russian Army for Unconventional Warfare* (Leavenworth: FMSO, 2014).

126. Ahmed Hashim, "From al-Qaeda affiliate to Caliphate," *Middle East Policy* XXi no. 4 (Winter 2014): 68.

127. Ibid., 70.

128. Ibid., 73

129. Ibid., 73

130. Ahmed Hashim, "The Islamic State: From al-Qaeda Affiliate to Caliphate," *Middle East Policy Council* 21, no. 4 (2016), http://www.mepc.org/islamic-state-al-qaeda-affiliate-caliphate.

131. Barbara Franz, "Popjihadism: Why Young European Muslims Are Joining the Islamic State," *Mediterranean Quarterly* 26, no. 2 (2016): 9–10.

132. Nikolas Busse, "Arbeitslose and Straftäter ziehen in den heiligen Krieg," *Frankfurter Allgemeine*, November 27, 2014, www.faz.net/aktuell/politik /dschihad- in- deutschland- zieht- arbeitslose- und- straftaeter- an-13287950.html, as quoted in Franz, "Popjihadism," 8.

133. J. Halverson, H.L. Goodall, and S. Corman, *Master Narratives of Islamist Extremism* (New York: Palgrave Macmillan, 2011), 14.

134. In this reading, the authors are drawing on the definition of propaganda as a "deliberate, systemic attempt to shape perceptions, manipulate cognitions, and direct behavior to achieve a response that furthers the desired intent of the propagandist." See G.S. Jowettand V. O'Donnell, *Propaganda and Persuasion*, 5th ed. (Thousand Oaks: Sage, 2012), 7.

135. Christopher M. Blanchard and Carla E. Humud, "The Islamic State and U.S. Policy," Congressional Research Service, February 2, 2017, https://fas.org/sgp/crs/mideast/R43612.pdf.

136. Jim Sciutto, Jamie Crawford, and Chelsea Carter, "ISIS Can 'Muster' between 20,000 and 31,500, CIA Says," CNN, September 12, 2014, www.cnn.com/2014/09/11/world/meast/isis- syria- iraq /index.html.

137. Samantha Mahood and Halim Rane, "Islamist narratives in ISIS recruitment propaganda," *The Journal of International Communication* 23, no. 1 (2017): 15–35.

138. Gilles Deleuze and Félix Guattari, *A Thousand Plateaus*, trans. Brian Massumi (London and New York: Continuum, [1980] 2004).

139. C.P. Meinel, "How Hackers Break in....and how they are caught," *Scientific American* (October 1998): 98–105.

140. Cronin and Hawford, "Information Warfare," 258.

141. Hashim, "From al-Qaeda affiliate to Caliphate," 78.

142. Ahmed Hashim. "The Islamic State: From al-Qaeda Affiliate to Caliphate" *Middle East Policy Council* 21, no. 4 (2016), http://www.mepc.org/islamic-state-al-qaeda-affiliate-caliphate.

CHAPTER 5

THE EMERGENCE OF
A HUMAN DOMAIN

In 1187, legendary commander Saladin placed a Crusader Army on the horns of a dilemma in the Battle of Hattin.[1] Similar to Hannibal's shaping actions before Cannae, Saladin exploited internal rivalries in the court at Jerusalem through attacking a series of fortresses belonging to different political rivals. The sieges baited Guy of Lusigan, the King of Jerusalem, into leaving his secure fortress, which had a critical resource water, to attack Saladin at Tiberias. Saladin set a tactical trap through understanding personalities, political rivalries, and the power networks that animated the court at Jerusalem.

This trap leveraged the center of gravity for desert warfare: water. Using local knowledge, Saladin's forces understood that the water supplies were insufficient to support the large Frankish force advancing through the desert. They baited the advancing Christian Army—using information warfare of the day, including prayers, chants, and burning smoke screens to demoralize the thirsty column—while arraying their forces to threaten Guy's flanks with skirmishers. As the Crusader force reached the Horn of Hattin, the famed site of the sermon on the Temple Mount, they faced a horrible choice. The army could either die of thirst or be cut down as they charged against defenders guarding every pass.

The idea that understanding human motives, connections, and interests as central to the conduct of strategy is not new. What is new is the sheer extent to which human connections make population-centric wars and subversive campaigns spread faster than they have historically. This shift necessitates new concepts and capabilities. States that singularly rely on combined-arms maneuver and fail to map the human terrain risk defeat in modern military campaigns.

Accelerated changes in communications technology eliminate the tyranny of distance and exponentially increase the momentum of human interaction. The world has become fast-paced, crowded, and as a result, increasingly prone to emergent complexity. Information is ubiquitous, presenting both opportunities and risks for major powers like the United States engaged in strategic competition, confrontation, and conflict with a range of actors around the globe. The new key terrain is connectivity: the connections groups make to mobilize local mass and challenge rivals. Social media networks and domestic politics were as important to the rise of Daesh, the so-called Islamic State, as controlling border crossing points into Syria to facilitate the flow of foreign fighters. Mapping human geography, understanding the interrelationships between people as they define spatial organization and interests, becomes as important as understanding how physical terrain shapes movement during military operations.[2]

In this fast-changing world, the organizing concepts that served humanity for centuries appear increasingly antiquated.[3] Modern staff organizations, the byproduct of post-Napoleonic reforms and indus-trial-era concepts of bureaucratic management, continue to lead forma-tions little changed since World War II and appear unable to translate tactical success in battle into enduring strategic outcomes in a hyper-connected world.[4] What started with newspapers shaping planning in the American Civil War through how television altered strategy in the

Vietnam conflict culminates in the postmodern web of connectivity that facilitates low-cost global reach for state and non-state actors alike.[5]

As discussed in chapter 2, our inability to understand local populations, much less how these places are situated in a global space of flows, sits at the crux of US military setbacks.[6] The world's largest superpower found it easy to take territory but struggled to hold terrain given the shifting alliances amongst local populations and the inability to understand this context. American efforts to adapt were often limited or too late to make a difference. Coalition forces created ad hoc structures (e.g. provincial reconstruction teams and village stability platforms) with some success, but lessons from those experiments were not institutionalized. Institutional preferences returned US military training, education, and concept development back to what it knew best: combined-arms maneuver and the technological aspects of war. Indeed, senior leaders saw nation building and stability operations as too costly, complicated, and more importantly, not politically palatable.[7] They chose to forget.

A growing number of studies show that increasing war costs combined with globalization and a decreasing ability of sovereign states to manage violence create an age of irregular conflict and "uncomfortable wars."[8] The changing character of conflict gives rise to new forms of competition. A hyperconnected world diffuses power across multiple actors and organizations forcing us to reexamine fundamental assumptions about security.[9]

In this world, the speed and velocity with which chaos emerges is alarming. Recounting Hurricane Sandy, Chief James E. Leonard of the Fire Department of New York City (FDNY) told a group of military fellows, "order collapsed quickly as citizens pulled guns on each other at gas pumps and looted stores."[10] The combination of a breakdown in essential services and how media outlets amplified fear caused social breakdown. Even the most developed sections of the United States proved vulnerable to the instantaneous spread of information, which sowed confusion and caused rapid distress amongst the populace. Studies on the collapse of states after the Arab Spring reflect this phenomenon as well.[11] Events spread rapidly leading to strategic compression. What starts as a local event can become a global crisis in less than a day.

The constant feed of information and 24-hour news cycle contributes to our collective forgetfulness of these past situations. We become lost in the information, chasing noise and defaulting to old habits to provide a false sense of certainty. The FDNY Chief's observations highlight a rapidly changing environment and encourage critical thinking about current operational constructs and intellectual frameworks—many of which are linear and anachronistic. How should a military understand the connections between people in a human domain and their role in shaping contemporary competition, confrontation, and conflict? How does a military with a conditional "license to kill" fashion an ethic of understanding and forbearance prior to action, with a constant eye on how their operations can cascade and make matters worse?

This chapter defines the human domain as the intersection of actors and interests, predominantly in the land and cyber domains, shaping modern competition and conflict. The following pages chart how the idea of a human domain emerged in US military circles following the end of the Cold War in response to the requirements of stability operations, foreign internal defense, and counterinsurgency—the preponderant missions of a modern military still disproportionately equipped for conventional battle. The chapter concludes with a discussion of how advances in data collection and analysis can help analysts better understand the human domain.

PIONEERS

The idea of an overarching human domain was first introduced in a 2010 speech delivered in Amman, Jordan, by then commanding general for Special Operations Command – Central (SOCCENT), Major General Charles Cleveland. For General Cleveland something fundamental had changed in the character of warfare causing increased unease within the US Army and Department of Defense writ large. This change required a new approach that accounted for the rise and success of terror groups and actors using unconventional methods. The speech also marked the beginning of intellectual introspection within the military. An experienced generation of warriors, who regularly found themselves working with the indigenous other, continued to experience frustration with an elusive enemy hiding in the population. Civilian and military leaders lacked conceptual structures to understand the changing character of war and the emergent conditions of the environment.

Paralleling the challenges of counterinsurgency and counterterrorism operations in the Middle East and South Asia between 2010 and 2015, a growing number of practitioners began to speak of a human domain. In 2013 Army Strategic Planning Guidance issued by the Honorable John M. McHugh and General Raymond T. Odierno, leaders argued that

> America's ability to deliver strategic landpower requires an improved understanding of the convergence of the human, cyber and geographic terrains we will operate in. Today's global connectivity and its effect on the changing environment reinforce that lasting strategic results can only be achieved by effectively influencing people. Success depends as much on understanding the social and political fabric of the situation as it does on the ability to physically dominate it...The Army's unique understanding and dominance of the land domain, as well as the factors that influence human behavior, enable it to shape security conditions favorable to US and allied interests.[12]

In October 2013, General Odierno joined Admiral McRaven and General Amos and published the Strategic Landpower White Paper.[13] The white paper argued for exploring new ways of employing military power at the "convergence of land, cyber and human domains."[14] The document illustrated a shift from decisive battle to shaping competition prior to conflict as well as identifying the interests and issues at the core of the clash of wills. In these reflections, leaders highlighted that tactical actions were not producing enduring outcomes, implying that much of the disconnect between ends, ways, and means revolves around a fundamental misunderstanding of the human domain. Yet, what is the human domain?

Revisiting table 1 in chapter 1, the traditional domains are all defined through a physical referent. The land domain is "the area of the Earth's surface ending at the high water mark and overlapping with the maritime domain in the landward segment of the littorals."[15] The maritime domain is similarly distinctly physical, denoting, "the oceans, seas, bays, estuaries, islands, coastal areas, and the airspace above these, including the littorals."[16]

As strategic competition, confrontation, and conflict took on new dimensions, military planners defined new domains. First, professionals separated the air and land domain, defining the air domain as "atmosphere, beginning at the Earth's surface, extending to the altitude where its effects upon operations become negligible."[17] As operations extended beyond the atmosphere, the domains expanded, resulting in a new space domain, "the environment corresponding to the space domain, where electromagnetic radiation, charged particles, and electric and magnetic fields are the dominant physical influences, and that encompasses the earth's ionosphere and magnetosphere, interplanetary space, and the solar atmosphere."[18] As the Chairman of the Joint Chiefs found it helpful to "treat cyberspace as an operational domain to organize, train, and equip," planners added a cyber domain and began to align force structure and organizations. [19] Therefore, as the military profession recognizes the importance of human interactions to operations, it should define a human domain and organize to achieve a position of advantage therein.

The human domain is the web of interactions that converge in cyber and geographic spaces to shape the ends and ways of competition, confrontation, and conflict. In many respects, highlighting the importance of a human domain pivoted on something old and something new. Following Clausewitz, military leaders held that war is at its core a clash of wills. [20] Yet, this clash of wills increasingly takes place along the connective tissue of the information age, what military planners call the cyber domain, "a global domain within the information environment consisting of the interdependent network of information technology infrastructures and resident data, including the Internet, telecommunications networks, computer systems, and embedded processors and controllers."[21] These cyber interactions create flows that change the spatial organization of entire communities, and by proxy, how the clash of will manifests in our world. Tweets spark protests. Election hacks undermine national institutions. The actor better able to understand relationships, issues, and interests in this emergent human domain gains a position of a relative advantage.

The need to understand the population is a first-order principle in the human domain. Understanding should precede action. Yet, a prime area of strategic weakness for the United States continues to be its inability to understand the local social-political context of conflict and war.[22] One young captain, Travis Patriquin, heroically challenged this convention prior to his death in 2006.

Dubbed "America's Lawrence of Arabia" in Iraq, Captain Patriquin is remembered for his efforts, which helped turn the tide of the insurgency in Al Anbar and spark the pivotal "Sunni Awakening."[23] Patriquin's combined understanding of local tribal society, political dynamics, and religious customs gave him a lens to interpret human activity with speed and clarity. His clear understanding of the environment and human geography instinctively allowed him to exploit a fissure that erupted from the death of a local sheikh.[24]

Patriquin understood that Al Qaeda's killing of a sheikh and the decision not to return the body dishonored the sheikh's family and gave the coalition a narrative to garner support from Sunni insurgents, redirecting their attacks on US forces toward Al Qaeda. This immediate shift in alliances created momentum and spread throughout Iraq.[25] Captain

Patriquin's efforts were remarkable, and his lessons from Iraq should be remembered to encourage the growth of more officers like him.

Technology can help foreign military actors understand the local dynamics that shape the human domain. For example, two students of the Naval Post Graduate School, Marine Corps Captain Carrick Longley and Army Special Forces Warrant Officer 4 Chad Michiela, developed an Android-based program, Lighthouse, to collect and depict demographic information geospatially. This social network map illustrated critical linkages between people and helped special forces teams in Afghanistan to identify tribal alignment and the human geography. This capability enhanced their understanding of the environment and improved the conduct of their operations amongst the populace.

In the Southern Philippines, Lieutenant Colonel Edward M. Lopacienski and Major Thomas Scanzillo, analyzed operations conducted by Joint Special Operations Task Force – Philippines (JSOTF-P) from 2004 to 2008 and captured the creative efforts taken to influence the population. They argued that operations should align "the preponderance of effort on influencing the human domain and integrating multiple lines of operation to include capacity building, civil-military engagement, information engagement, and intelligence support operations into that single focus."[26] For Lopacienski and Scanzillo the term "information operations" misrepresented the activities JSOTF-P conducted to shape local networks. In its place they proposed using the term "influence operations."[27] Taking this influence-to-shape mantra further, in 2008 Captain Arnel David and his civil affairs team shifted their civil-military operations from spending money on infrastructure projects to connecting with the populace through civil society organizations (CSO).[28]

This civil affairs team discovered vibrant networks of interconnected groups, capable of mobilizing masses of people to solve collective action problems, which they could harness to strengthen local governance and legitimize partner security forces. Like the aforementioned pioneers, this required an understanding of the local dynamics of the conflict. The group obtained an accelerated understanding of the human terrain by partnering early on with an Islamic Imam. Through the imam's religious and cultural expertise, they mapped the dizzying array of actors and groups operating in the environment. They discerned which groups in the network were potentially malign and leveraged partnerships with influential CSOs to win them over.[29]

Through collaborative activities with CSOs, this civil affairs team served as a catalyst for effective action on a scale disproportionately large relative to its small size. They worked with local governance, NGOs, CSOs (most of which were Muslim), and Philippine security forces to mobilize thousands of people to take part in peacebuilding events. Building powerful partnerships with small teams is *sine qua non* for special operators who operate in remote and austere environments. Another example is a small, special operations civil-military support element (CMSE) of four personnel in the hinterlands of Tajikistan, who pooled scarce resources and leveraged partnerships remarkably well.

Partnering with Spirit of America (SoA), this CMSE team led by Captain Wesley Strong and Sergeant First Class Nicholas Fitzpatric influenced communities in the Fergana Valley of Tajikistan, which were susceptible to radicalization by the Islamic Movement of Uzbekistan (IMU). With the help of SoA, the team brought a French film crew and cold-weather jackets to children in multiple villages. Gaining access to these contested spaces provided a richer understanding of the environment for the US Embassy team and other interagency partners. The activity resulted in the team finding a fascinating mix of actors and groups amongst the populace, expanding their network and identifying partners for future projects.[30]

Early on in his career, General Cleveland discovered the utility of working with an assortment of actors, some good and some bad. In Bosnia, General Cleveland's Special Forces teams worked with a set of unusual characters from religious leaders, business owners, and party functionaries to warlords and criminal syndicates. This network of influence agents gave his team early warning of unrest while providing a conduit through which to shape local and regional behavior and buying time for conventional peacekeeping forces to arrive and conduct stability operations.[31] Paul Staniland's work on wartime political orders emphasizes this point well. The interplay and "often surprising relationships between states and non-state violent actors emerge and change within internal conflicts: mainstream politicians build armed wings, states collaborate with militias against common foes, police ignore private counterinsurgent armies, militaries tacitly share sovereignty with insurgent enemies, and warlords place their loyalists inside state security forces."[32] Staniland proffers that the absence of a conceptual vocabulary to understand civil war causes one to overlook the diverse interactions that construct political authority and control. His most relevant finding is "that there are many ways of forging stability without creating a counterinsurgent Leviathan."[33]

Building on an understanding of local dynamics, Fotini Christia's *Alliance Formations in Civil Wars* challenges the common notion that groups align or form because of shared identity considerations (e.g., ideology and religion). After a close examination of Afghanistan and Bosnia, testing these two wars against fifty-three cases of multiparty civil wars, she makes a compelling case that group choices are driven by relative power considerations to determine alliance formations, shifts, and fractures.[34] The volatile and ambiguous regions in which US forces operate necessitate a holistic approach that not only integrates the whole-of-government but rather a whole-of-society approach, garnering multilateral partnerships to improve the efficacy of operations in the human domain. Concepts for achieving a position of advantage through the human domain, similar to Joint operations in conventional warfighting, require interagency collaboration and must include partners outside of the US government. Partnerships with nongovernment entities are expanding and evolving to employ other instruments of national power. The University of Notre Dame's Business on the Front Lines (BOTFL) is a good example of one of these partnerships.

Operating across the globe, graduate students in the BOTFL program leverage education to develop business incubators in countries predisposed to conflict. In places like Bosnia and Lebanon, BTOFL students transformed academic inquiry into businesses that created livelihood, opportunity, and in some cases, bridged sectarian divides. They carefully navigate complex religious, political, and social terrain to spur economic development. General Cleveland saw the positive effects of BOTFL and connected special operators with these students to cultivate best practices and enrich everyone's understanding of some of the world's most conflict prone areas. They developed a partnership to promote economic empowerment. Partnerships like this require mapping the human domain to identify key relationships and cultivate them to promote stability. Building and nurturing key relationships will be paramount as the United States fosters credibility and influence of legitimate authorities among pertinent populations.

Reflecting on the lessons of recent conflicts, General Martin Dempsey emphasized the importance of understanding "the science of human relationships."[35] These relationships move at the "speed of trust" and, as Special Operations Command (SOCOM) claims, "you can't surge trust."[36] You need to invest the time, personnel, and resources to engage tribal leaders, community influencers, key interlocutors, and civil society groups for mission success in modern war. Unfortunately, across the enterprise, cultivating and managing relationships is not a priority. Furthermore, there is currently no systematic way to track these partnerships and relationships. This concern is more fully addressed in chapter 6.

Without the recognition of a human domain, these pioneers' stories, successes, and novel theories fail to become institutionalized in doctrinal practice and fade away. To respond to the changing character of war, policymakers, strategists, and planners need a broader array of options and partnerships to better understand, influence, shape, mobilize, and empower local networks. They need to organize around the human domain.

These pioneers and many others like them have continued to innovate in the face of adversity. Their arduous work and sacrifice demonstrate what is possible in small numbers and with limited resources. The human domain concept is not a costly material platform nor a panacea for all operations, but rather a better balance of capabilities and allocation of minimal resources to provide options for gaining an advantage. The military needs to foment key partnerships and build forces to leverage tools that harmonize organs of society, exercise economies of scale with partners, and obtain greater synergies from collective actions that achieve strategic aims. However, before progress can be made with human-domain ideas, hurdles in how the military profession thinks about competition, confrontation, and conflict must be overcome.

The Pioneers meet the Leviathan

General Raymond Odierno, the 38th Army Chief of Staff (2011–2015), fully cognizant of the aforementioned challenges and emergent changes in the global commons, directed multiple efforts aimed at understanding the profound shifts in the character of the conflicts manifesting daily in Iraq and Afghanistan. To this end, he, Admiral McRaven, and General Amos commissioned the Strategic Landpower Task Force to define and delineate the boundaries of the human domain. General Odierno also approved the addition of engagement as the seventh warfighting function and ordered the development and implementation of a global landpower network for the United States Army, subjects explored in the next chapter.[37] Although separate, these efforts were interrelated in their purpose, which was to understand the shifts in the environment and the consequences on the ground. In 2014, the army published a new operating concept: *Win in a Complex World*. This work attempted to codify an approach for dealing with the new realities of war. It noted:

> Recent and ongoing conflicts reinforce the need to balance the technological focus of Army modernization with a recognition of

the limits of technology and an emphasis on the human, cultural, and political continuities of armed conflict.[38]

In November 2014, General Odierno asked his Strategic Studies Group two questions: how can the army adapt to a world characterized by diffusion of power, growing violence, and political competition from regional powers and persistent levels of conflict and violence? And more importantly, how can the army engage in this space without over-militarizing American foreign policy? [39] The engagement warfighting function, more aptly called interdependence and influence, and the use of a networked approach to conflict and competition provided partial solutions to the problem. Regrettably, the former was killed by Training & Doctrine Command (TRADOC), and the latter has yet to be codified into any enduring concept or doctrine.

However, if implemented, these ideas represent a radical shift in the army's approach to warfare. More than forty years ago, Russell Weigley published his seminal work, *The American Way of War*.[40] It characterized American combat preferences in terms of an attrition-based interpretation of Ulysses S. Grant's campaigns. The American military and the US Army, in particular, had shown a strong, consistent preference for this theory of victory, destroying enemy formations through superior firepower and mass.

In the wake of the American invasion of Iraq in 2003, Max Boot eulogized Weigley's work in *Foreign Affairs*:

> Its time is now past, however. Spurred by dramatic advances in information technology, the US military has adopted a new style of warfare that eschews the bloody slogging matches of old. It seeks a quick victory with minimal casualties on both sides. Its hallmarks are speed, maneuver, flexibility, and surprise. It is heavily reliant upon precision firepower, special forces, and psychological operations. And it strives to integrate naval, air, and land power into a seamless whole. This approach was put powerfully on

display in the recent invasion of Iraq, and its implications for the future of American war fighting are profound.[41]

Time has shown Boot's full-throated endorsement of the "quick victory" in Iraq to have been premature and his prognostications on the implications for American warfare to have been incorrect. For all its speed and lethality, American combat power missed the strategic mark in these struggles.

Antulio J. Echevarria goes further to claim the US military has "more of a way of *battle* than an actual way of war."[42] While exalting the tactical excellence displayed by soldiers in battle, retired three-star general Dan Bolger, laments that at the top, generals "yawned a howling waste" in the wars of Iraq and Afghanistan. His indictment of general officer leadership, to include himself, is rooted in one central premise: they allowed themselves to get surprised by the challenges of protracted irregular warfare.

The US military has shown unwavering preference for combined-arms maneuver and major combat operations *a la* prevailing narratives of World War II and Gulf War combat operations, rather than the messy wars it has found in Iraq and Afghanistan, not to mention in the jungles of Vietnam. The American military continues to seek decisive battle; conflict resolution resulting from military action in isolation of broader efforts to shape local social, political, and economic networks. As Freedman states in *The Modern American Military,* "there has long been a clear preference, reflected in force structure and doctrine, for big regular wars against serious great power competition."[43] In many respects, this is the right answer. America needs a force capable of seizing and holding terrain. What this book calls for is a new dimension to the traditional understanding of landpower: the addition of a human domain that shifts how we think about the spectrum of competition, confrontation, and conflict—and in the process—necessitates new concepts and capabilities for achieving a sustainable position of advantage.

As the recent conflicts have shown, America's *preferred way of war* does not match the character of contemporary conflict. As a result, the military needs a new construct suited to the interconnected and complex world in which it operates. The human cost of continued failure and wasted resources is unacceptable and weakens the nation. The next section highlights four mental pitfalls that must be overcome to enable broader strategic thinking about contemporary competition and conflict.

FALLACY OF THE LESSER-INCLUDED MINDSET

There is this misunderstanding that training for high-end warfare best prepares units for all forms of warfare. Military leaders assume a switch from high-intensity conflict to low-intensity, irregular war is easy. Doing the former good makes you better at the latter. This is a fallacy and past interventions demonstrate this mistake.[44] Some argue to just "mind the middle," and organize around hybrid warfare to prepare simultaneously for the high-end fight and low-intensity conflict.[45] While the United States does not have the luxury to subscribe to one typology of warfare, it must invest resources in those capabilities designed to do specific and necessary tasks. Secretary of Defense James Mattis sums it up best by warning that "we don't want or need a military that is at the same time dominant and irrelevant."[46] The United States may have lethal and "relentless strike" dominance on the battlefield but lacks capabilities to complement those efforts by operating in the human domain. As the adage goes, if all you have is a hammer, everything looks like a nail.

PERVERSE INCENTIVE MINDSET

The US military is plagued with perverse incentive structures, the biggest of which is an overwhelming reliance on attrition warfare through kinetic operations. Watching monitor feeds (often referred to as "kill TV") of ordnance delivery using aerial platforms has led to a narrow conduct of warfare that, according to some, is becoming an addiction.[47] The easy metrics of body counts and enemy killed in action are often mistaken as performance measures for strategic success.

Lieutenant General H. R. McMaster, the former national security adviser, once warned about the prevalent misbelief that "technology and firepower are sufficient to achieve lasting strategic results."[48] Put simply, targeting enemy organizations does not equal strategy. Logically, there is an incentive to use stand-off strike technology to avoid unnecessary loss of life. However, a path dependency forms and excessive use becomes habit. The capability to strike targets with precision from afar is useful in myriad situations but the unintended consequences of overuse should be examined. What does a joint direct attack munition (JDAM) do to village's embedded social and economic relations? Precision targeting may reduce threats but there are tertiary effects not seen on kill TV. In *The Thistle and Drone*, Akbar Ahmed explains the unheard narrative of tribal peoples' lives persistently shaken by drone strikes. Ahmed attributes the failure of the United States and Pakistan to deal with transnational terrorists to their ignorance of tribal lifestyles, patterns of behavior, and customs.[49]

For military personnel and diplomats alike, another perverse incentive is the need to demonstrate progress for individual evaluations during deployment. For government and perhaps other agencies, progress is often measured with project execution and dollars spent without regard to actual effects. The seventeen years of this repeated mistake in Afghanistan confirms this mindset remains inculcated within military and diplomatic thinking and is potentially harmful to desired objectives. Current interventions in places like Afghanistan are protracted struggles where the long-game requires persistent focus and continuity of effort. Unchecked, these perverse incentives grow to become ethical dilemmas harmful to the image of the American military and, worse yet, might create more enemies than they eliminate.[50]

LET THE DIPLOMATS DO IT MINDSET

Civilian organizations alone are not prepared or capable of operating in conflict zones on a sufficient scale over a sustained amount of time. Diplomats and civilian organizations are increasingly operating in seclusion in the world's conflict zones behind blast walls in secure compounds. This has created a growing disconnect between the civilian sphere and the environment in which they are operating, giving them less oversight, diminishing their understanding of complex conflict dynamics, and rendering them less effective. Working in contested and dangerous spaces will require some type of military support. Given that there is no substitute for ground context, this will be an enduring requirement for quite some time. The military must maintain a cadre of professionals capable of working with interagency partners to access far-flung hinterlands for local engagement. Adhering to the first-order principle of understanding is nearly impossible without access to the populace. The military must maintain a cadre of professionals capable of working with interagency partners to access these spaces.

FOCUS ON THE MACRO-LEVEL MINDSET

At its core, war is a political act and all politics are local. Both civilian and military leaders have a natural tendency to focus on the macro-level dynamics rather than the local drivers of violence and stability. Celestino Perez warns of this macro bias error contributing to strategic discontent.[51] He highlights work by Sèverine Autesserre that illuminates this local neglect by peace builders in the Democratic Republic of Congo, where tensions concerning political power, land rights, and ethnicity spur bottom-up conflict. General Cleveland has observed this need to "go slow, go long, go small and go local."[52]

These mental traps manifest a culture of thinking that plagues the defense establishment at all levels. Thankfully, through service and sacrifice, pioneers demonstrated the need for a human domain warfighting concept. They saw how an excessive focus on enemy forces has ignored the larger environment, which is replete with critical information on people and society that enables US forces and their local partners to achieve a position of advantage. The military needs large volumes of data revealing patterns in complex societies and illuminating key interactions and feedback loops driving phenomena ranging from financial crashes to popular uprisings. Data on human interaction and engagement is now central to understanding the environment.

EMBRACING THE HUMAN DOMAIN: BIG DATA AND THICK DATA

Mapping the human domain enables strategists and planners to visualize and describe shih. Shih, as discussed in chapter 4, is the interdependent relationship between actors and an environment that produces power and a position of relative advantage in context. Power is not fixed and constant, but varies according to the context. For example, in traditional relative combat power terms, an F-35 stealth fighter is more powerful than a small team of Hamas militants firing crude, improvised rockets. Yet, give that Hamas team an iPhone and let them upload fake images of F-35 strikes killing civilians along with the home addresses of Lockheed Martin executives, the manufacturers of the aircraft, and Israeli air crews, and you can tip the scales. How military power interacts with local dynamics matters and changes how we conceptualize advantage in modern conflict.

In a hyper-connected world big data rules. Information is ubiquitous. Large data sets reveal patterns and preferences that map the human domain.[53] The combination of data and new analytical methods like machine learning improve predictive analytics and help analysts forecast emergent trends.[54]

From predicting teenage pregnancies to stopping the spread of diseases, big data is rapidly changing the world.[55] Furthermore, the devices connecting humanity and creating new information flows are spreading. In 2012, the World Bank declared the "pace at which mobile phones spread globally is unmatched in the history of technology."[56] In studying areas of limited statehood, scholars found information communications technology (ICT) filling voids in governance.[57] The use of ICT and the spread of information prevented governments from controlling the narrative. For example, Moscow was unable to cover up the 2010 wildfires due to ubiquitious commmuninication pathways that made it difficult to hide the crisis. ICT enabled a non-state collective response and undermined the state's attempt to present a rosy account of the situation.[58]

In addition to mobile phones and ICT, the proliferation of other sensors provides a torrent of data that enables collective action. Web-connected cameras, bio-sensing devices, and the confluence of other connected devices and new analytical processes help people hold governments accountable, reduce corruption, enable crisis-mapping, strengthen civil society, and improve responses to humanitarian crises.[59] Understanding social relations is the first step to transforming them. We are entering a world of data-driven decision-making.[60]

While big data is crucial, military practitioners also require local understanding to address the complexities of the human domain. Scholars and development practitioners find an "eclectic combination" of diverse theoretical perspectives and research methods improve the chances of revealing hidden connections and dynamic patterns not visible with a single theoretical lens.[61] Thus mapping human geography and visualizing the human domain requires both *big data* and *thick data*.

Thick data is qualitative information that provides insights into the everyday emotional lives of people. It goes beyond big data to explain *why* people have certain preferences, the reasons they behave the way they do, why certain trends stick, and other such attitudinal and behavioral patterns.[62] Thick data is produced by experts who are adept at observing human behavior and underlying motivations. These experts span the fields of anthropology, ethnography, and even the military's special operations forces. Analyzing thick data illumines emergent human dynamics not immediately visible with big data alone.[63] Military forces can be more effective when they understand the emotional and visceral context of indigenous populations.

Organizations need strong ties to connect with stakeholders. Stories strengthen these connections. Stories contain emotions and larger narratives that make sense of the world.[64] While large data sets can capture patterns of human activity, these patterns exist in a larger context that often requires a careful human eye to interpret. It takes skilled and patient professionals to provide this critical insight, which allows units and organizations to adapt as circumstances change.

For example, while conducting ethnographic research for Nokia in 2009 Tricia Wang immersed herself into China's populace by selling dumplings as a street vendor near a construction site. She discovered that low-income consumers were ready to pay for the more expensive smartphones. This finding was contrary to Nokia's big-data analysis driving their business model. Given the small sample size of Wang's study, Nokia chose to ignore her recommendation of changing their product development strategy from making expensive smart phones marketed for elites to affordable smartphones for lower-income consumers. Their choice to rely on large quantitative studies over qualitative data was catastrophic and contributed to their downfall, missing the explosive wave of smartphones and leading to their buyout by Microsoft in 2013.[65]

Nokia was blindsided by a quantification bias absent an understanding of the larger social context in which people make choices. The military falls victim to this same bias and routinely confuses counting for context, from the body count obsession in Vietnam to the number of high-value targets prosecuted in contemporary counterterror campaigns.

Understanding the human domain requires more than counting the relationships revealed through analyzing big data. It requires understanding the emotional as much as the rational and seeing patterns of behavior as embedded in stories groups use to make sense of their world.

The act of collecting and analyzing these stories provides clues to the local context animating collective action. Rogers Smith highlights the importance of narratives defining power relations and creating political allegiances in identity groups. His concept of "ethically constitutive stories" help explain the ultimate values shared across generations and express the uniqueness of a people in specifically moral terms, where political and economic labels often fall short.[66] Narratives provide social networks with a logic that orders our world. Along these lines, Nicholas Christakis and James Fowler's research reveals how social networks influence virtually every aspect of our lives, many times in a subconscious way. [67]

Outsourcing complex problems to algorithms sorting big data absent an understanding of narrative and context renders an incomplete sight picture. Therefore, understanding the human domain requires both big and thick data. Table 7 shows the characteristics of these approaches.

Table 6. Comparison of Big Data and Thick Data.

Thick Data	Big Data
optimized for human learning	optimized for machine learning
reveals social context of connections between data points	reveals insights with a particular range of quantified data points
accepts irreducible complexity	isolates variables to identify patterns
smaller in scale and scope	large sample and scale

Source. Derived from Tricia Wang's website: https://medium.com/ethnography-matters/why-big-data-needs-thick-data-b4b3e75e3d7

The combination of big data revealing patterns and thick data describing the context in which they emerge illuminates the key relationships military professionals have to appreciate to be successful in contemporary competition and conflict. Understanding these relationships and finding the best way to shape them produces a position of advantage in the human domain. A theory of victory for the human domain requires rethinking how we collect and analyze data.

Most importantly, it is becoming increasing clear that successful use of these data approaches will require increased cooperation and engagement. Robin Chase emphasizes the value of cooperation and engagement amongst nontraditional partnerships forming a new collaborative economy.[68] She explains how the best of corporate power (industrial capacity and resources to scale) combines with people power (localization, specialization, and customization) to harness resources in new ways and creates new rules for value creation.[69] Chase's company Zipcar and Uber are examples of these types of businesses. Cooperation is key.

Pentland claims modern science is finding that cooperation is equally as important as competition. Cooperation requires purposeful engagement, and Pentland defines engagement as social learning, which typically leads to the development of behavioral norms and social pressure to enforce those norms within a group.[70] For example, groups with a high rate of idea flow among members of the work group tend to be more productive.[71] This form of engagement has similar implications for military practitioners who must connect with the populace in a meaningful way to gather essential data needed to foster an understanding of local dynamics.

The talent and skills to effectively harvest data are not immediately available or evenly distributed across DoD. Hence, engagement and cooperation with external elements is crucial for future interventions and requires mutually beneficial relationships. There must be incentives for outside agencies to partner with DoD, and this leads to a key recommendation of the book: human-engagement data must be a shared common resource for all to benefit.

DoD should lead the effort and manage this data to avoid what has been referred to as the tragedy of the commons, where people share a resource with no ownership, and self-interests prevail over common good to deplete and spoil a shared resource.[72] Leadership is essential to managing data. By providing access to data as a public good for all, DoD benefits most by gaining an understanding of environments where they are not present. Nonprofits, civil society groups, and a host of other agencies can provide context where DoD lacks access. This understanding will help decision makers, in collaboration with local stakeholders, understand how to prevent conflict, and when necessary, intervene alongside legitimate local partners.

Building this shared resource is not far from reality. There is an existing abundance of data available across the enterprise and through nonprofit and commercial channels. The DoD needs to champion a public-private partnership organizing and curating data while formalizing business practices to ingest more information as the world connects and our lives manifest in digital flows of information. Military organizations and a host of other civilian organizations (e.g. nonprofits, NGOs, IGOs) all stand to benefit from shared data repositories that use big data combined with local understanding to anticipate crises and coordinate responses.

A public-private partnership collecting and curating data on emerging crises will increase the efficacy of operations and promote conflict prevention over large military interventions. Across the globe, state and non-state entities will increasingly be held more accountable by citizens accessing data to identify corruption and injustice as well as coordinate humanitarian responses to complex emergencies. Democracy and development flourish with the exchange of ideas. Working with foundations and nonprofits to create a data repository mapping the human domain will improve how the world views the United States, whose reputation has been tarnished by mass surveillance and targeted raids. Beyond the moral and reputational stakes, the US military has incentives to harness the power of thick and big data to gain a position of advantage in twenty-first-century competition and conflict. For too long, garrisoned diplomats and constrained soldiers, who often only look for the enemy and miss the larger environment, have been unable to understand local context and align ends, ways, and means to win population-centric struggles.

Figure 3. Illustration of Data-Collection Dilemma and the Idea of a Common Shared Resource Pool for Human Data.

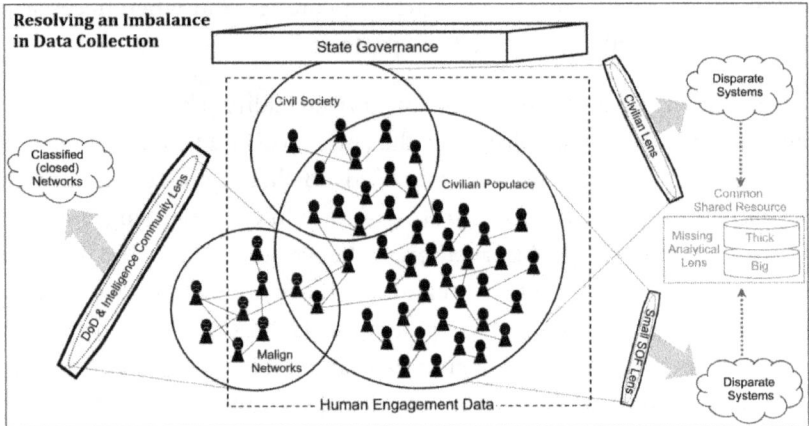

Source. Illustration by Arnel David.

CONCLUSION

> Knowing the human domain, therefore, gives commanders the ability to see, sense, anticipate, and maneuver through the complexity of peoples.
>
> —Patricia DeGennaro[73]

An enduring lesson from a series of interminable conflicts that continue to entangle the nation is that local struggles to consolidate political order require local understanding.[74] There is no substitute for ground context. Stories of pioneers in contemporary conflicts validate this insight and provide new tenets that reflect the importance of gaining a position of advantage in the human domain: understand, influence, shape, mobilize, and empower. Together, these evolving tenets illuminate the art of the possible. They remind us of the ingenuity of American soldiers, who are at this historical juncture are the most experienced combat force the nation has ever seen. However, these experiences and skillsets are fleeting if not codified.

Despite the military profession's efforts to develop new capabilities and concepts for population-centric conflicts, progress halted for a variety of reasons. New ideas met tremendous service pressure. Rather than frame the problem holistically, military services and the branches within those services, especially the Army and Marines, immediately debated ownership and resource allocation. The domain model—land, sea, air, cyber and space—secured dominance in what can best be termed traditional war (e.g., direct military confrontation between states). From major defense firms and their constituents to concept development within the military profession (e.g., AirSea Battle, Multidomain Battle), multiple incentives make the existing domain logic appear logical and absolute. As a result, the military profession did what it knew best and ignored the necessity of maneuvering within a new domain, the human domain.

The domains are at the core of how the United States organizes itself for war. However, this same model has proven increasingly inadequate for understanding and building the tools necessary to achieve US political objectives against seemingly less capable irregular enemies. We contend that a core problem is the failure of the current domain model to account for the most prevalent forms of conflict: resistance, rebellion, subversion and insurgency.

Recognizing the human domain and generating concepts and capabilities to gain advantage therein would be a disruptive innovation. Like cyber space, it would force changes across all branches of government. The United States has had the luxury afforded by its nuclear and conventional preeminence of avoiding the need to reorganize for irregular combat. Recent experiences in Iraq and Afghanistan are sobering reminders that the nation no longer has the luxury to subscribe to one typology of warfare. The US national security community squandered the initial victories of Iraq and Afghanistan and came up short providing capabilities and concepts for transitioning from combat operations to an acceptable level of peace and stability.

In an era before constant television war reporting and social media, states could wield violence with little worry of bad press, international condemnation, and a global network of recruits mobilized to fight back. These restraints on the nation state's use of violence in population-centric conflicts mean that unless the threat is existential, warfare will be limited, making investments in large conventional formations optimized for fighting other large formations suboptimal. The United States has come to realize that twenty-first-century irregular warfare is neither a smaller scale of traditional war nor the graduate level of conventional war. It is a different form of war, one in which information warfare, mobilized mobs, and other nontraditional forms of maneuver undermine US technological advantages. The weak will continue to win, the nation's resources wasted, and long irregular wars lost unless there is a considerable course correction to fully recognize the realities of the human domain.

Notes

1. For overviews of the battle and the campaign logic preceding it, see Steven Runciman, *A History of the Crusades: The Kingdom of Jerusalem and the Frankish East* (Cambridge University Press, 1968); *The Conquest of Jerusalem and the Third Crusade: Sources in Translation*, ed. and trans. by Peter W. Edbury (Aldershot: Ashgate, 1998); and *Saladin and the Crusaders: Selected annals from Masalik al-absar fi mamalik al-amsar*, trans. Eva Rodhe Lundquist (Lund: Studia Orientalia Lundensia v.5, 1992). For a general overview, see DRM Peter, "The Battle of Haitin: Four Accounts" *De Re Militari*, January 11, 2014, https://deremilitari.org/201 4/01/the-battle-of-hattin-1187-four-accounts/.

2. For an overview of human geography, see Martin Phillips, ed., *Contested Worlds: An Introduction to Human Geography* (Burlington: Ashgate, 2005); and Stuart Aitken and Gill Valentine, eds., *Approaches to Human Geography: Philosophies, Theories, People and Practices* (Los Angles: Sage, 2015).

3. Kishore Mahbubani, *The Great Convergence: Asia, the West, and the Logic of One World* (New York: Public Affairs, 2013), 1–3.

4. See Daniel Bolger, *Why We Lost: A General's Inside Account of the Iraq and Afghanistan Wars* (New York: Houghton Mifflin Harcourt, 2014); and Douglas Macgregor, "What Donald Trump Can Learn From Dunkirk" *National Interest* (August 2017), http://nationalinterest.org/feature/ what-donald-trump-can-learn-dunkirk-21761; and Douglas Macgregor, *Breaking the Phalanx: A New Design for Landpower in the 21st Century* (Washington, DC: Center for Strategic and International Studies, 1997).

5. On the American Civil War, see Harold Holzer, *Lincoln and the Power of the Press: The War for Public Opinion* (New York: Simon and Schuster, 2015). On Vietnam, see Robert Lester, ed., *Vietnam, the Media, and Public Support for the War* (Frederick: University Publications of America, Johnson Library Presidential Series, 1986), http://www.lexisnexis.com/ documents/academic/upa_cis/2292_VietnamMediaSuppWar.pdf.

6. Castells defines a space of flows as "the space of flows is the material organization of time-sharing social practices that work through... purposeful, repetitive, programmable sequences of exchange and interaction between physically disjointed positions held by social actors in the economic, political and symbolic structures of society." See *The Rise of*

the Network Society: The Information Age: Economy, Society, and Culture, vol. I, revised ed. (New York: Wiley-Blackwell, 2009), 408.

7. Anthony H. Cordesman, "Stability Operations in Syria: The Need for a Revolution in Civil-Military Affairs," *Military Review* (March 2017), http://www.armyupress.army.mil/Portals/7/military-review/Archives/English/Online-Exclusive/stability-operations-in-syria-by-anthony-cordesman.pdf.

8. Describing combat that defies AirLand Battle and U.S. technological strengths, these small wars were referred to as "uncomfortable wars" by General John R. Galvin. See Daniel P. Bolger, "The ghosts of Omdurman," *Parameters* 21 (Autumn 1991): 28–39; and Andrew F. Krepinevich, "Overhauling the Army for the Age of Irregular Warfare: The U.S. military isn't prepared to wage long fights against Islamic State and other enemies," *Wall Street Journal*, February 18, 2016, https://www.wsj.com/articles/overhauling-the-army-for-the-age-of-irregular-warfare-1455839486

9. Moisés Naím, *The End of Power: From Boardrooms to Battlefields and Churches to States, Why Being in Charge Isn't What It Used to Be*, (New York: Basic Books, 2013).

10. Authors' interview with James E. Leonard, New York, September 23, 2015.

11. Kurt Weyland, "The Arab Spring: Why the Surprising Similarities with the Revolutionary Wave of 1848?" *Perspectives on Politics* 10, no. 4 (2012): 917–934.

12. John McHugh and Raymond Odierno, Army Strategic Planning Guidance, 2013,http://usarmy.vo.llnwd.net/e2/rv5_downloads/info/references/army_strategic_planning_guidance.pdf.

13. Odierno, Amos, and McRaven, *Strategic Landpower*.

14. Ibid.

15. Deparment of Defense. JP 1-02: Dictionary of Military and Associated Terms (Arlington: Department of Defense, 2016), 141.

16. Ibid., 150.

17. Ibid., 7.

18. Ibid., 224.

19. Department of Defense Strategy for Operating in Cyberspace, July 2011.

20. Odierno, Amos, and McRaven, *Strategic Landpower*.

21. JP 1-02, 58.

22. Linda Robinson, Paul D. Miller, John Gordon IV, Jeffrey Decker, Michael Schwille, Raphael S. Cohen, *Improving Strategic Competence; Lessons from 13 Years of War*, (Santa Monica: RAND Corporation, 2014), 71.

23. Martha L. Cottam, Joe W. Huseby, Bruno Baltodano, *Confronting al Qaeda: The Sunni Awakening and American Strategy in al Anbar* (Lanham: Rowman & Littlefield Publishers, 2016).

24. William Doyle, *A Soldier's Dream: Captain Travis Patriquin and the Awakening of Iraq* (New York: Dutton Caliber).

25. Chad M. Pillai, "A Tribute to Captain Travis Patriquin: America's 'Lawrence of Arabia' in Ramadi," *Small Wars Journal* (December 8, 2010), http://smallwarsjournal.com/blog/a-tribute-to-captain-travis-patriquin

26. Thomas M. Scanzillo and Edward M. Lopacienski, "Influence Operations and the Human Domain," *Center on Irregular Warfare and Armed Groups Case Study*, (Newport: Naval War College, 2015), iv.

27. Ibid., iii

28. Arnel David, "Civil Society Engagement in the Sulu Archipelago: Mobilizing Vibrant Networks to Win the Peace" (master's thesis, Command and General Staff College, 2013).

29. Ibid., 48–52.

30. Arnel P. David, Wesley Strong, and Lucas Overstreet, "CA Forces in CENTCOM: Building the SOF Enterprise Through Partnerships," *Special Warfare* 25, no. 2 (April-June 2012):16–19; and Roger Jackson, "US Army and Spirit of America help villagers in Tajikistan," filmed November 2011, https://www.youtube.com/watch?v=gcARxTJ8qHk&index=17&list=FLsdxxxh2zYbxEBk4smjjCWA.

31. Charles T. Cleveland "Command and Control of the Joint Commission Observer Program: US Army Special Forces in Bosnia," (master's thesis, Army War College, 2001).

32. Paul Staniland, "States, insurgents, and wartime political orders," *Perspectives on Politics* 10, no. 2 (June 2012): 243–264.

33. Ibid., 243.

34. Fotini Christia, *Alliance Formation in Civil Wars* (New York: Cambridge University Press, 2012).

35. Sydney J. Freedberg, "Army Makes Case for Funding Culture Skills Beyond COIN," *Defense News*, July 2, 2012, http://defense.aol.com/2012/07/02/army-makes-case-for-culture-skills-beyond-coin/.

36. See Stephen R. Covey, *The Speed of Trust: The One Thing That Changes Everything* (New York: Free Press, 2008); and U.S. SOCOM, "Special Operations Forces 2020," Tampa: Government Printing Office.

37. The seventh warfighting function was codified in 2014. *TRADOC Pamphlet 525-8-5, the U.S. Army Functional Concept for Engagement* (Fort Eustis, VA: US Army Training and Doctrine Command, 2014), http://www.tradoc. army.mil/tpubs/pams/tp525-8-5.pdf. The call for the deliberate creation of a global landpower network was codified in the 2014 Army Operating Concept, *Win in a Complex World*, United States Army Training and Doctrine Command, *TRADOC Pam 525-3-1: The U.S. Army Operating Concept* (Suffolk VA: US Army TRADOC, 2014), http://tradoc.army.mil/ tpubs/pams/TP525-3-1.pdf.

38. *Win in a Complex World*, 8.

39. Chief of Staff of the Army Strategic Studies Group, "Expanding American Leadership Through Persistent Engagement," unpublished draft dated 2016, 13.

40. Russell F. Weigley, *The American Way of War: A History of United States Military Strategy and Policy*, 2 vols. (Indianapolis: Indiana University Press, 1977).

41. Max Boot, "The New American Way of War," *Foreign Affairs* 82 no. 4 (July/August 2003): 1, https://www.foreignaffairs.com/articles/united-states/2003-07-01/new-american-way-war.

42. Antulio J. Echevarria II, *Toward an American Way of War* (Carlisle: US Army War College, Strategic Studies Institute, March 2004), 1.

43. Lawrence Freedman, "Counterrevolution in Military Affairs," in *The Modern American Military*, edited by David Kennedy (Oxford: Oxford University Press, 2015), 13.

44. From early years in the Mexican-American War to present conflicts in Iraq and Afghanistan, Nadia Schadlow highlights a civil-military gap restricting successful political outcomes to be gained from tactical success; see *War and the Art of Governance: Consolidating Combat Success into Political Victory* (Washington, DC: Georgetown University Press, 2017).

45. David E. Johnson, "*The Challenges of the 'Now' and Their Implications for the U.S. Army*" (Santa Monica: RAND Corporation, 2016), 9–10, https:// www.rand.org/pubs/perspectives/PE184.html.

46. Jim Mattis, "A New American Grand Strategy," *Hoover Institution*, February 26, 2015), http://www.hoover.org/research/new-american-grand-strategy.

47. Micah Zenko, "Addicted to Drones: Is the allure of war by remote control the root cause of America's dangerously unbalanced foreign policy?"

Foreign Policy, October 1, 2010, http://foreignpolicy.com/2010/10/01/addicted-to-drones/.

48. H.R. McMaster, "Continuity and Change: The Army Operating Concept and Clear Thinking About Future War," *Military Review* 95, no. 2 (March-April 2015): 6–20.

49. Akbar Ahmed, *The Thistle and the Drone: How America's War on Terror Became a Global War on Tribal Islam* (Washington, DC: Brookings, 2013), 1–42.

50. See Douglas A. Pryer, "The Rise of the Machines: Why Increasingly 'Perfect' Weapons Help Perpetuate Wars and Endanger Our Nation," *Military Review* 93 no. 2 (March-April 2013): 14–24.

51. Celestino Perez, "Errors in Strategic Thinking: Anti-Politics and the Macro Bias, *Joint Force Quarterly* 81, no. 2 (April 2016).

52. Charles T. Cleveland, "Operating in Gray Zones," (speech, National Defense University, October 2015).

53. David Lazer, Alex Pentland, Lada Adamic, Sinan Aral, Albert-Laszlo Barabasi, Devon Brewer, Nicholas Christakis, Noshir Contractor, James Fowler, Myron Gutmann, Tony Jebara, Gary King, Michael Macy, Deb Roy, and Marshall Van Alstyne, "Life in the Network: The Coming Age of Computational Social Science," *Science* 323, no. 5915 (February 6, 2009): 721–723.

54. Pentland, *Social Physics*, 184.

55. Charles Duhigg, *The Power of Habit: Why We Do What We Do In Life And Business* (New York: Random House, 2012).

56. The World Bank, "World Development Indicators 2012" (Washington, DC: The World Bank).

57. Steven Livingston and Gregor Walter-Drop, eds., *Bits and Atoms: Information and Communication Technology in Areas of Limited Statehood* (New York: Oxford University Press, 2014).

58. Gregory Asmolov, "Natural Disasters and Alternative Modes of Governance: The Role of Social Networks and Crowdsourcing Platforms in Russia," in *Bits and Atoms: Information and Communication Technology in Areas of Limited Statehood*, edited by Steven Livingston and Gregor Walter-Drop (New York: Oxford University Press, 2014), 105–135.

59. Livingston and Walter-Drop, *Bits and Atoms*.

60. Alex Pentland, *Social Physics: How Social Networks Can Make Us Smarter*, reissue ed. (New York: Penguin Books, 2014), 263.

61. Rudra Sil and Peter J. Katzenstein, "Analytic Eclecticism in the Study of World Politics: Reconfiguring Problems and Mechanisms across Research Traditions." *Perspectives on Politics* 8, no. 2 (2010): 411–431.

62. Jess Cook, "The Power of Thick Data," BIGFish Communications, June 10, 2014, http://bigfishpr.com/the-power-of-thick-data/.

63. Tricia Wang, "Big Data Needs Thick Data," *Ethnography Matters*, May 13, 2013, http://ethnographymatters.net/blog/2013/05/13/big-data-needs-thick-data/.

64. Mikkel B. Rasmussen and Andreas W. Hansen, "Big Data Is Only Half the Data Marketers Need," *Harvard Business Review*, 2015.

65. Wang, "Big Data."

66. Rogers M. Smith, *Stories of Peoplehood: The Politics and Morals of Political Membership* (New York: Cambridge University Press, 2003).

67. Nicholas A. Christakis and James H. Fowler, *Connected: How Your Friends' Friends' Friends Affect Everything You Feel, Think, and Do* (New York: Back Bay Books, 2009).

68. Robin Chase, *Peers Inc: How People and Platforms Are Inventing the Collaborative Economy and Reinventing Capitalism* (New York : Public Affairs, 2015).

69. Ibid., 1.

70. Pentland, *Social Physics*, 414.

71. Ibid.

72. Elinor Ostrom, *Governing the Commons: The Evolution of Institutions for Collective Action.* (New York: Cambridge University Press, 1990).

73. Patricia DeGenarro, "Does the Human Domain Matter?" *Small Wars Journal* (February 23, 2017), http://smallwarsjournal.com/jrnl/art/does-the-human-domain-matter.

74. Lawrence Freedman, "Using Force for Peace in an Age of Terror," in *Leashing the Dogs of War: Conflict Management in a Divided World*, edited by Chester a. Crocker, Fen Osler Hampson, and Pamela Aall (Washington, DC: US Institute of Peace, 2007), 245–263.

CHAPTER 6

ENGAGEMENT AND THE
GLOBAL SECURITY NETWORK

Any successful strategy to ensure the safety of the American people and advance our national security interests must begin with an undeniable truth—America must lead. Strong and sustained American leadership is essential to a rules-based international order that promotes global security and prosperity as well as the dignity and human rights of all peoples. The question is never whether America should lead, but how we lead.

—President Barack Obama[1]

As long as we know our history, we will know how to build our future. Americans know that a strong alliance of free, sovereign and independent nations is the best defense for our freedoms and for our interests.

—President Donald Trump [2]

Despite vast differences in approach, every American president from Franklin D. Roosevelt to Donald J. Trump publicly recognized that the United States of America is strengthened by its connections. Major near-peer competitors like Russia and China can match American military technology. They cannot replicate the network of partnerships and alliances that allows US forces global access and the ability to aggregate combat power around the world. It is true that some presidents have come to this realization more grudgingly than others, but all have eventually accepted the fact that America's strength and reach is expanded by training and operating with partners rather than alone. Thus, the key question is not whether the United States should continue to build alliances and nurture partnerships, but how to sustain this global security architecture and convert it into strategic options to advance the national interest. How should the United States harness connectivity to prevent, deter, and ultimately win future conflict? How does the United States ensure that when it does take the field of battle the fight ends in victory fought through local partnership networks that facilitate access and help generate options faster than the adversary can respond?

The answer lies in networks. Understanding connections between groups and visualizing these networks through big data allows the United States to exploit, or if need be, destroy rival networks. Defense strategy becomes the art of mobilizing networks, whether making new connections or routing flows through existing connections, faster than your adversary. These network connections can range from activating basing and access agreements with partners to facilitate power projection to increasing your partner's combat power by helping them map local conflict dynamics and providing intelligence, logistics, and fires support. Military power can no longer be measured singularly by counting tanks and airplanes. Connections and how information and resources flow between actors across networks matter as much, if not more, than the number of individual fighting units. Therefore, military power becomes network power along two dimensions: 1) increasing the number of connections and your capacity to influence them and 2) ensuring interoperability and rules necessary to generate new network connections, and through them, combat power. These two dimensions, network power and network-making power, represent a new theory of victory that should drive twenty-first-century military strategy.

The strength and diversity of US networks are bolstered by America's free and open society. The US government's open approach to information underpins the vibrancy and complexity of its networks, which in turn allows ideas to flow freely and allows networks to thrive. This is a fundamental strength of American society, one that must be recognized and harnessed as a tool of influence and a means of defense in an era of Gray Zone competition, cyber war, and pervasive social media. In essence, the American strategic approach in the twenty-first century should be to capitalize on an inherent strength of the United States and that of its democratic allies: the free flow of information and ideas among its citizens. The United States should develop, nurture, and manage a global security network aimed at harnessing data and information flows to influence outcomes globally in furtherance of US strategic interests.

This chapter proceeds from the assumption that technologically-enabled human connectivity has changed the character of military power, and through it, strategic competition.[3] Nearly ubiquitous and instantaneous information flows that enable rapidly shifting connections produce profound shifts in the concepts and capabilities required to "win" in the current era. The conflicts in Iraq, Afghanistan, and Syria, as well as the events of the Arab Spring serve as ample evidence that this shift has occurred. The new key terrain is not just based on physical geography. It is based on identifying key relationships and using the data to mobilize networks that place your adversary on the horns of a dilemma.

To develop this proposition, the chapter proceeds as follows. First, we will reflect on how connectivity alters strategy. From this vantage point, the chapter will consider two forms of power: networking and network making.[4] *Networking power* is the capacity an actor has to influence the flows from connections in a network, to include influencing which connections form while disrupting others. For example, at the strategic level China's One Belt One Road initiative to build land and sea-based trade routes connecting coastal China through Central Asia and Southeast Asia to Europe and Africa represents a bold geopolitical strategy predicated on networking power. Investing in trade infrastructure gives China the ability to influence local politics by connecting economic and political networks. To the extent Beijing can harness the power of big data to map the multiplicity of human connections across this trade network, they will gain a position of continuous advantage that crowds our US interests slowly but surely.

Network-making power is the capacity for influence that results from generating rules and standards (i.e., protocols) governing which actors connect and how they interact. Returning to One Belt One Road, to the extent China can create common transportation standards or get countries to adopt their currency, Beijing translates network power into network-making power. They gain a position of continuous advantage by governing how resources and ideas flow along the network. Military power in the traditional sense becomes reduced to controlling key nodes along the network and through engagement, ensuring interoperability with new partners thus creating a rival to the US-led liberal order. Put another way, the battle for the flanks in Asia concerns economic networks more than the placement of aircraft carrier battle groups.

Finally, the chapter will discuss the unique role the US military can play as a network hub in the twenty-first century. The US military and the US Army, in particular, currently sit astride a vast array of networks that can be used for both networking and network-making power. For example, the NATO alliance not only requires collective defense under Article 5, it also requires all members adhere to common standards of interoperability—STANAGS—which shape defense procurement and how the alliance fights.[5] Similarly, the United States, through its military, has significant networking power available through foreign military-sales programs. That said, a recent CRS report contends that the post–Cold War conventional arms transfers have tended to be economically motivated rather than policy determined.[6] The United States must understand the extensive untapped networking and network-making power available through these transfers and craft their use more deliberately for strategic ends. These two examples illustrate the depth and complexity of the networks in which the US military wields network-making power. It should be harnessed for its strategic potential.

How Connectivity Shapes Strategy

The world is connected. The number of devices connected to Internet Protocol (IP) networks was double that of the global population in 2015.[7] In 2015, mobile and Wifi data passed fixed internet traffic in terms of volume.[8] That means more people are connected and on the move. The young are more eager to connect than the old. According to a 2014 Pew Research Center study, people in the 18–29-year-old group are adopting social media and mobile technologies faster than earlier generations.[9]

This connected world is home to big data, the growing volume of information transforming our economic, social, and political lives.[10] New analytical techniques allow actors to find signals in the noise, searching messy, heterogenous flows of data for emergent patterns. This trend—the growing volume, velocity, and variety of data—is likely to continue.[11]

The new connectivity is not just a function of cyberspace networks. It takes spatial dimensions in increased trade, connecting global supply chains with megacities that act as regional economic, social, and political hubs.[12] These hubs facilitate the exchange of ideas and resources, even between strategy competitors. For example, the United States and China engage in more than half a trillion dollars in trade annually.[13]

This web of global connectivity does not necessarily herald a new era of peace. Interdependent great powers engaged in crisis brinksmanship prior to World War I, leading to arms races, shifting alliances, and a security dilemma. In the twenty-first century, powerful states use the anonymity of cyber and Gray Zone activity to challenge each other short of war. Increased global connectivity creates an opportunity for extremists, rogue states, and criminals to create "dark networks" that operate along transnational illicit pathways and undermine state governance.[14] According to Seth Jones, increased connectivity "will likely have a notable impact on insurgent operations and tactics, making it easier for insurgents to recruit, distribute propaganda, and communicate."[15] States leverage these dark networks to wage a new form of political warfare as seen in the Russian use of criminal networks to facilitate cyberattacks against Estonia, Georgia, and Ukraine.[16]

Military leaders speak not only about the volume of social interaction but also their velocity. Army War College Professor Steve Metz argues that "connectivity and the technology that enables it have increased the velocity of change in human society."[17] Velocity in combination with magnitude changes the way that human beings learn and also increases the rapidity with which they adopt new positions. In his work, *Social Physics*, MIT professor Alex Pentland opines:

> To understand our new hyper connected world, we must extend familiar economic and political ideas to include the effects of these millions of digital citizens learning from one another and influencing one another's opinions.[18]

Both the speed and the magnitude of interactions are critical factors for understanding the changing character of power. As an example, Google currently answers questions for half the planet every day.[19] There is significant power associated with these information flows. They influence both ideology and action. As Pentland explains:

> We must stop thinking of people as independent decision makers and realize the dynamic social effects are equally important at shaping our ideas and are the driving force behind economic bubbles, political revolutions and the internet economy.[20]

The connections between agents, seen as networks, determine how ideas, goods, and people circulate. They are a space of flows.[21] Networks of states and non-state actors have ties that, "determine how information and influence flow in the global village."[22] Drawing on social network theory, Zeev Maoz defines a network as a "set of units (nerves, species, individuals, institutions, states), and a rule that defines whether, how, and to what extent any two units are tied to each other."[23]

There are two types of networks: relational and affiliation. Relational networks connect units based on rules defining the "presence, direction and magnitude" of a relationship.[24] Affiliation networks organize around rules that "define an affiliation of a unit with an event, organization, or group."[25] How goods and ideas flow in these networks shapes behavior. Variants of social-network theory have been used to test propositions from world-systems theory about center-periphery political relationships and economic inequality, status inconsistency, network centrality as a source of cooperation and conflict, and how the interdependence shapes trade and war.[26]

Increasing network connectivity is shrinking the world. In the 1960s, researcher Stanley Milgram showed that the median distance through networks between anyone in the American population was six degrees.[27] That is, it only took six different people, as nodes in a relational network, to connect any two Americans. By 2016, Facebook researchers found that the degrees of separation dropped to 3.46 for the United States, and 4.5 for every connected human in the world.[28] To put that in perspective, humans across the world with access to cell phones or the internet are more connected to each other than the American population was in 1967.

For Parag Khanna, a Senior Fellow at the Lee Kuan Yew School of Public Policy at the National University of Singapore, the increasing density of these global connections shifts the epicenter of international politics and strategy.[29] The organizing principle is no longer sovereign territory. Rather, the new geography and resulting geopolitics are organized around supply chains. In this world, the goal is not to control key territory—the proverbial heartland in H.J. Mackinder's early twentieth-century treatment[30]—but to be the central hub through which ideas, goods, and people flow. In this world, "thanks to global transportation, communications, and energy infrastructures—highways, railways, airports, pipelines, electricity grids, internet cables, and more—the future has a new maxim:

connectivity is destiny...global infrastructures are morphing our world system from division to connections and from nations to nodes."[31] As a result, "we are moving into an era where cities will matter more than states, and supply chains will be a more important source of power than militaries."[32]

What does strategy look like in a world built around connections as opposed to states? For many countries, markets are already the domain of foreign policy competition, not battlefields. According to Robert Blackwell and Jennifer Harris, "many states today are as likely...to air disagreements with foreign policies through restrictions on trade in critical minerals or through buying and selling of debt than through military activities."[33] The art of competition is thus not limited to political intrigue, propaganda, or military formations alone. Gaining a position of advantage is shifting from geopolitics to geoeconomics. Building on earlier work on economic statecraft,[34] geoeconomics represents the art of using economic instruments to advance geopolitical ends and promote national interests.[35] This competition leverages global connectivity first, putting a premium on understanding local contexts and gaining access, while military might, the number of carriers and armored brigades, come second.

Anne-Marie Slaughter sees network connectivity as grand strategy.[36] Failures in foreign policy are often a result of an inability to grasp that global connections, not narrow national interests, produce a new form of bargaining power. According to Slaughter, "we have no playbook for strategies of connection, or for creating the tools we need to implement them. To create it, we must turn to network theory as Schelling once turned to game theory."[37]

In networks, power does not flow from hierarchy; it flows from connectivity. A network perspective on grand strategy sees new sources of power: information, adaptability, and scalability.[38] The speed of information gives unique advantages by revealing risk and opportunity. An example of this is cyber conflict. Networks provide even weak states and non-state actors with cheap access to the domain, as well as the means with which to conduct attacks.[39] Conversely, networks and the ability to map them also provide the capability to identify malicious actors even before they can act. Thus, the use of network power provides both increased risk and increased opportunity for both sides. It is incumbent on the government and the military to use networks to their full advantage to mitigate risks and exploit opportunities. Not doing so cedes "terrain" to our adversaries.

The number of connections and the rate at which they can exchange ideas and resources (including people) increases their adaptability. An example of this can be seen in global networks focused on preventing and controlling the spread of epidemic disease outbreaks. The Center for Disease Control is plugged into a global response network that shares information and best practices to combat the spread of deadly infectious diseases.[40] Although not foolproof, the network, run through the World Health Organization, is strengthened by the number of members, or connections, within the network. Once again, one can see that a globalized world is a double-edged sword when it comes to disease transmission. Increased mobility and travel can spread the disease more quickly, but conversely, networks aimed at prevention and early response can combat their spread. In fact, epidemiologists are harnessing network science specifically to understand transmission patterns, as well as critical nodes of immunization in order to stop outbreaks.[41]

Last, scale—the ability to grow rapidly at low-cost—allows actors to maximize adoption and achieve not just a momentary but also a long-term advantage. The United States continues to project military power in the Asia-Pacific rim to deter growing North Korean aggression, as well as to counter growing Chinese military power and influence within the region. From a conventional perspective, China's military rise and North Korean threats should be met with traditional military capabilities, such as a carrier-strike group in the Taiwan Strait or a conventional military buildup on the Korean Peninsula. However, these capabilities come at increasing cost.

America's newest aircraft carrier, the USS Gerald R Ford, which was commissioned in 2017, is expected to deploy in 2021 at a price tag of $12.8 billion to build, along with an additional $4 billion in research and development costs. [42] To deploy this carrier and its accompanying ships (five surface vessels, an air wing and an attack submarine) would cost the American tax payer $2.5 million per day.[43] Deterring North Korean aggression with traditional capabilities could mean stationing more forces in South Korea. According to the Congressional Budget Office, the cost of a single armored brigade combat team is approximately $500 million a year, while an F-35 squadron costs $570 million per year to operate.[44] Adding to this, the cost of replacing a single lost F-35 is just short of $95 million.[45] Further, there is no guarantee that these exorbitantly priced, exquisite military capabilities will have the desired effect.

Networks provide an alternative. Making use of the United States' networking and network-making power to positively influence the security architecture of our Asian alliance system would be a far less costly as well as less escalatory alternative. Returning to Robert Blackwill and Jennifer Harris' geoeconomic arguments, a network approach could contain favorable trade agreements with Asian nations along with increased military exercises and military exchanges in the region. These efforts would be bolstered by coercive diplomacy, including targeted and escalating sanctions. The combined effect would be a carrot-and-stick approach, shaping the decision calculus of rivals. Through the development of a multipronged network approach, integrating all of the instruments of power, the United States can potentially achieve all of its security objectives without the outlay of hundreds of billions of dollars in military equipment it can no longer afford and with much less risk of inadvertent escalation to war.

Seeing strategic competition through the prism of networks introduces new theories of victory and changes the focus of military operations.[46]

For Slaughter, in a networked world, victory becomes less about subjugation, or power over, and more about power with.[47] Similar to the aforementioned example about Asia-Pacific strategy, measuring relative capabilities does not capture the ability to leverage connections and create emergent effects. For Slaughter, it is the difference between the power of a mayor and the power of a mob. Network strategy therefore revolves around brokerage, the ability to connect as opposed to the traditional use of signaling capabilities and resolve to coerce rivals. Network strategy offers new theories of victory. States orchestrate new connections, isolate malign actors, and focus on engagement to increase information exchange, adaptability, and scalability.

Adapting network theory to conflict prevention and brokerage is a slow process, one that requires the deconstruction of prevailing cultural norms. That said, the US military is taking strides to adapt to this reality. The US Army has recently stood up the first Security Force Assistance Brigade (SFAB) at Fort Benning, Georgia. It is one of six such brigades scheduled for activation. Their mission will be to advise and assist foreign security forces.[48] In addition to the skills that these SFABs will provide to partner military forces, they will also extend the network connections of US military and US security networks more generally. Partner militaries will receive American military equipment, as well as training, thus increasing the supply-chain requirements and brokerage aspects of the relationship. In short, network membership will come with benefits and the United States will be in position to determine membership requirements. This is the essence of network-making power.

These connections are not just physical linkages in our world; per Khanna's supply-chain map, they are virtual. In a world where the internet of things and proliferating access define connectivity, the cyber domain merges with physical reality. Connections carry with them ordering architectures. The flow of goods and ideas creates points of advantage even in physically distributed networks. Therefore, technologies of connection—whether increasing information exchange or shipping standards that enable global trade—alter the speed and circulation of goods and ideas, and in the process, create new modalities of power and governance. For French philosopher Paul Virillo, this speed of exchange is the foundation of human history:

> ....modernity is logistical. It doesn't directly deal with war, but with everything that makes it possible. Logistics is the preparation for war through the transfer of the nation's potential to its armed forces in time of peace as in times of war. Modernity is a world in motion, expressed in translations of strategic space into logistical time, and back again. It is a history of cities, partitions, trading circuits, satellites, and software; of a political landscape governed by competing technologies of surveillance, mobilization, fortification, and their interdependent administrations. It begins as an archaeology of naval routes, strategic techniques and urban distributions, and becomes an integrated world of events reduced to shapes and symbols, viewed and manipulated instantaneously on screens.[49]

Virillo's modernity is perceptual as much as it is material. Thus, an aspect of networking power can be found in manipulating the information found on the billions of screens human beings interface with hourly through news feeds to understand the world around them. "Reality," by virtue of technology, has become more of a postmodern matter of perception than ever before. The US government has been learning this the hard way in the wake of the 2016 presidential elections.

Although the cries of "fake news" reverberating through mainstream media are relatively new to most Americans, the use of subversion, deception, misinformation, and influence operations aimed at undermining the legitimacy of political adversaries is as ancient as it is a constant of human behavior. What is new is the impact technological advances have had on these tactics. According to Laura Daniels, a Senior Fellow at the Global Public Policy Institute in Berlin, "social media shortens the response window and allows disinformation to evolve as events unfold on the ground." [50] She further asserts that "technological advances have amplified the effectiveness of instruments that were in play during and well before the Cold War."[51]

Information is increasingly central to competition, confrontation, and conflict. This observation is not new. Strategic studies scholars began to entertain the possibility of a new form of war linked to increasing connectivity in the early 1990s. According to John Arquilla and David Ronfeldt, the information revolution altered the character of conflict by increasing the importance of "network forms of organizations" and information as a form of power.[52] War is waged by networks who often leverage "information operations" and "perception management" to both influence and coerce targeted populations.[53] In this realm of competition, "psychosocial disruption may become more important than physical destruction."[54]

Both sides attack connectivity because it is a force multiplier. Conventional military power is generating diminishing returns, which renders the fight for information more critical in an age of network power. As described in chapter 4, the United States pioneered subversive attacks on elections and engaged in influence operations to contain the spread of communism and advance a liberal democratic international order. It is time to resurrect these techniques, albeit in a more ethical fashion, in order to protect and expand America's network power in the twenty-first century.

Arquilla and Ronfeldt defined netwar as a mode of conflict and crime at "societal levels involving measures short of traditional war, in which the protagonists use network forms of organization and related doctrines, strategies, and technologies attuned to the information age."[55] Russia has engaged in "netwar" during its interventions into both Georgia in 2008 and the Ukraine in 2014. In "Russia's Improved Information Operations: From Georgia to the Crimea," Emilio Iasiello contends that the 2008 Russian invasion of Georgia saw increasing instances of "cyberattacks and conventional operations work[ing] together."[56] In conjunction with its invasion of Georgia, agents of the Russian government denied service to more than fifty websites linked to government, finance, and communications.[57] These tactics were used to greater effect in Crimea in 2014 when Russian forces entered the peninsula on March 2, 2014 after "they had already shut down Crimea's telecommunications infrastructure, disabled major Ukrainian websites, and jammed the mobile phones of key Ukrainian officials."[58]

Connectivity does not replace war, but it alters how groups engage in a contest of wills. Connectivity has increased the number of strategic actors, from states to issue-groups and businesses, while lowering the cost of mobilization creating a new complexity.[59] A connected world may limit the utility of conventional conflict, but it empowers states in the shadows and non-state actors to continue politics by other means through network competition.

Modern military organizations have difficulty achieving political ends in these wars of connectivity. The Evolved Irregular Threat Project noted critical gaps existing in "information operations, situational awareness, especially in the urban environment; and geography, culture and language knowledge"[60] in combating irregular threats. A central premise of the study was that these actors were evolving as "armed sub-state or non-state actors such as military units, terrorist networks, insurgent movements, militia groups, or armed criminal actors (including piracy networks, human/drug/arms-trafficking rings or urban gangs)" applied emerging off-the-shelf technology to enhance their ability to adapt "from coercive (combat capabilities) through administrative (governance capabilities) to persuasive (political and propaganda capabilities)."[61] Similarly, Seth Jones argues that "threats are increasingly networked, adaptable, and empowered by cyberspace to find new ways to recruit, collect intelligence, train, distribute propaganda, finance, and operate."[62]

Connectivity levels the playing field. It allows actors with fewer traditional capabilities to mobilize resources, spread their narrative, and recruit forces to challenge more powerful actors.[63] In his article "Communication, Power and Counter-power in the Network Society,"

Castells theorizes that "media has become the social space in which power is decided."[64] The rise of "self-radicalized" lone-wolf actors perpetrating low-tech attacks underscores his point.

Extremist networks use "social media outlets" to achieve "global reach for organizing, planning, and conducting operations. They instill loyalty among their followers through near constant, clear communication."[65] Operating in cyberspace makes it difficult to identify and target these networks "using conventional military power."[66] State actors similarly leverage cyberspace to wage global, irregular warfare. Patrick Michael Duggan argues that Russia and Iran use dispersed groups leveraging new technologies and operating along networks to gain a position of advantage over their adversary in the information domain. Specifically, they use, "groups of special operators armed with asymmetric cyber tools, irregular warfare tactics, and mass disinformation" to achieve strategic effects.[67]

The United States has yet to embrace the benefits of leveraging connectivity and exploiting it to gain a position of strategic advantage. The biggest deficit is building a capacity to see and influence actors in open sources. Numerous studies cite a need to reorganize the intelligence community and Cold War–era analytical processes in order to deal with the new environment.[68] According to John Mackinlay, connectivity creates an "information anarchy" that gives violent extremist networks an advantage over government actors.[69] Insurgents appear to be better at exploiting user-generated content and social media to wage information warfare.

Connectivity also enables positive forms of influence. For example, development activists use a combination of crowd sourcing, remote sensing (i.e., commercial satellites), and social media—all combined to form data rich representations of human environments—for activities ranging from public health to peacebuilding. The Swedish NGO, Flowminder, uses narrow artificial intelligence to predict epidemiological patterns and the spread of disease.[70] The Map Kibera Project uses a big data approach to map urban slums and underdeveloped areas in Nairobi, Kenya.[71] Crowdseeding initiatives, such as distributing cell phones to enable local reporting in the Democratic Republic of Congo, help activists and relief agencies track political violence in real time.[72] Collecting the digital footprints we leave as we wander the web of connectivity provides social radars mapping the habits, preferences, and relationships of a population in real time.[73]

In summation, connectivity alters strategy. Seeing the world as networks requires strategies that focus more on building relationships than combat power alone. The actor who builds more connections along a global network of relationships creates a position of advantage. In addition, shaping the volume and velocity of ideas and material flows along these network connections creates options faster than a rival can respond. The two objectives—increasing the balance of connections and shaping flows between them—requires network power and network-making power. These concepts in turn explain how the United States can generate favorable points of interdependence and influence within the human domain.

NETWORK POWER: INCREASING CONNECTIVITY

There are two key components to increasing connectivity: understanding and engagement. First, increasing connectivity requires understanding each actor, their interdependent interests, and shifting relationships in context. As discussed in the last chapter, this situational awareness is the crux of the human domain. With this understanding, the US military should reinvigorate the push to make engagement a warfighting function focused on identifying favorable points of interdependence and influence vectors in relational networks. Without managing relationships, the access points to a global network of flows, the United States will decrease the probability of achieving a position of advantage in future crises and conflicts.

Understanding

Taking a network approach to strategy formulation entails compre-
hending power as an ephemeral information flow, not a tangible thing or
object. Joshua Cooper Ramo, describes the phenomenon in *The Seventh
Sense*:

> power operates as much through light pulses running inside
> fiber optic webs as it does in any physical sense. Think of the
> most influential geo-political forces, the most lethal militaries,
> the greatest new commercial or financial efforts. All now depend
> on and are nearly defined by their fluency with different sorts
> of connection.[74]

The idea of a global security network is about harnessing the power of
network science to track the social information flows that are currently
ongoing to identify key nodes and influencers. In plain English, we must
study connections and determine their implications. This will allow for
the development and maintenance of these nodes through regular contact
in order to improve engagement, trust, and open communication. For the
military this includes exploiting existing partnerships and alliances, as
well as extending their reach. However, it also requires thinking about
nontraditional networks and undertaking data collection and analysis
on them.

Currently, there is little social network analysis occurring within the
military. Most of the relationships and the networks they illuminate
remain fleeting and unstudied. Further, as individuals are themselves
transitory within positions, the strength of interorganizational bonds
ebb and flow with personnel transition. To capitalize on its influence and
to develop greater partnership capacity, the US government and the US
military must manage networks purposefully and thoughtfully. These
are assets that have yet to be harnessed.

In certain respects, this is akin to an intelligence function. However,
there are significant differences. Since the 9/11 attacks, the military
and the intelligence agencies have placed significant resources against

tracking and destroying terrorist networks. In effect, certain portions of the US government are very adept at social network analysis and using a network approach for kinetic targeting.

The idea of a network approach and developing a strategic defense network is far broader. It is also much more reliant on open source, publicly available information. The vast majority of this network mapping can come from unclassified data. A network approach for the military requires integrating the intelligence, civil affairs, and key leader engagement functions into a single system of reporting and systematically analyzing it using big and thick data.

In her 2015 work, *Thieves of State,* Sarah Chayes makes a compelling case for the need of social network analysis directed far more widely than threat networks. Regarding a decade-long nation-building effort in Afghanistan, she contends that:

> Despite the thousands of intelligence professionals spread throughout the country, not to speak of the hundreds of diplomats and intelligence practitioners, the international community knew almost nothing useful about the government officials or contractors we were dealing with.[75]

In this case, network analysis of the partner government in Kabul could have illuminated the fundamental corruption issue years earlier and the United States and its International Security Assistance Force (ISAF) allies could potentially have changed tactics as a result or, at a minimum, been much more clear-eyed about the end states and the reliability of partners. This is merely one example of the utility of social network analysis combined with the power of big data within an operational theater.

A critical problem to date has been managing data volume and generating analytic capacity. Social network analysis on the scale required to maximize US networking capacity globally has historically been beyond our ability. This is changing. Currently, the Department of Defense is attempting to grapple with this problem through using narrow artificial intelligence applications to help sort through large volumes of data, and in the process, make sense of the world. Project Maven, launched by former Deputy Secretary of Defense Robert Work, was tasked with "turning the enormous volume of data available to DOD into actionable intelligence and insights at speed."[76] The work combines artificial intelligence and machine learning to analyze full motion drone footage.[77]

This groundbreaking approach could be extended to analyze key relationships in the human domain and create new US networking and network-making strategies. Returning to chapter 5, new public-private partnerships could collect and catalogue publicly available information to map the human domain. Using social network analysis and narrow artificial intelligence applications, analysts could identify key relationships and variables associated with instability. They would understand who the key influencers were and what stories they told to mobilize the population. This information would help nonprofits and local partners address the root causes of unrest and, done correctly, prevent conflict escalation.

Engagement

Translating situational awareness, mapping the human domain through big data and machine learning, into a position of advantage requires a deliberate scheme of engagement. Engaging partners and building trust facilitates network access and flows thus creating options faster than a rival can respond. This idea is not new.

In 2011, the US Army flirted with updating its doctrine to include "engagement" as a new warfighting function. Military operations are guided by doctrine. Doctrine is designed to describe how forces should operate, and serves as a, "guide to action," rather than a list of rules to follow.[78] Currently in its nineteenth edition in 2016, Army Doctrine Publication (ADP) 3-0 *Unified Land Operations* serves as the primary text on how the army operates or fights. The 2016 edition of ADP 3-0 defines the army's operational concept, Unified Land Operations (ULO), which is executed through the application of combat power and comprised six warfighting functions: mission command, movement and maneuver, intelligence, fires, sustainment, and protection.[79] These functions are defined as a "group of tasks and systems united by a common purpose that commanders use to accomplish missions."[80] The warfighting functions provide army professionals with an intellectual organizing construct to frame action. Adding engagement to the warfighting functions would place managing relationships across the range of military operations on par with gaining intelligence or sustaining deployed troops. It would also serve to expand the current definition of warfare beyond combat operations.

The desire to elevate the status of managing complex local relationships grew out of the lessons learned in Iraq and Afghanistan reviewed in chapter 2. The paradox of military intervention in Afghanistan and Iraq, similar in some respects but not all to Vietnam, is that the US military could win every battle and still fail to achieve its strategic ends. The intellectual organizing construct—the warfighting functions—did not produce plans that led to operational or strategic success. Combined arms, what Stephen Biddle calls the modern system,[81] alone was insufficient to the problem at hand. This deficit led to significant introspection within the ranks of the military profession.

Sustained counterinsurgencies and the fight for information (as discussed in chapter 3) led practitioners to seek new ways of gaining access to and understanding local populations including efforts to under-stand the human domain discussed in chapter 5. However, unlike prior conflicts this effort to understand the local population intersected with a change in the volume, density, and velocity of global connections.[82] Technology-enabled connectivity, from social media to cell phones, created new networks that made it difficult to keep local conflicts isolated. From foreign fighters to transnational advocacy networks restraining the use of force to advance political objectives, the struggles were increas-ingly transnational. The number of actors connected to any one conflict seemed to increase exponentially. The question then was how to manage these connections beyond destroying identified combatants. How could a force gain situational understanding and isolate adversaries faster than the enemy could generate new combatants?

These questions formed the core of the push to create a new warfighting function: engagement. When the discussion to add a seventh warfighting function began in the US Army in 2011, there was considerable debate on what it should be called and what it should include. There was an argument made for elevating special operations as a warfighting function, as well as an argument for the addition of an influence operations warfighting function.[83] Despite disagreements over the name and exactly what activities it should encompass, there was a consensus among senior leaders that something critical was being missed and that missing piece was inextricably linked to the human dimension of conflict. The idea of "war among the people" and the link to politics, networks, and the new weapon of choice—social media—abounded.[84]

In the end, senior leaders chose engagement as the umbrella term under which to gather a profusion of tasks and activities that "influence the behaviors of a people, security forces and governments."[85] Although somewhat amorphous, there was a growing appreciation amongst senior leaders that growing connectivity increased the importance of engagement. Pentland captures this logic, noting that "there is growing evidence that the power of engagement—direct, strong interaction between people is vital to promoting trustworthy, cooperative behavior."[86]

The engagement warfighting function was qualitatively different from the other six. It was designed to recognize and elevate the human dimension in warfare. The difficulty it faced in gaining acceptance was primarily cultural. Current Army doctrine includes information as an element of combat power and a key enabler for successful operations. Doctrinal publications also acknowledge cyber operations as an element of combined arms.[87] However, these publications do not specifically acknowledge a human domain. In fact, the concept of a human domain remains controversial and the term is unacknowledged outside of some segments of SOCOM. There is no current doctrinal acknowledgement of the existence of a human domain. In short, the army has returned to its comfort zone and ended further discussion of a seventh warfighting function.

However, the operational and strategic need that began the conversation remains. It is most comprehensively outlined in *The US Army Functional Concept for Engagement:*

> Future leaders must understand the human aspects of conflict and ways to achieve outcomes consistent with national interests. Inform and influence activities, military support to governance, development and establishing rule of law will be central to achieving ends across the range of military operations. [88]

The logic of engagement is not limited to irregular warfare. It is far more encompassing. Engagement is tied to the increasing connectivity of human relations and velocity of interaction. For the United States, engagement is also foundational to its continuing role as a superpower. So long as the United States seeks to maintain global leadership, it must maintain a robust strategy of engagement both within its military as well as more broadly. For the military, it is imperative to engage with partners to build and maintain coalitions. This goes beyond diplomacy to encompass generating access. The TRADOC concept for engagement describes:

> the need for army forces to enter an area of operations on foreign soil; communicate with local leaders and populace; assess needs; understand the situation; and develop capacity building programs; and direct efforts towards achieving outcomes consistent with US interests.[89]

Engagement is about network power, although those words were not used to describe it. It was also intended to combat the problem with conflict below the threshold of warfare. In testimony before the Senate

Select Intelligence Committee, Eugene Rumer, a former member of the National Intelligence Council, argued that:

> While the public's mood for involvement in further overseas adventurism is less than sanguine, it still remains important for the United States to be able to shape events on the ground overseas with as little force as possible.[90]

The president and national-level decision makers require options at thresholds lower than major theater war. The architects of the engagement warfighting function operationalized the concept to organize an integrated response to contemporary struggles. Although this discussion began within the army, it has much broader applicability. Properly implemented, it could use a network approach to increase the US government's ability to strengthen and influence partners to manage and attain shared security objectives. It could also allow the United States to increase both its networking and network-making power by managing interoperability requirements for partners and allies, as well as by deliberately linking foreign military sales to expanding American network power.

Engagement could also extend the reach of America's international networks, improving situational understanding in both military and nonmilitary arenas. Improved network connections via deliberate engagement could also help identify emerging crises. Done correctly, engagement increases the scope of the United States' networking and network-making power.

A consistently derided limitation of the United States' current diplomatic and military networks is that they are neither congruent nor complementary. One need only look at the maps of the Department of Defense's Geographic Combatant Command structures in comparison with those of the Department of State's geographically organized bureaus to see the evidence. The seams are obvious and exploitable. A more holistic approach is needed to optimize and integrate the sources of America's network-making power. But the problem is larger still.

A strategy predicated on networks and engagement requires an even larger focus. To fully implement a strategic approach to networking, the United States must also incorporate nongovernmental and commercial networks. There must be a fundamental shift in the way that power is understood. Taking a network approach to strategy is about brokerage rather than ownership. Information is exchanged rather than compartmentalized. This is a profound cultural shift for US government agencies and departments. It requires greater analysis and greater inclusivity.

NETWORK-MAKING POWER: SCALABILITY

Unmistakably, global security networks currently exist. The components of a defense network exist as a subset of other networks. Formal networks, ranging from NATO to the African Union, rely on official state commitments to promote interoperability and collaboration. Other less formal networks coalesce around emerging threats or crises and shared interests (e.g., combating the Ebola outbreak, countering maritime piracy). The networks vary in size and structure. The operative question then is how to think about them in a manner that enables the US military to gain a position of advantage in long-term competition and conflict.

The work of Sir Julian Corbett, the famed sea power theorist, provides a conceptual blue print for thinking about network power and network-making power. Corbett, a lawyer by training from a wealthy family, began his study of sea power through a series of biographies on famous naval leaders from British history.[91] These biographical sketches evolved into his seminal book *Some Principles of Maritime Strategy*, published in 1911.[92]

For Corbett, the theory of victory revolved around command of the sea. Specifically, Corbett held that control of sea lines of communication enabled the protection of commerce, which was a center of gravity for the British Empire. The empire faced the dilemma of having to be everywhere and protect a global network of flows. Therefore, the British needed a network of staging areas, friendly ports and supplies, to operate a fleet of cruisers that could act as maritime skirmishers covering the nerves of empire. These skirmishers would buy sufficient time to mobilize combat power, larger battleships, in the event someone challenged British command of the commons. Furthermore, a smart adversary used a "fleet in being"—such as combat power in fortified ports—to occupy adversaries while smaller forces harassed the enemy's lines of communication, buying time to mobilize the fleet for decisive battle.

Corbett's entire concept looked at how to minimize the costs and risks associated with maintaining a global security network in the late nineteenth and early twentieth century. As such, it provides a guide for thinking about twenty-first-century network power. According to Corbett, "the object of naval warfare must always be directly or indirectly either to secure Command of the Sea or to prevent the enemy from securing it."[93] The object of competition, confrontation, and conflict in a hyper-connected world, both physically and virtually, similarly is to increase your connectivity while limiting your strategic competitor's connectivity. You create options while limiting the options available to your rivals. You cannot control a network, but you can shape interactions across it through having more access points than your opponent.

Shaping network flows requires network power, increasing the number of connections and your capacity to influence them, and network-making power, ensuring interoperability and scalability to generate combat power. First, you must understand your partners. That is the crux of engagement. Engagement is a precursor to network power. To operate along a global network of flows requires working through partners, both state and non-state, as nodes. These nodes, based on trust and shared interests, can increase or decrease your tempo. You must manage your relationships as deliberately as you would your fires plan or maneuver forces. That requires elevating the status we give to engagement in the US military.

Next, you must invest in partner capability and capacity, interoperability, and scalability as much, if not more, than your own systems.

This is the crux of network-making power. Building exquisite systems that do not connect to or work well with partner capabilities is a self-imposed constraint. The balance of investment should favor enablers (i.e., intelligence, fires, sustainment) as well as those concepts and capabilities that make it easier for our partners to threaten strategic competitors along a global security network. For example, ensuring that our network of Asian allies and partners that will respond to a Korean crisis have interoperable communications, are able to shoot standardized munitions (including air defense assets), and can share targeting information is the key to increasing options for shaping the initial stages of a conventional conflict, if not deterring an escalating crisis outright. Your goal, similar to Corbett's skirmishers, is to tie down an adversary and buy time and space for political leaders to determine the optimal strategy.

Furthermore, partner capability and interoperability provide scalability. That is, they allow you to generate local mass more quickly than your adversary can shift forces. In the event of a conflict, more capable partner forces absorb the initial shock while you escalate vertically, by standing up a Joint Task Force, and horizontally, by pressuring your adversary in other geographic areas through your network. North Korea knows that they face a blockade waged not just by the United States and South Korea, but by the Japanese air and naval forces. These air and maritime forces free up naval assets to threaten amphibious assault along North Korea's coasts while US and South Korean ground forces mobilize along the Demilitarized Zone. There is a reason North Korea's only option is nuclear, chemical, biological and cyber blackmail. They are isolated in terms of their network connectivity and face an adversary network that can generate options faster than they can respond, buying time for strategic mobilization.

Creating partner capability, capacity, and interoperability requires investment in theater shaping and aligning ends, ways, and means. For example, take defense commitments to the Philippines and Chinese activities in the South China Sea. The end is not winning a war with China.

The strategic end is maintaining a vibrant economic relationship with the world's second largest economy while sustaining a rule-based regional order that limits crisis escalation. The strategic end requires increasing the cost of Chinese coercive action without incurring significant escalation risk.

The way to achieve this end, consistent with Corbettian principles, is network power and network-making power. The United States should combine security force assistance and security cooperation in a more deliberate manner. Rather than conducting training exercises firing mortars or practicing rifle marksmanship, focus on selling, if not outright providing, the Filipino military optimized commercial off-the-shelf cybersecurity software and integrate these cyber defenses into military exercises that test air defenses around key airfields. Identify the key nodes, not just in terms of partners, but terrain required to increase flows and generate combat power in a future crisis. Create your network of skirmishers and test it to signal capability and resolve. Security force assistance and security cooperation become a core—not a peripheral task—of a military strategy built around networks.

In an era of persistent, low-level conflict, the US Army should serve as a focal point for coordinating connections across a global security security network, including both formal military ties and informal ties to civil society actors. By using the US Army as a super connector for the broader collection of networks, it can be an instrumental connection for shaping the environment and preventing the escalation of conflict to a point that requires costly military intervention.

In his groundbreaking work *The Rise of Network Society,* Castells develops the ideas of key nodes and mega nodes. He states that different types of activities develop different global key nodes. For example, he asserts that Silicon Valley exists as a key node for information and communication technology, while New York and London are key nodes for financial flows. [94] He explains:

> when these multilayered networks overlap in some node, when there is a node that belongs to different networks, two major consequences follow. First economies of synergy between different networks take place in that node [...] Second, these become mega-nodes. Mega-nodes are switching nodes for the entire global system connecting various networks.[95]

For the United States, the US Army is uniquely positioned as a mega node, a place where multiple different networks come together and can be synergistically harnessed as result. The US military, with the army most often at the forefront, participates in such diverse activities as disaster relief and humanitarian intervention, as well as more traditional international and training activities and military operations. The expanse of the army's extant landpower network and the range of preexisting networks it connects with on a daily basis should not be ignored or dismissed. Rather, these relationships should be purposefully harnessed, by both military and civilian leaders, in order to achieve strategic ends.

While the conventional force should remain focused on its core mission, segments of the broader force, including special operations forces, remain uniquely positioned to thrive in network environments, given the breadth and depth of their preexisting connections. A dose of patience coupled with long-term, interoperable relationships with partners and allies, will promote strategic access, increase multilateral relationships, and may ultimately reduce the necessity of future US military intervention. Furthermore, should military intervention become necessary, the benefits garnered from a robust landpower network will increase the likelihood of coalition support and interoperability while improving our capacity to shape the environment and set the theater. Developing a network approach to the existing vast array of interorganizational relationships and tracking, analyzing, and maintaining them are the keys to success. This will allow staffs to assess and prioritize relationships with strategically significant partners based on environmental considerations and identify the type of relationship to build based upon a partner's capabilities.

CONCLUSION

In *Thinking Beyond War,* Isaiah Wilson asserts the American definition of war is incomplete.[96] He states that,

> war as we know it is a sign of the times....the present and prevailing US (Western) construct of what constitutes "war" is rapidly being overruled by the contemporary realities of twenty-first-century warfare.[97]

War, as it is most commonly understood in the United States, brings to mind uniformed military forces fighting major combat operations *a la* World War II or Desert Storm. If prodded, Americans will also conjure images of Vietnam and potentially Fallujah. Few would think of John Arquilla's vision of netwar and fewer still would refer to Sun Tzu's "acme of skill"—winning without fighting.[98]

To attain a position of relative advantage, the US military should expand its definition of core tasks beyond conventional warfighting. Specifically, leaders should incorporate an understanding of conflict as waged between competing networks in the human domain. This perspective puts a premium on the fight for information and understanding the power of networks and network-making power in the current international system. To do this, one must look beyond battles to network connections that animate human society throughout all phases of competition and conflict. For the US military and the US government, this means presence, both virtual and physical, as well as robust engagement with both our partners and adversaries.

Connectivity has changed the character of power. To maintain its ability to provide relevant options for policy makers, the US military must adapt to these changes. Connectivity will put a premium on the fight for information and the ability to leverage networks to operational and strategic advantage. In his book *Connectography,* Parag Khanna argues that, "today, we don't get to choose between a world of great power competition, globalized interdependence, and powerful private networks. We have all three."[99]

This means that the military must be able to function with equal alacrity in all the domains of conflict, including the human domain. Declining military budgets do not obviate the requirement to adapt to this changing environment. It merely means the tradeoffs involved are more difficult and more critical. To maintain our military overmatch and America's position of global leadership, the US defense establishment must adapt to the changing calculus of conflict. To paraphrase former Secretary of Defense Donald Rumsfeld, we must fight the war we have, not the war we want. This means understanding and leveraging the power of connectivity through the purposeful development of a network maintained through engagement. The technology is extent. The difficulty is cultural. The next victory is as dependent upon a mindset shift as it is upon conventional military capability.

Notes

1. *The National Security Strategy of the United States* (Washington, DC: The White House, 2015) 1, http://nssarchive.us/wp-content/uploads/2 015/02/2015.pdf.

2. Donald Trump, *Remarks by President Trump to the People of Poland* (Washington, DC: The White House Office of the Press Secretary, July 6, 2017), https://www.whitehouse.gov/the-press-office/2017/07/06/ remarks-president-trump-people-poland-july-6-2017.

3. This argument proceeds from the argument promulgated in the book by Joshua Cooper Ramo, who argues that connectivity fundamentally changes the nature of power; see *The Seventh Sense: Power, Fortune and Survival in the Age of Networks* (New York: Little, Brown and Company, 2016), 36.

4. Manual Castells, "A Network Theory of Power," *International Journal of Communication* 5 (2011): 773–787. The definitions here merge Castells' larger taxonomy.

5. Cihangir Aksit, "Smart Standardization: A Historical and Contemporary Success at NATO," North Atlantic Treaty Organization: Topics, May 28, 2014, https://www.nato.int/nato_static_fl2014/assets/pdf/pdf_2014_05/2 0140528_140528-smart-standardization.pdf.

6. Catherine Theorhary, *Conventional Arms Transfers to Developing Nations: 2008-2016* (Washington, DC: Congressional Research Service, 2016), https://fas.org/sgp/crs/weapons/R44716.pdf.

7. Cisco Systems, *Cisco Visual Networking Index: Forecast and Methodology, 2010–2015* (San Jose: Cisco, 2011);

8. Cisco Systems, *Cisco Visual Networking Index: Global Mobile Data Traffic Forecast Update, 2011–2016* (San Jose: Cisco, 2011).

9. Pew Research Center, *Emerging Nations Embrace Internet, Mobile Technology,* February 2014, 12–13, http://www.pewglobal.org/files/2014/ 02/Pew-Research-Center-Global-Attitudes-Project-Technology-Report-FINAL-February-13-20147.pdf.

10. For an introduction to Big Data, see Kenneth Neil Cukier and Viktor Mayer-Schoenberger, "The Rise of Big Data: How It's Changing the Way We Think about the World," *Foreign Affairs* (May–June 2013) and Viktor Mayer-Schoenberger and Kenneth Cukier, *Big Data: A Revolution that*

will Transform How We Live, Work and Think (New York: Dolan/Mariner Books, 2014).

11. General Keith Alexander, USA (Ret.), "Closing Remarks at Accumulo Summit, June 2014," June 12, 2014, http://accumulosummit.com/archives/2014/program/ talks/.

12. John P. Sullivan and Adam Elkus, "Command of the Commons: Towards a Theory of Urban Strategy," *Small Wars Journal*, September 26, 2011, http://smallwarsjournal.com/printpdf/11533.

13. Office of the United States Trade Representative, "The People's Republic of China: US China Trade Facts," Office of the United States Trade Representative Resource Facts, https://ustr.gov/countries-regions/china-mongolia-taiwan/peoples-republic-china.

14. Kilcullen, *Out of the Mountains*, 34.

15. Seth Jones, *The Future of Irregular Warfare* (Santa Monica: RAND Corporation, 2012).

16. Andrew F. Krepinevich, *Cyber Warfare: A Nuclear Option?* (Washington, DC: Center for Strategic and Budgetary Assessments, 2012), 22–23; Brandon Valeriano, Benjamin Jensen, and Ryan Maness, *Cyber Strategy: The Changing Character of Power and Coercion* (New York: Oxford University, forthcoming).

17. Steven Metz, "Strategic Horizons: The U.S. Military Can't Ignore the Deep Future," *World Politics Review* (blog), April 3, 2013, http://www.worldpoliticsreview.com/articles/12842/strategic-horizons-the-u-s-military-can-t-ignore-the-deep-future.

18. Pentland, *Social Physics*, ix.

19. Ramo, *The Seventh Sense*, 116.

20. Pentland, *Social Physics*, 3.

21. The idea of seeing networks of spaces of flows comes from the work of Manuel Castells. For an overview, see Felix Stalder, *Manuel Castells* (Cambridge: Polity Press, 2006).

22. Zeev Maoz, *Networks of Nations: The Evolution, Structure, and Impact of International Networks 1816–2001* (New York: Cambridge University Press, 2011), 5.

23. Ibid, 7. Maoz bases this definition on Stanley Wasserman and Katherine Faust, *Social Network Analysis: Methods and Applications* (New York: Cambridge University Press, 1997); John Scott, *Social Network Analysis: A Handbook*, 2nd ed. (Thousand Oaks: Sage, 2000); and Matthew Jackson, *Social and Economic Networks* (Princeton: Princeton University Press, 2008).

24. Maoz, *Networks of Nations*, 7.

25. Ibid.

26. These examples are drawn from Maoz, *Networks of Nations*, 1-32.

27. Stanley Milgram, "The Small World Problem," *Psychology Today* 2 (1967): 60–67.

28. Smriti Bhagat, Moira Burke, Carlos Diuk, Ismail Onur Filiz, Sergey Edunov, "Three Degrees of Separation" Facebook Research, February 2016, https://research.fb.com/three-and-a-half-degrees-of-separation/.

29. Parag Khanna, *Connectography: Mapping the Future of Global Civilization* (New York: Random House, 2016).

30. H.J. Mackinder, "The Geographical Pivot of History," *The Geographical Journal* 23, no. 4 (April 1904): 421–437.

31. Khanna, *Connectography* , 5.

32. Ibid., 6.

33. Robert Blackwill and Jennifer Harris, *War by Other Means: Geoeconomics and Statecraft* (Cambridge: Harvard University Press, 2016), 6.

34. Baldwin reference, seminal historical work is Lambert; for a recent policy statement see Hillary Clinton Delivering on the promise of economic statecraft

35. Blackwill and Harris, *War by Other Means*, 8.

36. Anne-Marie Slaughter, *The Chessboard and the Web: Strategies of Connection in a Networked World* (New Haven: Yale University Press, 2017).

37. Ibid., 13

38. Ibid., 161–182.

39. For an overview of cyber conflict and strategy, see Valeriano, Jensen, and Maness, *Cyber Strategy*.

40. Centers for Disease Control and Prevention, "CDC Global Rapid Response Team," The Center for Disease Control and Prevention, August 8, 2017, https://www.cdc.gov/globalhealth/healthprotection/errb/global-rrt.htm.

41. Davide Castelvecchi, "Strategy to Stop a Pandemic," *Science News* (July, 4, 2008), https://www.sciencenews.org/article/strategy-stop-pandemic.

42. George Will, "Is It Time for the Navy to Reassess the Importance of the Aircraft Carrier?" *The National Review*, September 30, 2015, http://www.nationalreview.com/article/424870/it-time-navy-reassess-importance-aircraft-carrier-george-will.

43. Ibid.

44. Congressional Budget Office, *The U.S. Military's Force Structure: A Primer* (Washington, DC: Congressional Budget Office, 2016), , 28, 86,

89, https://www.cbo.gov/sites/default/files/114th-congress-2015-2016/reports/51535-fsprimer.pdf.

45. Christopher Drew, "Lockheed Lowers Price on F-35 Fighters, After Prodding From Trump," *New York Times*, February 3, 2017, https://www.nytimes.com/2017/02/03/business/lockheed-lowers-price-on-f-35-fighters-after-prodding-by-trump.html.

46. On the concept of a theory of victory, see Jensen, *Forging the Sword*.

47. Slaughter, *The Chessboard and the Web*, 172–173.

48. C. Todd Lopez, "Security Force Assistance Brigades to Free Brigade Combat Teams From Advise, Assist Mission," US Army.mil, May 18, 2017, https://www.army.mil/article/188004/security_force_assistance_brigades_to_free_brigade_combat_teams_from_advi

49. Benjamin H. Bratton, "Logistics of Habitable Circulation" in *Speed and Politics*, ed. Paul Virillo and trans. Mark Polizzotti (Los Angles: Semiotext(e), 2006), 7.

50. Laura Daniels, "Russian Active Measures in Germany and The United States: Analog Lessons from the Cold War," *War on the Rocks*, September 27, 2017, https://warontherocks.com/2017/09/russian-active-measures-in-germany-and-the-united-states-analog-lessons-from-the-cold-war/.

51. Laura Daniels, "Russian Active Measures in Germany and The United States: Analog Lessons From the Cold War," ibid.

52. John Arquila and David Ronfeldt, *Advent of Netwar* (Santa Monica: RAND Corporation, 1996), 7. See also, John Arquila and David Ronfeldt, *Networks and Netwar* (Santa Monica: RAND Corporation, 2001).

53. Arquila and Ronfeldt, *Advent of Netwar*.

54. Ibid., 8

55. Ibid., 9

56. Emilio Iasiello, Russia's Improved Information Operations: From Georgia to Crimea" *Parameters* 47, no. 2 (2017): 51–63, esp. 52.

57. Ibid. Although agency has not been incontrovertibly identified, there is reasonable certainty that these attacks were perpetrated by agents of the Russian government.

58. Azhar Unwala and Ghori, Shaheen, "Brandishing the Cybered Bear: Information War and the Russia-Ukraine Conflict," *Military Cyber Affairs* 1, issue 1, article 7 (2015), http://scholarcommons.usf.edu/mca/vol1/iss1/7.

59. David Betz, *Carnage and Connectivity: Landmarks in the Decline of Conventional Military Power* (New York: Oxford University Press, 2015), 180

60. Noetic Corporation, *The Evolved Irregular Threat Project* (Washington: Noetic Corporation, 20xx), 6.

61. Ibid., 5
62. Seth Jones, *The Future of Irregular War* (Santa Monica: RAND Corporation, 2012), 2.
63. Manuel Castells, "Communication, Power, and Counter-Power in Network Society," *International Journal of Communication 1* (2007): 238–266.
64. Ibid., 238.
65. Robert William Schultz "Countering Extremist Groups in Cyberspace" *JFQ 79*, (4th Quarter 2015): 54.
66. Ibid., 54.
67. Patrick Michael Duggan, "Strategic Development of Special Warfare in Cyberspace" *JFQ 79* (4th Quarter 2015).
68. Catherine Johnston, Elmo C. Wright, Jr., Jessica Bice, Jennifer Almendarez, and Linwood Creekmore, "Transforming Defense Analysis" *JFQ 79* (4th Quarter 2015).
69. John Mackinlay, *The Insurgent Archipelago* (New York: Columbia University Press, 2009), 94–95.
70. Benjamin Jensen and Ryan Kendall, "Waze For War: How the Army Can Integrate Artificial Intelligence," *War on The Rocks,* September 2, 2016. https://warontherocks.com/2016/09/waze-for-war-how-the-army-can-integrate-artificial-intelligence/.
71. Jiri Panek, "The Commercialisation of Public Data – How Does Participatory Data-Mining Look on a Global Scale?" *South African Journal of Geomatics* 2, no. 3 (June 2013): 234.
72. Peter Van der Windt and Macartan Humphreys, "Crowdseeding in Eastern Congo: Using Cell Phones to Collect Conflict Events Data in Real Time," *The Journal of Conflict Resolution* 60, no. 4 (November 4, 2014): 748–781.
73. Michael T. Flynn, James Sisco, and David C. Ellis, "'Left of Bang': The Value of Sociocultural Analysis in Today's Environment," *Prism: A Journal of the Center for Complex Operations* 3, no. 4 (September 2012): 121–137.
74. Ramo, *The Seventh Sense*, 33.
75. Sarah Chayes, *Thieves of State: Why Corruption Threatens Global Security* (New York: W. W. Norton & Company, 2016), 45.
76. Tasha Chappelet-Lanier, "Project Maven Right on Schedule, Air Force's Shanahan Says," Fedscoop, November 2, 2017, https://www.fedscoop.com/project-maven-dod-machine-learning/.
77. Ibid.

78. Headquarters, Department of the Army, *Army Doctrine Publication 3-0: Unified Land Operations* (Arlington: Headquarters, Department of the Army, 2016), https://www.otc.army.mil/ADP3-0.pdf.

79. Ibid., 13.

80. Ibid., 12.

81. Biddle, *Military Power.*

82. On dynamic density, see Hugo Meijer and Benjamin Jensen, "The Strategist's Dilemma: Global Dynamic Density and the Making of US China Policy," *The European Journal of International Security* 3, no. 2 (2018): 211–234.

83. Bennet S. Sacolick, MG and Grigsby, Wayne W. Jr., BG, "Special Operartions/Conventional Forces Interdependence: A Critical Role in 'Prevent, Shape, Win,'" *Army,* June 2012.

84. This paragraph was written from the personal experience of the author serving as the Division Chief for Strategy, Concepts and Doctrine on the Army Staff at the time.

85. *TRADOC Pamphlet 525-8-5, the U.S. Army Functional Concept for Engagement,* 5.

86. Pentland, *Social Physics, 65.*

87. Ibid.

88. *TRADOC Pamphlet 525-8-5, the U.S. Army Functional Concept for Engagement,* 6.

89. Ibid. page 1.

90. Eugene Rumer, *Russian Active Measures and Influence Campaigns* (Washington, DC: Testimony before the U.S. Senate Select Committee on Intelligence, March 30, 2017), http://carnegieendowment. org/2017/03/30/russian-active-measures-and-influence-campaigns-pub-68438.

91. For an overview of the context in which Corbett wrote, see D. M. Schurman, *The Education of a Navy: The Development of British Naval Strategic Thought, 1867–1914* (Chicago: The University of Chicago Press, 1965); and LCDR Ian C.D. Moffat, "Corbett: A Man Before His Time," *Journal of Military and Strategic Studies* 4, no. 1 (2001): 10–35.

92. Julian S. Corbett, *Some Principles of Maritime Strategy* (London, Longmans, Green & Co,1911).

93. Ibid, 87.

94. Manuel Castells, *The Rise of Network Societies,* 2nd ed. (Chichester: Blackwell Publishing, 2010), 772.

95. Ibid. 784.

96. Isaiah Wilson, *Thinking Beyond War: Civil-Military Relations and Why America Fails to Win the Peace* (New York: Palgrave MacMillan, 2007), xiv.
97. Ibid.
98. Sun Tzu, *The Art of War* (Oxford: Oxford University Press, 1971).
99. Khanna, *Connectography,* xviii.

CHAPTER 7

CONCLUSION

This book argues for seeing crisis, confrontation, and conflict in terms of networks connecting local actors. Connectivity changes strategy. Achieving a position of advantage in modern military art requires mapping the human domain and increasing the number of connections in a global security network that allows the United States to project power and influence. Seeing the shifting network of relations in the human domain—from the local to the global—will allow US forces to tailor their operations to the context and find the right balance of cooperation, influence, manipulation, and targeted violence to achieve national security objectives. The network connections required to operate in the human domain are not just with states or exercised through military power alone. Rather, wielding network power and network-making power requires mobilizing local populations through civil society, as well as economic and political relationships, to achieve a position of advantage often before the first shot is fired.

As practitioners, our collective experiences suggest that US military power will produce declining marginal returns until we change how we see the map. Since the Napoleonic era our concepts and processes emphasize a friendly, "Blue" force and an enemy, "Red" force. These forces had different capabilities, which could be independently quantified. The only context that mattered was terrain and its effects on those capabilities. These simplifications allowed strategists and planners to think about the correlation of forces and maneuver options, the hallmark of operational art.

In a connected world, even more than before, the correlation of forces and our very understanding of military power is emergent. Red and Blue collide with Green, the population, in both the physical and virtual contexts creating positions of advantage not reducible to weapons alone. Power is best understood as the Chinese concept of shih, situational advantage. This world requires that we think more like Hannibal and Saladin and see how social, economic, and political networks create opportunities to influence our rivals and shape their decisions.

The stakes are high. The United States continues to invest a significant share of its budget in military resources without a corresponding return. Victory is fleeting. Worst still, the capabilities American tax payers do buy have increasing price tags. The United States is buying smaller numbers of expensive equipment that can make it more difficult to work with our partners. We are closing ourselves off rather than reaping the benefits of engagement and a global security network. Even the F-35, which multiple partners are buying, does not necessarily ensure interoperable communications and targeting between allies. This book starts a dialogue about a way out of this trap.

The US national security community must reorient how they think about power and influence in the twenty-first century and embrace a view of the world as a series of interconnected networks. This shift rests on two pillars: embracing the idea of the human domain and changing how we think about engagement.

The logic of networks rests on two concepts: network power and network-making power. Network power is the capacity to influence that emerges from the connections between actors. The more connected you are and the less connected your rival, the more likely you are to achieve a position of advantage. You generate options while closing them off to your rival.

Network-making power involves increasing the interoperability between connected actors to generate local mass and enable scalability. Network-making power involves the less glamorous, and often under-appreciated, task of standardizing munitions and communication frequencies alongside logistics agreements. Most do not join the military to write SOPs for alliance communication, targeting, rearming, and refueling, but these tasks create significant returns on investment. The fact is that America fights with partners. Increasing the capability and interoperability of that partnership network creates options our rivals cannot match.

Understanding competition, confrontation, and conflict as they exist within rival networks creates a new demand signature for US military modernization. First, it requires new concepts. The US military at large and the US Army in particular should move to acknowledge the human domain and engagement as a warfighting function. Revitalizing these initiatives, but at the level of the Secretary of Defense, would pull the services away from the petty competition over defense dollars for modernization priorities still connected to the Third Offset strategy and shift the focus back to war as a contest of wills. Understanding the human domain and embracing engagement and influence as a viable warfighting function reinvests America in its core strategic asset: the global network of partnerships built since World War II.

Next, mapping the human domain and generating local mass through network and network-making power requires capability investments. The US military should build an open-architecture platform that aggregates unclassified data to help map the human domain. This data should be publicly available to nonprofits. The purpose would be to identify instability and crisis, similar to existing work on early warning in the development communities, before a crisis emerges. By collecting and curating data, the United States offers a global public good that facilitates local solutions to local problems before they require US military forces.

Second, the baseline data, when integrated with machine learning applications could facilitate increasing situational awareness. As small teams begin to respond, they will have a map of existing grievances, concerns, and interests that helps operators engage with the right local partners.

Third, the US national security community must shift our defense procurement paradigm from exquisite, expensive, and exclusive to include cheap and accessible platforms that our partners can use. Increasing partner combat power is an investment in a Corbettian network of skirmishers that provides US strategists and planners options in a crisis. Service modernization programs, particularly within the US Army, should start to prioritize systems that are easier to integrate with our allies. The next section visualizes these recommendations through two future vignettes.

PROXY WAR ALONG ECONOMIC NETWORKS

It is 20XX. Trouble is brewing along the One Belt One Road trade network in Central Asia. As part of a coalition, a new US Corps headquarters comprised SOF and conventional forces, integrated with an interagency and non-profit network, deploys its forward command team to form a headquarters. The headquarters, along with a SOF group and a Brigade Combat Team with additional aviation, civil affairs, military police, engineering and logistics units from the National Guard and Army Reserve form the Combined Forces Land Component Command (CFLCC). These units link up with local partners based on habitual training relationships and previous engagements by Special Forces. The CLFCC staff runs a series of machine-learning programs on five years of data scraped from social media, municipal governments, and commercial platforms, creating a picture of the local dynamics. Partners provide thick data and context that helps prioritize leadership engagements and isolate malign actors.

The coalition's mission is to secure a humanitarian corridor covered by a no-fly zone in order to support ongoing peace negotiations designed to end a civil war in the CENTCOM AOR. Groups from each side of the conflict are in the process of negotiating their position in a new transitional government. Hostile forces operate through proxies using aerial ISR and attack drones integrating commercial-off-the-shelve technology and leftover ordnance from the civil war. They field semi-autonomous T-72 tanks, hidden SAMs capable of operating autonomously, and automated mortars that use low power sensors through a commercial wireless network with machine-learning firing solutions to adjust fire. Their operatives intermingle with refugees, using mobile phones with commercial encryption to target coalition forces with indirect fire and drone attacks while mobilizing insider attacks and sabotage. Coalition forces have a limited ROE and cannot attack formal units in the process of negotiating. Proxies for these units have set up smart IEDs capable of interdicting ground and low-flying aerial targets around the coalition perimeter in order to limit freedom of action. They conduct GPS denial, harassing cyberattacks and use improvised ground drones for limited EW attacks designed to erode situational awareness and maneuver.

The coalition establishes a local WiFi network using cheap, high altitude balloons to help refugees and other parties affected by the conflict contact loved ones and seek relief. This connectivity also allows the coalition to optimize its engagement strategy while providing the development community a better understanding of local needs and wants. This situational awareness helps the coalition leadership develop their engagement strategy and understand each side of the conflict, gaining access to information they need to isolate malign actors and any foreign backers. At the same time, using tailored social media ads, the coalition activates a tip line that helps refugees identify insider threats. Through scraping social media content, the coalition gains an understanding of shifting population sentiment and uses this insight to tailor its messages. Key influencers are identified through combining big-data hits on references with thick-data engagements with a broad network of actors.

Coalition partners operate with US advisors, using partner equipment kits that make it easier for them to shoot, move, and communicate. These teams increase the operational reach of the coalition and produce a tempo that overwhelms adversaries in limited engagements. The equipment is simple and easy to use but capable of integrating into US systems.

PEER COMPETITION

It is 20XX. Protests erupt in the ethnic Russian enclave in Riga, and Latvia has NATO on edge. Russian units in the Western Military District are on alert, conducting snap exercises involving autonomous ground- and air-attack systems. Airborne and Spetsnaz forces from the Central Military District are radio silent and believed to be assembling near the Latvian border where a large rally by Russian nationalists is underway. The Russian president makes a speech, promising to protect Russian citizens wherever they live with military forces if necessary.

As part of a Joint force, USAREUR tasks elements of the 2nd Cavalry Regiment, 12th Combat Aviation Brigade, 66th MI, and 10th Air and Missile Defense Command to reassure Latvian forces, deter Russian aggression, and on order conduct a mobile defense. They link up with a Security Force Assistance Brigade currently on rotation in the Baltics. Using big data, the task force processes terabytes of unclassified social media posts. Machine-learning software agents isolate images of potential Russian covert elements agitating protests, cross referencing cell-phone pictures posted on social media with police traffic cameras and more sensitive military collection platforms. US forces provide the images along with an analysis of likely movements over the next 48 hours to Latvian police forces. The Latvians distribute the images on a fifth-generation cell-phone alert network that lets concerned citizens turn their cell phones and other personnel devices into civil-defense sensor networks. Cyber-defense teams work with Latvian government agencies and citizen hackers to identify existing malware and future cyberattack vectors. The task force deploys low-cost autonomous drone defenses along MSRs that lead from the Russian border to NATO bases and urban areas. Optionally manned ground combat vehicles integrate with forward deployed Latvian formations in prepared defense positions. They are controlled remotely while their crews assess the situation and man the reserve and QRF elements. These paired combat formations provide the task force a 1-crew-to-4-vehicle ratio.

CONCEPTS AND CAPABILITIES FOR TWENTY-FIRST-CENTURY MILITARY STRATEGY

This book is a clarion call for the US national security community to organize for population-centric competition, confrontation, and conflict in the twenty-first century. While the conventional force should retain its advantage in combined arms maneuver, more resources should be invested in capabilities and concepts required to operate in the human domain. Achieving a position of advantage in future struggles will require understanding the network of social, economic, and political interests that create incentives to challenge US interests. This information advantage will help strategists and planners mobilize countervailing coalitions that isolate adversaries. If you increase your connectivity while limiting your adversaries, you set the conditions and define the tempo. Done right, you "win" before the first shot is fired and limit the risks and costs associated with large-scale combat.

Military power, coercion, and traditional approaches to inform and influence populations take on new meanings when viewed through the human domain lens. Power is better thought of as shih, contextual advantage, than a standalone capability or force ratio. Rather than singularly imposing your will on an enemy, you generate network connections that limit their freedom of action while giving your coalition additional pathways through which to influence, and if necessary, manipulate and destroy an isolated enemy. This position of advantage only emerges if you see the networks that constitute the human domain and understand their connectivity in terms of network power and network-making power.

To this end, the US national security community should work across bureaucratic lines and with partners in the private sector to develop a new operational concept for the human domain. This concept, at a minimum, should revisit foundational works on Strategic Services from World War II as well as political warfare from the earlier Cold War while taking an inventory of how our rivals use the operations in the human domain to limit US power. An effort along these lines would will help clarify how to operate in a human domain and identify the types of organizational structures and authorities required to achieve a position of advantage.

At a more micro level, the concept of seeing human interactions as intersecting networks in a connected world should become part of education and training. The military profession needs to create the space to think about the human domain and population-centric warfare, given its prevalence, and the necessary adaptations to address it at echelon. As veterans of decades of struggle that saw stalled American military power fail to reach strategic objectives, it is our sincere hope that this book starts that larger professional discourse.

Once the US national security community defines the concepts and organizational structures necessary to operate in the human domain, strategists and planners should develop a capability set that enables maneuvering in the human domain. These capabilities will almost certainly involve entirely rethinking how we stovepipe information between enemy and the population as well as identify opportunities to integrate commercial off-the-shelf big data and machine-learning solutions.

The fact is that the US national security community has an information problem. Bad processes, legacy bureaucracy, and outdated, risk-averse approaches to data management limit America's ability to convert information into power. Worst still, despite leading the world in the development of the big data and artificial intelligence social and economic revolutions, the United States has yet to unleash their potential in its national security enterprise.

The defenders of the Republic need a data revolution that fundamentally alters how we look at empirical data to visualize the human domain. A data revolution in government is long overdue and opens the prospect of finding ways to integrate machine learning and alternative approaches such as Bayesian updating. These new methods of describing probabilistic futures and how to solve national security problems will complement our traditional understanding of military judgment, rooted in historical perspective, and help overcome pervasive bias. Embracing data requires more than just buying servers and software. It will require retraining the military professional, along with the broader network of security practitioners, in basic statistics and decision science, especially recent insights from behavioral economics and cognitive psychology. These are subjects lacking in most professional military education and training establishments. The future force needs data scientists as much it needs aviators and infantry. Failure in current conflicts continue to be human rather than technological and the social sciences are therefore pivotal in twenty-first-century strategy.

Appendix

People, Connectivity and Competition Policy Brief

Connectivity changes strategy. The US national security community must reorient how they think about power and influence in the twenty-first century and embrace a view of the world as a series of interconnected networks. This shift rests on two pillars: embracing the idea of the human domain and changing how we think about engagement.

In the twenty-first century, strategic advantage will emerge from how we engage with and understand the political, economic, and social networks that connect humanity. This connectivity defines an emergent human domain that transcends the physical characteristics of traditional military domains (land, air, sea, space) to embody the web of network relations defining power and interests in a connected world.

The state that bests understands the human domain gains an enduring position of advantage in twenty-first century competition and conflict. Traditional military power used in isolation produces decreasing marginal returns in population-centric struggles that constitute the majority of modern conflict. In these struggles information becomes paramount as states and non-state actors seek to undermine adversary resolve and mobilize the populace.

Therefore, the US military should optimize for operating in the human domain and prioritize understanding social relations, influence operations, and engaging with partners to generate local mass faster than an adversary can respond. Achieving a position of advantage in modern military art requires mapping the human domain and increasing the number of connections in a global security network that allows the United States to project power and influence. If you increase your connectivity while limiting your adversaries, you set the conditions and define the tempo.

Seeing the shifting network of relations in the human domain—from the local to the global—will allow US forces to tailor their operations to the context and find the right balance of cooperation, influence, manipulation, and targeted violence to achieve national security objectives. The network connections required to operate in the human domain are not just with states or exercised through military power alone. Rather, wielding network power and network-making power requires mobilizing local populations through civil society, as well as economic and political relationships, to achieve a position of advantage often before the first shot is fired.

Table 7. Policy Recommendations.

1. Definitions	Define the human domain in military doctrine and use the definition to conduct DOTMLPF-P analysis optimizing the military for the most likely 21st century contingencies.
2. Data	Develop a public-private partnership that collects data and maintains an analytical repository - to include machine learning and other narrow AI applications - that nonprofits, international organizations, and the military can use to map the human domain and understand the roots of instability.
3. Partnerships	Make engagement a warfighting function and shift the US defense procurement paradigm from exquisite, expensive, and exclusive to cheap and accessible platforms that our partners can use. Increasing partner combat power is an investment in a Corbettian network of skirmishers that provides US strategists and planners time and options in a crisis. Service modernization programs, particularly within the US Army, should start to prioritize systems that are easier to integrate with our allies.

Index

ABOUT THE AUTHORS

Lieutenant General Charles Cleveland (U.S. Army, Retired) left active duty in 2015 as the Commanding General of the U.S. Army Special Operations Command. His ARSOF 2022 rejuvenated U.S. Army unconventional warfare capabilities and institutionalized the Human Domain as an organizing concept for Army SOF. He also commanded SOCCENT, SOCSOUTH, and the 10th Special Forces Group (Airborne) and has operational experience in Iraq, Afghanistan, Yemen, Lebanon, Pakistan, Panama, El Salvador, and Bolivia. He began his career in Special Operations and Army intelligence units during the Cold War.

Benjamin Jensen, PhD, holds a dual appointment as an associate professor at Marine Corps University and as a scholar-in-residence at American University, School of International Service. He is also a senior nonresident fellow at the Atlantic Council. Dr. Jensen's previous publications including *Forging the Sword: Doctrinal Change in the U.S. Army* (Stanford University Press 2016) and *Cyber Strategy: The Evolving Character of Power and Coercion* (Oxford University Press 2018). He has published in several academic journals such as the *Journal of Strategic Studies* as well as major media outlets like the *New York Times*, *Washington Post*, and *Financial Times*. He writes the "Next War' column for *War on the Rocks*. Outside of academia he is an officer in the U.S. Army 75th Innovation Command.

Susan Bryant is a retired Army Colonel who served 28 years on active duty, including tours in Afghanistan, the Middle East and the Korean Peninsula. She holds a doctorate in liberal studies from Georgetown University, where she currently teaches Grand Strategy and Military Operations, as well as American Military History. She is also a Visiting Fellow at National Defense University's Institute for National Strategy

Studies and a Visiting Lecturer at Johns Hopkins University's School of Advanced International Studies.

Lieutenant Colonel Arnel David is a Civil Affairs officer and Army Strategist still serving on active duty. He has served multiple tours of duty in both conventional and special operations units where he deployed to the Middle East, Central Asia, and Pacific. He is currently the Chief of Staff for the Army Future Studies Group and recently deployed as the Commander's Initiative Group Chief for Special Operations Joint Task Force – Afghanistan. He is a distinguished military graduate from Valley Forge Military College and was a Local Dynamics of War Scholar at the U.S. Army Command and General Staff College.

CAMBRIA RAPID COMMUNICATIONS IN CONFLICT AND SECURITY (RCCS) SERIES

General Editor: Geoffrey R. H. Burn

The aim of the RCCS series is to provide policy makers, practitioners, analysts, and academics with in-depth analysis of fast-moving topics that require urgent yet informed debate.

Since its launch in October 2015, the RCCS series has the following book publications:

- *A New Strategy for Complex Warfare: Combined Effects in East Asia* by Thomas A. Drohan
- *US National Security: New Threats, Old Realities* by Paul Viotti
- *Security Forces in African States: Cases and Assessment* edited by Paul Shemella and Nicholas Tomb
- *Trust and Distrust in Sino-American Relations: Challenge and Opportunity* by Steve Chan
- *The Gathering Pacific Storm: Emerging US-China Strategic Competition in Defense Technological and Industrial Development* edited by Tai Ming Cheung and Thomas G. Mahnken
- *Military Strategy for the 21st Century: People, Connectivity, and Competitipauon* by Charles Cleveland, Benjamin Jensen, Susan Bryant, and Arnel David

For more information, visit www.cambriapress.com.